Asylum

A Survivor's Flight from Nazi-Occupied Vienna
Through Wartime France

MORIZ SCHEYER

Translated, with an epilogue, essay
and notes, by the author's grandson

P. N. SINGER

LITTLE, BROWN AND COMPANY
New York   Boston   London

Little, Brown and Company
Hachette Book Group
1290 Avenue of the Americas, New York, NY 10104
littlebrown.com

First North American edition, September 2016
Originally published in Great Britain by Profile Books, January 2016

Little, Brown and Company is a division of Hachette Book
Group, Inc. The Little, Brown name and logo are
trademarks of Hachette Book Group, Inc.

The publisher is not responsible for websites (or their content)
that are not owned by the publisher.

ISBN 978-0-316-27288-9
LCCN 2016932793

10 9 8 7 6 5 4 3 2 1

RRD-C

Printed in the United States of America

Contents

Introduction

Asylum is an extraordinarily tense, painful, dramatic – and at times almost miraculous – account of an Austrian-Jewish writer's persecution, flight and rescue, first in Vienna and then in wartime France. It was written at the time of the actual events: drafted in hiding in a convent in the Dordogne from 1943 to 1944 and finally completed after the end of the War in Europe, in 1945.

The account is the memoir of Moriz Scheyer, who before being driven out of Vienna in 1938 was the arts page editor for one of the city's principal newspapers, the *Neues Wiener Tagblatt*. As such, he was a personal friend of Stefan Zweig, acquainted with Arthur Schnitzler, Gustav Mahler and Bruno Walter, and himself the author of several volumes of essays and travel writings. So, despite his own protestation that this is not 'a literary work', it is a recollection of the Holocaust by a prominent, published writer.

The manuscript was discovered by chance – by my brother and myself – in the loft of my father, Konrad Singer, Scheyer's stepson, when he was in the process of moving house at the age of eighty-nine. Scheyer seems to have made some attempt at publication: what we found was a typescript, contained in a folder inscribed with the address of Stefan Zweig's first wife, in America. However, Scheyer died in 1949 and my father, who inherited his original typescript, did not pursue publication; indeed, he strongly disliked the book and its intensely 'anti-German' sentiments, and believed himself to have destroyed it. The typescript that I came upon was, it seems, a carbon copy kept by my grandmother – Scheyer's wife, Margarethe (Grete) – and had found its way into the loft amongst other of her possessions.

Scheyer's memoir has a number of unique features, even among Holocaust survivors' accounts. First, as noted, it was written at the time, with the events fresh and raw; almost a diary, it rivets the reader with the actual perspectives and minute details of those days. Secondly – just because of the events that happened to him – it covers an unusually wide range of experiences: the Anschluss in Austria; Paris during the 'phoney war' and under German Occupation; the Exodus from Paris; life in two different French concentration camps; an attempt to escape to Switzerland; contact with the Resistance in the Unoccupied Zone; and, finally, a dramatic rescue, and clandestine life in a convent in the Dordogne. Thirdly, there is the distinctive voice: Scheyer, who had been a serious Viennese literary journalist, dissects what is happening to him with a relentlessly acerbic critique.

The text that follows is a faithful – unedited – translation of Moriz Scheyer's typescript, which was written in German and entitled, simply, 'Ein Ueberlebender' (A Survivor). I have kept footnotes to a minimum but have added relevant biographical notes in an appendix of 'People mentioned in the text', as well as an epilogue giving further information on the narrative's events and its characters' subsequent history, and a summary of Moriz Scheyer's life and career.

P. N. Singer, London, 2016

STAATSOPER

hne Stempel der Staatsoperndirektion ist
die Karte ungültig.

Moriz Scheyer in 1937. This is the only surviving image of Scheyer from
the 1930s and is reproduced from his press pass for the Vienna Opera.

Grete (Margarethe) Scheyer, painted in 1923 by the Austrian
artist Anton Faistauer, probably at Salzburg.

Sláva Kolářová, the Scheyers' Czech-born housekeeper and faithful companion throughout their wartime experiences.

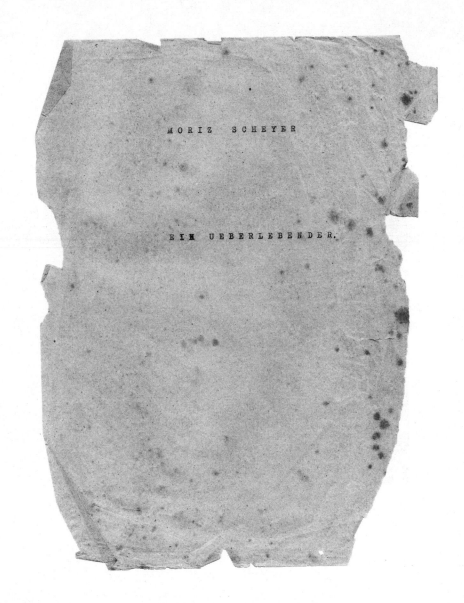

Title page of Scheyer's original manuscript, which he entitled EIN UEBERLEBENDER (A Survivor).

Asylum

*Written in hiding at the Convent of
Labarde, Dordogne, 1943–44,
and revised at Labarde in 1945*

* CHARACTERS (AND ORGANISATIONS) identified with an asterisk are noted with brief biographies in the Appendix 'People mentioned in the text' (pp. 293–300).

Foreword

THIS BOOK HAS NOTHING to do with 'literature' as normally understood: the circumstances of its composition preclude that from the outset.

To begin with, there was everything that happened to me before November 1942, the date when I found refuge in the Franciscan Convent of Labarde. It was while I was in hiding there that two friends, Pierre Vorms* and the great writer Jean Cassou* – who had himself just come out of prison – finally persuaded me to undertake the project. Even then, though, our salvation from the Germans was still a long way off. The Gestapo headhunters were going to their sport more energetically – and the fate of any Jew that they tracked down was more gruesome – than ever.

There were many times when, even if by good fortune I managed some work on this book, I did not know whether I would be delivered into the clutches of the Germans the very next day. Many times when I was forced suddenly to suspend work for an indefinite period – to bundle the papers up hastily so as not to put the Sisters of the Convent in serious danger. Many times when – to put it bluntly – the end seemed to be before me. In such circumstances you do not think in terms of creating literature out of all this material, or of having a 'good story'. If I did have such thoughts, indeed, I would hardly deserve to have survived the persecution.

It may be that the way in which the words, the sentences, the pages of which this book consists have been put together is the result of a certain intellectual effort. But their content, their essence, has a quite different source. And that source is a profound emotional anguish. An anguish in which the wretched sufferer is able only to keep repeating the same, stammering question: *How could it all have happened?*

Any answer to this question would have to address the guilty – all the guilty – and would entail an appropriate punishment. In this case, however, a true 'day of reckoning' of that kind is highly unlikely: the more time passes, the less importance the world will attach to such a notion. People will have more important concerns than the responsibility for war crimes in general, and the suffering of the Jews in particular.

But that does not make it any less necessary to pose the question – and to keep posing the question *'How could it all have happened?'* even if all one may hope to achieve by doing so is to stir the conscience, the thoughts, the anger of just a few individuals. There is, too, an inescapable duty to bear witness, to play one's part, however modest that may be. This book has no ambition beyond that of recording the witness of a Jewish refugee.

I have absolutely no pretension to be a historian. If I touch upon wider events, I do so only inasfar as I experienced them myself. It would be wrong, too, to characterise the work as a 'memoir': my own life is only of importance to the extent that it was dragged into the stream of world events – the opposite of the case with a memoir.

Besides, memoirs aim to be as 'interesting' as possible. I have made no attempt to be interesting – only to be truthful. Nor have I been principally concerned with accounts of external events – even with the description of atrocities – but rather with the attempt to express an internal condition: a state of the soul. My deepest desire has been to portray the mental misery that the German persecution created in us Jews. Even among the survivors, many – so many – have carried on, but with their souls broken: maimed for life.

I know that I will provoke the criticism in some quarters that I talk too much about Jewish refugees – as though nobody else existed, as though others had not suffered too.

It is absolutely true that others – innumerable others – were made to suffer, no less than we. And I have not failed to make mention of that. I myself happen to be both a refugee and a Jew; and one who bears witness must bear witness to his own personal experiences. But there is another point, too; and that is that whatever those others were made to suffer at least had some connection – direct or indirect – with the War. Their treatment at the hands of Germany was unprecedented and absolutely without justification. But, for all that they suffered, at least it was not the case that their freedom, their existence, their lives, were forfeit – forfeit from the very outset – simply by virtue of their birth. Even Hitler did not have the audacity to question whether they were actually human beings.

Whereas Goebbels, Hitler's official cultural spokesman, stated quite baldly in a speech immediately after the 'Advent' of the Third Reich: 'If I am asked whether the Jews are not also human beings, I can only reply: are not bugs also animals?'

What was perpetrated against the Jews, moreover, had nothing to do with the War. The project was undertaken long before the War, and would have been carried out systematically – in accordance with a clearly laid-out programme of extermination – even if there had been no War. And it was perpetrated against unarmed, defenceless people, who were unable to mobilise themselves, unable to resist. Perpetrated against powerless victims, who had already been deprived of their rights, despised, insulted, and humiliated in both body and soul. Perpetrated as a result of the impetuosity – as cowardly as it was crazy – of a madman, with the willing, happy participation of his 'Comrades of the People'.

It was perpetrated, too, without the civilised world daring to demand that it be stopped, or at least daring to make clear its abhorrence. Only later, much later – only when it was already far *too* late – did we begin to get all those fine expressions of solidarity, which came in the context of general war propaganda. And, while it was being perpetrated, states which had every opportunity to do so, and could have done so without cost, failed in their duty to open their gates to the persecuted. The granting of a visa was a process invariably attended with all manner of obstacles, restrictions, provisos and caveats, before – through a grate in the wall, reluctantly, like alms to a troublesome beggar – the document was finally dispensed. Or not dispensed, as the case might be. The lowliest consular official was suddenly a god.

No: others had to undergo all kinds of trials, certainly. But our journey of *spiritual* misery – to speak of nothing else – was without parallel. You have to have been a refugee yourself, to have lived as a Jew under the sign of the Swastika, to know what that really meant. And whatever anyone might say with regard to that ... it would still be too little.

How could it all have happened? We survivors – we who went through it – we, surely, have the right to keep asking that question. While at the same time bearing witness – in our name, and in that of the silenced six million. The martyrs: men, women and children, whom the 'Führer' – the Leader of his murderous Germany – hounded to their deaths.

If this book had the effect of making a few of those who were spared the fate of being refugees, of being Jewish, in the Hitler era, ask themselves the question, *How could it all have happened?*, that would be the best reparation I could receive – the greatest achievement of my life.

1

The 'Anschluss'

ON 7TH FEBRUARY 1938 COUNT G., of the Bundeskanzler's office, had lunch with me in my apartment in the Mariahilferstrasse in Vienna.

It was shortly after Schuschnigg's* return from Berchtesgaden. Count G. gave us an account of the reception that Schuschnigg had been accorded: how Hitler had first of all kept the Austrian Chancellor waiting for hours in an antechamber; how, in response to any mild attempt at counter-argument, he had resorted to shouting in the most vulgar way imaginable; how Schuschnigg, a hardened smoker, had not been allowed to touch a cigarette for the entire duration; and how, that evening, by the time he arrived in Salzburg, he was in such a state of nervous collapse that he had to break his onward journey to Vienna.

G. ended his account with these words: 'There can be no doubt about it. In spite of any assurances to the contrary from Hitler, we are going to be swallowed up by the Germans. Still, we should have at least a year till that happens.'

That was the 7th of February.

On the evening of 9th March I left my office at the *Neues Wiener Tagblatt** to return home. In the Rotenturmstrasse I encountered a group of white-stockinged adolesecent lads, barking 'Hitler!' and 'Sieg Heil!' alternately. (The white stocking, being a sign of affiliation to the Nazis, was supposedly illegal.) Two policemen on patrol at the corner of Brandstätte and Rotenturmstrasse gave the group clear indication of their approval. Schuschnigg was still the chancellor of Austria. But, even now, both policemen were displaying Swastikas openly on their uniform.

Near me, an old woman shouted excitedly at the demonstrators: 'Austria!'[1] At this, one of the youths went up to her and laughed in her face: 'Don't fret yourself, granny. Your Austria's had it. Heil Hitler!' The old woman burst into tears.

Two days later the 'Anschluss' was a *fait accompli*. Whatever political events took place in between were in a sense no more than directorial details in the staging of the Tragedy of Austria.

The outrage had been carried out overnight. And all that remained of the famous 'face of Austria' was an unpleasant leer. No one could have imagined such a swift transformation possible. Within the physiognomy of Vienna, it was only lifeless objects that retained their previous appearance; but even these appeared somehow changed from within. The very air seemed to have acquired a different taste.

Everywhere you went there was a rabble. People who suddenly felt they were someone – who saw that this was their chance. People who looked on the Anschluss, first and foremost, as an opportunity to get involved in the witchhunt. Everywhere the triumphant grins of those traitors, with their 'illegal' party insignia, hitherto carefully hidden but now worn proudly and openly. Everywhere the vulgar hubbub of a provincial market. In short, there was a gross, ugly 'Teutonification' of the city, which felt like a punch in the face. If we were not talking about a terrible catastrophe, the whole thing would have resembled nothing so much as an elaborate festival

---

1. 'Austria' (accompanied by a particular form of salute) was the official greeting sanctioned by the government as the Austrian patriot's alternative to 'Heil Hitler'.

of bad taste. Language itself became a caricature overnight. In the press, on the radio, in every announcement, a ghastly sort of jargon had already appeared along with the goose-step, emanating from the Nazi mania for neologisms and abbreviations, for Germanification in all things. Austria became 'the Ostmark' (*Eastern Province*); Vienna, the capital of the 'Lower Danube Area'.

And for whole weeks the incessant, painful noise of the loudspeakers and chants in the streets. It was quite impossible to escape from them.

The fact that the great and the good in other countries, who had stood by and observed the shameless Rape of Austria without lifting a finger – the fact that these people attached no significance to such chants as 'Sieg Heil, Sieg Heil' or 'One People – one Empire – one Leader', was no longer a surprise. That they were totally unaffected by such heroic battle-cries as 'Jew – perish!'[2] or 'When Jewish blood spurts from the knife', was quite natural. We were only talking about Jews, after all. The anti-Semitic persecutions in Germany had never previously troubled these 'representatives of world opinion'. That they were not prepared to take notice of a chant like 'Today Germany – tomorrow the whole world', on the other hand – that was something that would cost them dear. They simply refused to take any notice, too, of the fact that – as early as March – high-ranking German officers in Vienna could be heard to declare openly: 'Now we have got Austria. But in a few months we will be in Prague. After that – well, after that, we shall see.'

We saw, all right.

'Jew – perish!' From the first day of the invasion, the 'Comrades of the People' started to put this programme into action.

---

2. 'Juda – verrecke!' was the first line of a chant popular with Nazi activists. The verb, 'verrecken', is a vulgar one, and might be used in relation to vermin.

Bürckel, the first Gauleiter of the 'Ostmark', had given an assurance immediately after his arrival in Vienna, that the Austrian Jews would feel a much sharper wind blowing than the Germans had. And Seyss-Inquart* – who had hitherto been a supporter of so many 'non-Aryan' businesses, and been a charming dinner-guest and bridge-partner in so many Jewish households renowned for their cooking – this same Seyss-Inquart made the following pronouncement at a meeting: 'We are indebted to our brothers from the Reich for everything. But there is one respect in which they may learn something from us, and that is how to deal with the Jews.'

Actually, they had nothing to learn in this respect, these brothers from the Reich. And the brothers from the Ostmark had nothing to teach. They were exactly on a par – the Heroes of the North and the Golden Heart of Vienna.

If, nonetheless, a certain unhappiness began to be felt on the part of the 'Comrades of the People' in the Ostmark, then this was only because the 'Master Race' from the Reich, quite naturally, kept the lion's portion of the Jewish booty for themselves, while the Austrian hyenas had to content themselves with the crumbs that fell from the table of the Feast of Aryanisation. They were quite substantial crumbs, to be sure, but they were still only crumbs.

It would require a separate book to enumerate the crimes perpetrated against the Austrian Jews from the day of the 'Advent' up to 15th August 1938, the day on which I was finally able to leave Austria. What a tortuous journey, even to reach the point where finally – after the payment of a sum which the Bandits of the Swastika had the nerve to call a 'fine for flight from the Reich', after being robbed down to the shirt on your back, abased and humiliated to the very depths of your soul – where, finally, after all this, you were actually able to have in your hand a passport and a permit to leave the country. From one day to the next I had become an outcast, someone who was fair game: a Jew. Against a Jew, now, everything was permitted, and nothing was forbidden. Or, to look at it another way, nothing was permitted any longer: even my best 'Aryan' friends took every imaginable precaution before daring to telephone – or, if they were particularly brave, to visit me in person.

I was not – in contrast with many other writers and journalists – immediately arrested and placed in a concentration camp. That was a fate that was to befall me a little later, after my emigration. I was left in 'freedom' – unlike, for example, the venerable chief editor of the *Neues Wiener Tagblatt*, the highly respected Hofrat Dr Löbl, who was locked up, along with his wife and daughter. I was extremely lucky. Still, at this time it was only the thought of my wife and children that kept me going. In these first five months alone, nine thousand Viennese Jews could not resist the temptation to escape to their deaths.

Nine thousand suicides in the first five months. While the 'Comrades of the People' looked on and laughed.

The door to the apartment of a well-respected Jewish family – parents and three children – who had 'exterminated' themselves was decorated, before the funeral, with a placard bearing the following inscription from the hands of the Nazis: 'Five Jews, who have killed themselves. Course of action highly recommended to others.'

Nine thousand in five months. And, even so, these nine thousand could never have imagined all that would have lain before them, if they had not found the courage to commit suicide.

It was not simply physical, material things that led these nine thousand to prefer to pay the 'tax for flight from the Reich' with their own lives. They had had enough. It was not just that the brown-shirted German heroes made a sport of tying together male and female Jews on the open street; making them crawl on all fours, and then finally trampling their victims' hands to a bloody pulp with their boots. It was not just that they thought it amusing to freeze Jewish café owners in their own refrigerators. It was not just that they enjoyed burning holes in the cheeks of defenceless Jews in the prisons with their cigarettes. Nor was it just that Jews were deprived, at a single stroke, of any possible means of making money; that every public space, every bench was daubed with the warning: 'Jews strictly forbidden'; that the trams were decked out with huge posters declaring: 'Jewry is criminality'; that ... the list could be continued *ad infinitum*.

No: what drove so many to death was the spiritual, the mental abuse. And the embittered, disgusted sense of disappointment at the cowardice and meanness of spirit of 'friends', who suddenly did not know us – who denied us, betrayed us, who were greedy for the booty that we would leave behind us, or who – in the best cases – dared to show themselves only from far off, their face covered with a protective mask. One day they were greeting you with open arms; the next day – well, they still stretched out their arms towards you, but this time in an anxious attempt to ward off any possible contact. You were an outlaw, something contaminated.

Mixed marriages alone provide a miserable chapter in this story. There were many (legal as well as illegal) partnerships in which the 'Aryan' partner, in many cases after decades of a close relationship, not only brutally severed himself from his 'non-Aryan' companion, but even used the sanctions of the Nuremberg laws for the most appalling blackmail. The fabrication of a 'crime of racial impurity' could in certain circumstances be a profitable business.

It was pitiable, too, to see how willing the vast mass of people was to take on board the most absurd terms of insult, as well as the most stupid anti-Semitic slanders. I remember one portly working-class woman, a nice, friendly-looking type, sitting opposite me in the tram with a female friend, and studying the *Stürmer* newspaper intently. Suddenly she turned to her companion and, with a sad shake of the head, said: 'I really had no idea that the Jews were as bad as that.'

'Jew – perish!' Of those who died of their own accord, many were really killed by mental anguish, by disgust, by horror. They could simply not bear the ghastliness of Hitler's world any longer. And all the while they had no idea that all this was actually a relatively harmless overture; had no idea what unprecedented pinnacles of devilish sadism would yet be achieved by German culture and science, by the German spirit of enquiry and invention, in its noble struggle to find ever new, ever more gruesome types of torture to accompany that catchy folksong, so full of true German sentiment: 'When Jewish blood spurts from the knife'.

As for the others – those who had steeled themselves to emigration, to a 'new life' somewhere abroad – somewhere where a visa had finally managed to open the door for them – those others of course had no inkling that Hitler would catch up with so many of them and get them in his grasp again. If they had, even more would have chosen emigration into the Beyond.

Those of us who contemplated emigration were certainly not in any mood to laugh. And yet perhaps nothing encapsulates the tragedy of our situation – and also the world's indifference to our fate – better than this little selection of anecdotes that did the rounds among Viennese would-be émigrés at that time. Gallows humour of the Emigration.

Three Jews, who are considering emigration, meet on a street-corner. 'I'm going to England,' says the first. 'I'm going to America,' says the second. 'And I'm going to Australia,' declares the third. 'Such a long way!' cries the first, in amazement. To which the one destined for Australia simply replies: 'A long way from *where*?'

Four Jews, this time. The same old question about destination. The first replies: 'China.' The second: 'New Zealand.' The third: 'Bolivia.' 'Well,' says the fourth, 'I'm staying here.' The others look at him for a moment in silence. Finally one says, in a tone of admiration: 'My God: that *is* adventurous!'

And finally: one Jew, who has walked his feet sore in the futile effort to get hold of some kind of visa, finally goes into a travel agency. 'I *must* get out,' he tells the man at the desk, in desperation. 'But where to, where to? Can *you* give me any advice?' The man fetches a globe. 'Here,' he says, 'here you have all the countries in the world. You must be able to find something here.' The Jew turns the sphere this way and that for a long time, shaking his head the whole time. Finally, crestfallen, he puts it to one side. 'Well,' says the man behind the desk, 'what have you found?' 'Oh, sir,' says the Jew very diffidently, 'you wouldn't possibly have another globe, would you? There's no room for me on this one.'

To this day I cannot rid myself of a feeling of bitterness, when I think of the endless forest of red tape that was put in our way by most states at that time, as we begged for visas. With a little good will, it would have been possible to save everyone.

Meanwhile Goering – the stout, jovial Goering – had announced even in those days, in Vienna: 'For Jews who are not able to leave, there are only two possibilities: to die of hunger or to be rooted out by fire and sword.'

Emigrating: that was the Act I of the tragedy. But once this problem had been solved, there began the second act: Being an Émigré.

To begin with Act I, let me give just a very brief summary of my experience of it.

Since 1914 I had been on the staff of the *Neues Wiener Tagblatt*, as essayist and critic. In 1924 I was recalled from Paris, where I had been working as a correspondent for the paper, to take over the post of head of *feuilleton* after the death of Paul Busson.[3]

---

3. The writing of *feuilleton* was Scheyer's main literary activity. The *feuilleton*, a characteristic element of continental quality newspapers (then and now) is essentially an essay, often prompted by a particular cultural event but going well beyond a review. Typical themes of the pre-war *feuilleton*, and Scheyer's output in particular, were reflections on moments, or characters, in world history – as it were, historical novels in miniature. See appendix, 'Moriz Scheyer: Writer'.

It goes without saying that after the completion of the Anschluss I was immediately back on the street. As a 'non-Aryan', I received not a penny of the severance money promised me in my contract, nor of the amounts owing to me from my pension and insurance funds. The investments I had in a deposit account, and the author's royalties held by my publisher, were also both frozen.

It was very simple. Anything I possessed – and could still get access to – had to be spent in obtaining permission to leave the country. To get what I needed for everyday living expenses, I was forced to sell valuable objects, furniture, books, and so on.

We were allowed to take with us ten marks per person, with which to start our 'new life' abroad.

And yet the actual, physical robbery – the poverty – was not the worst of it. Much worse, as I have already said, was the impoverishment – the degradation – of the soul. No reparation could ever compensate for these experiences.

Few are born with the capacity for loyalty. Few, even, with the courage to behave decently. As regards Hitler's 'Comrades of the People' in the Reich, there was no depth that would surprise me. Yet all too many Austrian 'Aryans', too, of my immediate and not-so-immediate acquaintance, were every bit the equal of their brothers from the Reich. Intellectuals, especially – even people who owed me some kind of debt of gratitude. If I have any positive memory of individuals in Vienna at that time, they were with few exceptions the ordinary people: a waitress, who sobbed uncontrollably when I left the *Neues Wiener Tagblatt* building for the last time; a compositor, who even dared to look me up in my apartment; our porter in the Mariahilferstrasse.

Others – people who had worked alongside me daily for decades – people who just a short while before had been unable to do enough to show their friendship and intimacy with me …

It is better not to dwell on such things. Although it is also important not to forget them. These people at least made my leavetaking from my homeland easier. 'A long way from *where*?' It was an observation that applied to the spiritual aspect of emigration too. Even homesickness had lost its home.

On the evening of 15th August 1938 I was finally able to leave Vienna. My elder stepson, Stefan, a medical student, had been taken in by a wonderful woman, Miss Marian Dunlop* – who had not previously even met him – in the most magnificent spirit, and was already in England. My wife had to wait a few days longer in Vienna with my younger stepson, Konrad, who was waiting to obtain a transit visa for Switzerland, in order to be able then to go to Scotland, where he would be enabled to continue studying for his degree in chemistry at the University of Glasgow, thanks to a grant from the International Student Service.* For my wife and myself I had obtained visas for France – with great difficulty, in spite of the fact that I had for decades been an active and enthusiastic propagandist on behalf of French literature and culture. But that was all in the past …

The afternoon before my departure I made a last visit to a friend, the well-known architect Dr Hans Berger, to say goodbye to him. At the end of the visit Dr Berger went with me as far as the tram stop. As the tram came into view, I said to him: 'Look at this. This is the last time that I shall be able to buy a ticket out of my own pocket. From the moment that I cross the border, I shall have to live on … on … charity. That is something I shall have to get used to.'

To be, suddenly, in the position of a poor relation who lets people thrust money into his hands (even if those people happen to be your best friends); to be compelled to accept invitations which you will never be able to return and which must therefore be regarded as a subsidy, as a merciful bounty – this is among the most painful things contained within the concept 'refugee'. To be a beggar you have to be born to it.

The facts of my situation, though, would be brought to my attention with absolute clarity the very next day, even before I crossed the border at Feldkirch.

A few minutes before the train's departure, the boy in the Storm-Trooper uniform who had taken my passport at Innsbruck returned, holding it in his hand. Apart from me, the compartment was occupied by three Swiss people.

'So: you are the Jew Scheyer,' he said. Then, looking at the passport: 'Fifty-one years old.'

I wondered where he was going with this.

'Fifty-one,' he continued. 'Not as old as all that. And ten marks in your pocket. So – how are you going to live, now, with your ten marks? Can you tell me that?'

I ground my teeth together and said nothing.

'These Jews,' he shouted furiously, 'these Jewish pigs! You can take everything away from them and they'll still find someone to take them in.' And with that he threw the passport down at my feet. The train started. One of the Swiss people stood up and grasped my hand, silently.

How are you going to live ... Jewish pigs ... take them in ... These were the last words of comfort – the provisions with which my homeland sent me off into the unknown.

They have lasted me up to the present day.

2

Breathing again:
Switzerland

THE TRAIN ROLLED OVER the bridge above the Rhine: it had crossed the Swiss border. Buchs. Switzerland. Noble land. No more 'Heil Hitler!' No more Swastika. No more Brown Shirts. No 'Jew – perish!' Saved. Free. The land beneath my feet is a land where Jewry is not, after all, criminality.

How I had dreamed of this moment. How I had looked forward to it, as to a transport of joy. Homelessness, poverty, uncertainty – all the anxieties and questions about the future – how unimportant that all seemed, put alongside the sensation of being free of the constant mental presence of Hitler. That, at least, is how it was in my dreams, my longings.

Now, however, in the very moment of fulfilment, to my own surprise and dismay, the expected, longed-for euphoria did not come. How was that possible? What had happened? Some kind of nervous response, perhaps – a reaction to all the tensions and let-downs of the last five months? There was this terrible feeling of disappointment, of irritation – irritation with myself. A feeling of being cheated of a priceless, unique, once-in-a-lifetime experience.

But the more time passed in the new surroundings – the closer I got to Zurich on this stretch of track, so familiar from previous journeys – the more clearly I understood the reasons for this apparently inexplicable, unforgivable mood.

Here you had the Swiss landscape – houses, people: peace, strength, solidity, the sense of well-established contentment and security. The whole scene – you would have thought – balm for a wounded spirit, for shattered nerves.

And yet, this time, there was this simultaneous feeling of being irrevocably distant – on the opposite bank of the river. On *that* side stretches another world – near enough to touch, yet at the same time unattainable. A world in which the present is still the legacy of the past and the future still the legacy of this present. Where I am standing now, on the other hand, is a No-Man's-Land – the desolate land of a person with *no* legacy.

I am sitting in a railway train with other people. To all external appearances, I am no different from them. My destiny is not inscribed like a sign on my forehead. I read the newspaper, just as they do. I glance at the wonderful scenery, at the comings and goings at the stations, just as they do. Inwardly, though, a huge gulf divides us. A gulf as wide as ...

The only real answer to that comes from that same question: 'A long way from *where?*'

In Zurich I was expected by my old friend Victor Sax.* Ours was a friendship of decades: it went back to our early youth. Many were the happy months I had spent on holiday with him, first in the house of his late parents at Kreuzgut Goldbach near Zurich; and later, after his marriage, in his own house in Zollikon. I had been his best man. He and his wife Sylvia greeted me with the same warmth as always. And yet something has changed between us.

Something? No, not some *thing*: what has changed is myself. I have lost any spontaneity in my reactions; worse than that, I catch myself feeling distrustful, almost suspicious, in my relations with this old, trusted friend. I find that I am actually on the lookout for anything in his behaviour – a word, a look, a thought – that might offend me, that might reinforce the consciousness of my outcast status.

The fact that I am no longer in a position to buy a tram ticket from my own resources threatens to become a barrier between us.

In the evening we go to the same old restaurant I know from my previous visits. But now I feel like someone who has no business in establishments of this kind any more – almost like a gatecrasher, some down-and-out who is being given an inappropriately grand meal, out of pure kindness. Every word is an effort; every mouthful chokes me; and the moment when my friend settles the bill brings the colour flooding to my face.

The next day, too, when I visit Victor's brother, Erwin Sax, and another old friend, the university professor Dr. [] (who has since died), this inner feeling of constraint, this depressing sense of dependency, will not leave me. Every perfectly well-intentioned question seems to my over-sensitive spirit to be a wounding reference to my situation.

I should have been wallowing in relief at being able to breathe freely again; at being surrounded by friends; at being able to walk down the road without the constant assault of 'Jew! Jew!' I should have been enjoying the sense of freedom and normality afforded by this wonderful country. I should at least have been able to take refuge in forgetfulness for a few short hours. Instead, all these things came across, in my mind, as a constant, dull reminder: 'You are not part of this any more. It's over.'

Now I realised all too clearly what it was that had robbed me of that happiness that I had so keenly expected on stepping upon Swiss soil – robbed me, even, of some small interval between Acts I and II of The Refugee's Tragedy. Previously,

18

when I still had a home, and a homeland, saying goodbye to Switzerland and Swiss friends was always difficult. This time ... well, this time I almost felt relief when I was finally alone again in the train taking me to Paris and the unknown.

3

France: beloved France

As he returned my passport, the guard at the checkpoint on the French border smiled at me and said: 'Maintenant vous pourrez respirer.' Now you will be able to breathe again. I was grateful to him, not just for those few friendly words themselves, but because they seemed to me to be a confirmation of precisely the qualities that I expected in France.

I had loved France since my early youth. For me it had achieved the status of an emotional construct – the home land of my ideals, my fantasies. Other countries that I had visited had given me pleasurable holidays. But France – however many times I visited – was always the fulfilment of a passion. And I had never tired of praising the country's delights, in conversation and in print. To me France was like a lover to whom you enslave yourself willingly, and who is quite incapable of disappointing. Even her little weaknesses are things that, if anything, only enhance the charm. Austria was where my home was. But France was where I felt *at home*.

That was my mental picture of France – even before emigration. No wonder, then, that I did not hesitate even for a moment when the problem of emigration presented itself. I could probably have got a visa for England, or for the United States. But in my mind no other country on the globe was even worth considering. Any vacillation would have seemed like doubt of my beloved – like infidelity. France was not only going to take me in and put up with me; she was going to set me straight again, to stand by me. She was going to do everything possible to make the process of 'recommencer à zéro' – starting again from nothing – an easier one, if not in fact to spare me it altogether. Yes: in my wilder fantasies I even gave in to the madness of imagining that emigration would in the final reckoning turn out to be actually just the fulfilment of my long-treasured desire to live permanently in France. That, in my personal case, the catastrophe of Austria's invasion would actually be the occasion of a great joy.

Of course, alongside this symphony of hope I did hear another sound, too: a tiny whisper, warning me that this was all a delusion. But I did not want to listen to that whisper. I blocked it out. Even the huge difficulties I had encountered in obtaining a visa did not give me pause for thought.

There was another respect, too, in which I felt like an especially privileged kind of refugee. When, on 18th August 1938, I arrived in Paris, I knew immediately where to go in order to have a roof over my head. So many of my fellow sufferers did not have that good fortune.

My old friend, the art publisher Pierre Vorms, and his wife, received me into their home with the warmest of hospitality, giving my wife and myself two rooms to live in in their charming home on the Quai Louis Blériot. Another old friend, Emil Kofler,* arranged (in the most tactful manner possible) that I could draw money at his bank. And my niece, Louise Schwarzmann, who at that time lived in Lausanne, also made some money available to me. In short, I was not compelled to engage in the harsh struggle for the daily crust from the very first moment. I had been granted a breathing space, which I wanted to use to look up old acquaintances and reestablish contacts. I had also taken it upon myself to keep on drawing people's attention to the Brown Peril, whenever the opportunity arose. My experiences, I thought, should at least entitle me to do that.

'Today Germany – tomorrow the whole world.' This threat, after all, applied to the people of my beloved France too.

Why had France not reacted in any appropriate way when Hitler simply grabbed Austria? ... Still, you forgive many things, with a lover ...

Before continuing with my personal story, I should like first to say a few words about the climate of opinion at that time – hardly more than a year before the outbreak of the War. What I shall say applies to the situation in Paris. I doubt, however, whether the climate of opinion in the country as a whole was significantly different. If it had been, subsequent events might have been a little different.

At a very simple, basic level, the mentality can be summed up by an expression which one used to hear all the time: 'Pas d'histoires!' 'No stories!' Let's have no trouble – no unpleasantness. In other words, we want a peaceful life and we aren't going to trouble ourselves about things that don't concern us in the least. We eat well, we drink well, our women are beautiful, our businesses are prosperous; anything else is just about as important as Hecuba. It doesn't bother us what happens outside France. As long as Hitler doesn't interfere in *our* affairs – and he has no intention of doing so – we don't need to interfere in his.

'Pas d'histoires': a carefree indifference, a lightheartedness verging on frivolity; a cynical self-centredness that hardly even bothered to conceal its true nature with specious justifications; the politics of the ostrich, hiding its head in the sand of everyday life and refusing to see or hear anything. At all costs, let's have no unpleasantness! The rape of Austria, the shameful betrayal of the Czechs? How can that affect us? ... The Germans roar in chorus: 'Today Germany – tomorrow the whole world!' So? They're welcome to it! France is surely not included in this 'whole world'. We've happily gone along with everything that Hitler wanted. He can have the whole world – the rest of it – just so long as we carry on eating well, drinking well, loving well, earning well. Pas d'histoires!

What, then, of the younger generation – surely *they* saw things differently? I have to say that among the younger generation, too, there was all too often a terrifying materialism, a cynical rejection of all ideals, a desire to get ahead that was directed at purely financial and hedonistic goals, and that saw education or culture solely as means to the end of acquiring sinecures in the civil service or in political life. This section of the younger generation looked up only to the *débrouillards*, the people who knew how to get on in life, to 'arrange' things – people who have brought to a pitch of perfection the techniques of *pistonnage*: of patronage, of creating and exploiting a network of influential individuals.

In every kind of social context, I attempted to open people's eyes to the reality of Hitler and Germany. And everywhere I encountered one of two reactions: an attitude of sympathy mixed with total disbelief; or one of bored indifference. If, that is, they were prepared to listen at all: sometimes I even provoked a degree of irritation.

One reaction that comes vividly to mind was at a party which included people from a wide range of professions, among them influential journalists. The host – normally a quite amiable individual – cried with unconcealed anger: 'But why are you *telling* us all these tales?' He was right.

In this context, particular mention should be made of the attitude among French Jews. I have to say that, in spite of the fact that they had every reason to open their eyes and ears, they for the most part were even less keen to know than the French 'Aryans'.

To add to 'Pas d'histoires!' this group had another refrain, too: 'Chez nous en France, tout cela serait impossible.' 'Here in France none of that could ever happen.' And woe to the man who dared to admit the slightest doubt as to the certainty of this categorical pronouncement. One could make oneself quite unpopular even by the subtlest reference to their Jewishness. This would tend to be seen as rather tactless – a *faux pas*. And any mention of the word 'anti-Semitism' was greeted with a dismissive wave of the hand – if, in fact, its existence was not explicitly denied. The notion that there might ever be discrimination between 'Aryans' and 'non-Aryans' in France, too, was to them unimaginable.

In relation to us refugees they observed a certain distance. There was a definite anxiety not to be mixed up with us, not to be tarred with the same brush. They were 'long-standing' or 'settled' inhabitants. While the other French citizens had no desire to hear what was happening outside France, the French Jews clamped their ears shut whenever anyone started talking about Hitler and his unhealthy obsession with the Jews.

One of them once said to me straight out: 'On en marre de vos histoires juives.' 'We're really fed up with all your Jewish stories.'

The attitude of those Jews resident in France who were foreigners, but not refugees, meanwhile, was no better. These individuals preferred to regard themselves as little outposts of their various home countries, and were keen to make clear the distinction between them, with their affiliation to a native land, and us, with our affiliation to a No-Man's-Land. They had a right to be considered as guests; we had to consider ourselves lucky to be put up with.

And yet none of this prevented Charles Maurras* (who had been presented with a valuable sword by his Jewish admirers on the occasion of his election to the Académie Française) from writing that it was the Jews who were responsible for forcing France to attack the peace-loving, well-intentioned Hitler. Why, Jewish refugees had even had the nerve to celebrate France's declaration of war with champagne!

4

Earning the first hundred francs

I HAD ARRIVED IN PARIS, then, on 18th August. My wife joined me a few days later.

For the first few weeks, everything seemed to be going well. Everywhere I went I was greeted with the most encouraging words. The important thing for you now is to have a bit of a break. Everything else will fall into place in due course.

Jules Romains,* the president of the French PEN, received me in the friendliest manner and opened doors for me immediately. My wife and I were invited to a dinner held specially to greet us at the headquarters of the PEN in Rue Pierre Charron. Speeches, heart-warming words, tears in the eyes. I felt like the prodigal son who has at last come home.

At the end of this wonderful, unforgettable evening I was left with the definite impression that, as far as starting a new life here was concerned, my only problem would be to know which of the many offers to take up.

But as the days, and then weeks, went by I was unable to convert any of all those beautiful promises into reality. Only Benjamin Crémieux* – a good man – did something concrete to back his willingness to help: by his personal intervention with the police chief he succeeded in having me issued with – wonder of wonders! – an identity card valid for three years.

I had already gone here, there and everywhere in my search for some kind of starting point. Some way into the 'recommencer à zéro'. I was forced with ever greater clarity to the conclusion that as far as France was concerned – the France of my dreams – I was just some refugee in search of a job. A poor wretch that the Beloved has tired of. She very politely offered me a chair, but she placed it outside the door. My time was up. Everywhere I came up against a sort of rubber wall – an elastic form of refusal – especially in places where in earlier times I had always found the doors thrown open for me; places where I used to encounter that particular kind of helpfulness that is only offered to those who are independent and are not asking for anything.

There is a French saying: 'On ne prête qu'aux riches.' You only lend to a rich man.

One day, I finally said farewell to any attempt to see the present in the same terms as the past. Time, I decided, to draw a firm line under it. Armed in this way, I set out again.

Purely on the off-chance, I called in at a translation service not far from the Trinité, and asked to speak to the manager. I was mistaken for a new client, and brought immediately to the *patronne*, Madame F., a powerfully built woman already in her maturer years.

Well, first of all I had to clear up the misunderstanding: I was not a client. In fact, I was looking for work.

The charming smile on the face of Madame F. transformed itself instantly into the haughty demeanour of the potential employer. She examined me, hesitated, then asked me a few questions. 'Austrian ... refugee ... there are so many of them these days ... Writer, you say? Well, wait a moment ... perhaps I do have something for you.'

She disappeared and returned with an envelope, from which she took out a thick letter.

'I have here a letter,' she said to me. 'Your job would be to translate it from German into French, but ... we are not talking about a *literal* translation. What I need is ... how can I put it? ... more of a ... free version. A reworking.'

I must have reacted with a certain air of bewilderment, because Madame F. smiled in amusement, before adding: 'You'll soon see what I mean. This is a love letter. A love letter from a lady, who has entrusted it to us to be translated, because she knows that she can rely on our absolute discretion. Some time ago this lady became acquainted with a Viennese gentleman here in Paris, who subsequently returned home. They write letters to each other. But the gentleman speaks not a word of French and the lady not a word of German.'

I began to understand, though still only imperfectly. 'The lady,' Madame F. went on, 'is an excellent client, and I consider it of the utmost importance to keep her happy. I have a number of highly efficient translators at my disposal – but in the present case that is not sufficient.'

Madame F. lit a cigarette. A naughty, knowing smile spread over her already somewhat flushed face. She continued her explanation.

'The lady, you must understand, is terribly in love. The more passionate, the more thrilling, the letters that she receives, the better for her – and the better for us. You say that you are a writer. I suppose, then, I may take it that – in addition to your linguistic abilities – you also have imagination and ... panache.'

I gave a flattered bow.

'Well, then,' Madame F. concluded. 'Give your imagination and panache free rein. Use them to your heart's content. Exaggerate, embellish – beef it up – in fact, add whatever words of your own you think necessary. Be lyrical, pathetic, tender, passionate ... and above all let us have no false modesty. Don't be embarrassed to call certain things by their names. The lady is not only very much in love, she is also of a very passionate disposition. The usual fee for the translation would be fifty francs. But if you do the job well, you can have a hundred. And for every subsequent letter too.'

Next day I presented Madame F. with my concoction. After checking it over, she gracefully handed me a one-hundred-franc note. And from then on, regularly, every eight days, I received a letter to ... adapt.

After a while I got so much into the swing of it that I could probably have satisfied our client's taste even without reference to the 'original'. And secretly I hoped that this was the love that – at one hundred francs a week – would last forever.

This glorious state of affairs, however, was destined for an early end. Not that the passion of my Viennese friend was ever going to let up. I would have made sure of that. But war came, and with it the end of the idyll.

A real shame, that.

In January of 1939 we were able to rent a small apartment in the 15th *arrondissement*. Shortly after that we were joined by our beloved friend Miss Sláva Kolářová. From Czechoslovakia, where, as a one-hundred-per-cent Aryan, she could have lived undisturbed with her mother and siblings, she came to us, a voluntary refugee, if you like – and even a voluntary Jew, as will be seen in what follows.

If a novelist had decided to invent a woman like this, readers would shake their heads cynically. 'Far-fetched,' they would say. 'The sort of thing you only get in novels.' Well, we got it in 'real life' too – this miracle of goodness and loyalty. It actually happens. And the fact that it *can* happen is more than a consolation; it is a light in the darkness, a light from above.

Sláva Kolářová had shared our life for nearly thirty years. She had brought up our children, and was my wife's closest friend. Life without her would have seemed unimaginable to us. And yet, when we were forced to emigrate, we insisted that she must be separated from us and us from her. To bring her along with us on our journey of uncertainty, trouble, hardship – how could we have that on our conscience?

It was almost by force that we finally made her return to her family in Bohemia, who took her in with open arms. The moment when we had to say goodbye to her in Vienna was one of the hardest of our lives.

And then, one fine day – here she was again. With us in Paris. She had simply not been able to take it any more. Always so shy, so helpless – she had managed to get herself a permit to travel and a visa. Not only that – she had brought a few thousand francs, too … She not only wanted to share in our destiny, to take our woes upon herself, to help us to get our daily bread. She had also already sacrificed her last savings for us.

It happens.

So there were three of us, now: in it together. I did my translations, published an article occasionally in this or that newspaper or magazine, and busied myself in my free time as a delivery boy. My wife and Sláva made Viennese cakes and pastries that became quite popular; and I used to take them to the relevant houses. On several days of the week Sláva also did housework for a family at five francs an hour. And the two women also had knitting to do in the evening – or often at night. There was of course no question of going for a walk, of doing something for pleasure.

But we were content. We had a roof over our heads, and a few good friends. Our sons were able to complete their studies in England. And we had something else, too, that made up for all the trouble and fatigue: we could breathe freely. We did not have to jump whenever there was a ring at the door.

If anyone could have told us then what the future held …

5

The men in berets

SEPTEMBER 1939.

For an unconscionable time France had had her head buried in the sand, in spite of the shameful tragi-comedy of Munich and everything which followed from it. 'Pas d'histoires.' Meanwhile Hitler was allowed to plan his next attacks as calmly and thoroughly as he liked. Within France itself, the 'Fifth Column', that admirably well-developed organ of Nazi espionage and propaganda, was able to carry out its sinister poisonous underground activities almost openly.

And now the Brown Reptile thought that the time was ripe. The War had come.

The émigré body in France was both able and willing to undertake work which could have been of value for the country's defence in all kinds of ways; in fact, they desired nothing more. All that would have been necessary was to bring that body together and use their resources in appropriate ways. But – as a good Frenchman, François Crucy,* put it to me at the time, with bitter irony – 'En France, on s'organise toujours après.' In France we always organise after the event.

What was the first thing that happened? A brief account of my personal experience may serve better than any general summary.

On 12th September, at ten in the evening, the doorbell of our apartment rang. I opened the door. Two burly individuals with berets entered. 'Police. You're under arrest.'

'Under arrest – why?'

'You'll see soon enough. Take a blanket, some linen and provisions for two days. But quick! Quick! We don't have any time.'

Quarter of an hour later I was standing on the street, in pitch darkness, holding my bundle and flanked by my two guardians. They took me to the police station in Rue Lecourbe.

The brigadier demanded to see my identity card. I had the audacity to enquire as to the grounds of my arrest.

The great man appeared initially to have been struck dumb by my cheek; but in the end he condescended to give an explanation. 'Why have you been arrested? You must take that up with Monsieur Hitler. You are an Austrian, a *ressortissant hitlérien* (a subject of Hitler). That's why you are being locked up. Is that clear enough for you?'

I attempted to protest, objecting that it was grotesque to hold Hitler's victims responsible for Hitler, instead of ...

This met a less than favourable reception. The brigadier thumped the table furiously with his fist and roared: 'Pas d'histoires! Germany shouldn't have declared war, that's all. Take him away!' And I was taken to a cell where I spent the rest of the night in the company of several pickpockets and burglars, who, I have to say, showed markedly more understanding of my situation than the brigadier.

At eight in the morning a minibus arrived; two policemen got in with me, and they took me to the Stade de Colombes, the assembly point for 'enemy aliens'. Here there was already a fight underway between refugees and genuine 'subjects of Hitler'. The latter had started singing the Horst Wessel* song, to which the former had responded with the Marseillaise. This was too much for the 'Comrades of the People' of Hitler (and of his pimp, Horst Wessel), who proceeded to attack the Jews. On this occasion, however, the Jews were able to defend themselves.

Only after this incident did the camp command take the trouble to separate the two categories of *ressortissants hit-lériens*, at least physically.

Around midday I was taken before a captain, who told me simply: 'You may go home.'

Only one who has experienced what it means to be imprisoned can say what it means to be free again. Blissfully – deliriously – happy, I leapt into a taxi (there were still a few in those days), so as to be home again as quickly as possible.

From my wife I learned that Benjamin Crémieux and Crucy had interceded for me 'with a higher authority'. This contact was the reason for my release: other 'enemy aliens' of my kind – Austrian and Czech refugees – still remained in captivity.

On the next day another man in a beret appeared at my door. All friendly smiles, this time; and the man presented me with an invitation to the Prefecture of Police. There a higher official revealed to me that it had been decided, on the grounds of my services to France, to allow me to remain at home indefinitely. A note to that effect was entered on my identity card, which the official handed back to me with the words: 'This is a very special favour that you are being accorded.' He even shook my hand as we parted.

I do not believe that any of my 'services to France' would have helped much, without contacts.

In view of my age and the state of my health, there was no question of active military service, though I had immediately enrolled myself in the 'Austrian Legion'.[4] Crucy and Crémieux

---

4. The reference is presumably to the 'Association pour la libération de l'Autriche' (of which Scheyer's membership card survives).

exerted themselves to have me employed by the propaganda department; and to that purpose an elegant file was deposited at the Hotel Continental, where they had their headquarters. I was assured that my valuable services would definitely be employed, at the appropriate moment. I would just have to be patient for a little.

And so I was patient – throughout the whole of the 'Drôle de Guerre'.

6

The 'Drôle de Guerre'

A GHOSTLY TRAGICOMEDY; a state of war whose lethargy (one is almost tempted to say, euphoria), hidden behind a façade of lying phrases and slogans, followed on perfectly from the prewar politics of 'Pas d'histoires'.

It was a state reminiscent of those deceptive periods of remission sometimes experienced by the terminally ill – periods in which the patient apparently feels well, is full of confidence, takes the doctor's assurances at face value, makes plans – in short, is totally unaware of his true condition. Until one day comes the final crisis, bringing in its wake a swift and inexorable death.

The very fact that this despicable phrase 'Drôle de Guerre' – phoney war – could be used at all was a shocking symptom of the dissolution that held sway between September 1939 and June 1940, in an atmosphere of carefree frivolity and gay *rodomontades*.

Well, yes, of course: we were at war. Somewhere or other there were the daily tears, the suffering, the death, the prayers wrung from the very heart. These would be the unavoidable side-effects of war. All very sad, of course.

But, given that one had to have a war, didn't this war – if you were very honest about it – have its good side, too? The 'artists of life', the *débrouillards*, were given their first real opportunity to display their talents; and, while others fell on the field of honour, these fellows at home asserted themselves ever more effectively in the field of business and profit. Wasn't the War a once-in-a-lifetime opportunity for countless individuals to walk away with honours, titles and profits? Every last soldier in this army of self-enrichment carried a marshall's baton in his knapsack.[5]

Sorrow, bloodshed, death. Yes – somewhere. A long way away. Back here, in Paris, the War was the inspiration for a thousand delightful, original, and at the same time patriotic, innovations – in *haute couture*; in the jewellery trade; in luxury goods in general. Identity tags, for example, like those worn by our brave men on the front so as to be identifiable in case of their death – but adapted for the ladies in Paris: in gold or platinum and studded with jewels. Or there were charming miniature sub-machine guns and tanks that hung from 'good-luck bracelets'; shoes which were based on uniform; evening outfits in matching combinations of blue, white and red; expensive 'Musette' handbags; distinctive leather cases for gas masks, etc., etc.

These Roxanes of the Drôle de Guerre would have needed a new Rostand, with a new *Cyrano de Bergerac*, to give them their full due.

The War also provided an excellent excuse for all kinds of galas, parties and functions, organised in the name of charity: they became practically a patriotic duty. And more than that: the War was a sort of admonition to pleasure, a sexual stimulus to seize the moment. The uncertainty of the morrow provided an atmosphere of romantic gloom in which certain

---

5. The reference is to a motto that Napoleon used of his army: 'every soldier carries a marshall's baton in his knapsack', signifying his encouragement of their individual sense of worth and potential for leadership.

inhibitions could be swept aside.

'Il faut se serrer les coudes' – we must stick close together – was the watchword. And so that is precisely what people did: stuck close together, at dinner- and supper-parties, in the cosy intimacy provided by windows veiled in accordance with the *défense passive*. Housewives who thought highly of themselves had even transformed the cellar space belonging to their apartments into tastefully decked-out *boudoirs abris*, underground 'cosy corners' where, in the case of an alert, you could enjoy all the appurtenances of drinks cabinet and cocktail shaker, ready to prepare the Drôle de Guerre cocktails. This *défense passive* certainly had its attractive side.

Theatres, too, revue bars and nightclubs – as well as those houses which offered the other, more secret pleasures – all did very well out of it. They did record business.

As for those who had opted for voluntary 'evacuation' right at the beginning of the War – those who had a chateau or a place in the country, or perhaps just accommodating relatives – well, for them the War was just a splendid opportunity to grant themselves an indefinite holiday.

And then there was that élite that could afford to stay in a luxury hotel by the sea or in the mountains for the duration. Cannes, Nice, Biarritz, Chamonix – all had an unprecedented season. The society world – as well as the demi-monde, and indeed the nouveau-riche underworld – had set up their headquarters in the various palaces, and communiqués from this army's front were published with appropriate respect in the daily newspapers. Those other warriors, on that other front, would have been able to follow to the last detail which individual was undergoing the *tourmente* on the Côte d'Azur, which on the Côte d'Argent, or in the Alps – each of them draining his cup of sorrow in draughts of champagne.

Because officially, of course, we were in the middle of the *tourmente* – we were in the thick of it. This was the constant theme, repeated daily in the newspapers with a thousand variations; confirmed by the radio; and shrilled by the orators of every party. And yet, at the same time, the propaganda was using every opportunity to inject the masses with the narcotic: 'Nous vaincrons, parce que nous sommes les plus forts.'

We shall win, because we are stronger. Because – this was the truth didactically expounded by every leading article, radio talk, military authority, by every possible type of expert – because we are, in a clear mathematical sense, superior to the enemy in every respect. Here – just look at this, please ... and they would proceed to a triumphant deployment of figures, calculations, demonstrations, statistics. It was not just deception by words – what one might call the metaphysical side of propaganda. No: here we had the lies of a pseudo-science; the whole apparatus of an apparently exact methodology of proof and falsifiability was brought into play. The rational *bourrage de crânes*[6] had become a kind of encyclopedic science, which had usurped all other branches of science and whose apparently objective method of reasoning reached its conclusion in the irrefutable logical proposition already mentioned: We shall win, because we are stronger.

Moreover, this certainty was given support by another circumstance. Although we were in the middle of the *tourmente* – the horrors of war – the communiqués almost every day ended with the comforting phrase 'rien de spécial à signaler'. Nothing special to report.

And, after all, what could happen to France, barricaded as she was by her impenetrable Maginot Line?

True, the soldiers on the front line might not have been too well equipped. There were all too frequent requests to families for blankets, linen and woollens. That was regrettable, the pundits admitted, but not of fundamental significance. In fact, it was rather encouraging that the men complained not only

---

6. The expression – literally 'skull stuffing' – means a kind of propaganda or brain-washing and apparently derives from the specific context of the French army in 1914, among whose ranks it was used in reference to the misleading information then being sent back from the Front.

of cold but also of boredom: the clearest proof, surely, that the Germans did not dare to attack the Maginot Line.

And so the weeks went by; and the weeks turned to months. The *tourmente* gradually became no more than a conventional, tired phrase. It was used rather in the way that one says 'terrible' when one hears of a stranger's misfortune, which, a few moments later, one has forgotten.

There was not much in the way of serious privations – although there were great sacrifices, it is true, in particular Parisian circles. There was the newspaper write-up, for example, by a very well-known female novelist, of a sensational première mounted with highly patriotic intentions in the Théâtre des Ambassadeurs; a write-up which she used to give a particularly stirring account of how, at the end of the performance, ladies dressed in the absolute latest chic suffered in silence the terrible provocation of having to wait in the middle of the street, in the pouring rain, for one of Paris' ever rarer taxis; or even that of taking the metro or the bus like any plebeian.

The *tourmente* – the 'storm' – was now hardly distinguishable from a state of total calm. There were always, of course, the messengers of doom: those who were not comfortable with this 'peace within war'; those who were uneasy about the brooding calm of the Nazi Monster. These were dismissed as defeatists. They were tedious troublemakers, disrupting the peace of the Drôle de Guerre. Here, too, the watchword was: 'pas d'histoires!'

The enslavement of those countries already occupied by the Germans, the atrocities committed by their troops at every brutal step; these gave rise to retaliation – at most – in the press and on the radio, in the form of patriotic expressions of indignation. But behind these official statements, the attitude was one of somnolence. This is how one of the few voices in the wilderness put it to me in that period (in tones of bitter resignation): 'How would you expect us to be bothered about the fate of others? If the enemy march through the Porte Maillot in Paris tomorrow, then people at the Porte de Versailles will still say: "How does that affect us? Thank God, it's still a long way from the Porte Maillot to the Porte de Versailles."'

The tormenting question 'What are Hitler's intentions?' had achieved the status of a challenging brainteaser, which virtuoso players delighted in solving afresh each day – the solution being always one of universal comfort and consolation. Whatever the variations, the basic result was, naturally, always the same: 'Nothing can happen to us. To others, maybe. But not to *us*.'

And so it went on until, in May 1940, the true situation could no longer be concealed from the country; and the idyll of the Drôle de Guerre came to a sudden and terrible end.

It is not necessary for me to go over the actual events. One by one, like the messengers in the Book of Job, came the series of blows which were to lead to the end – an end which was all the more dreadful after the false security of that 'rien à signaler'.

The myth of the impermeability of the Maginot Line: collapsed like a house of cards. Belgian refugees who had managed to make their way to Paris, with terrible stories to tell. (Their appearance alone told volumes.) And the Germans over the border – in France.

Step by step, step by step they advanced. They advanced with mechanical consistency. The rousing extract from the Marseillaise which was used by French radio to punctuate its broadcasts began to sound like a ghastly parody.

The people of Paris, usually so open and voluble, had become suddenly taciturn and reserved. It was as if everyone was afraid to express his thoughts aloud. Life went on – as the saying is – and on the surface nothing had changed. But already everything had a death-mark inscribed upon it: *so far* nothing had changed. But for how much longer?

'But' – this was the line from the official organs of mendacity – 'all is not yet lost.' The most brilliant army in the world had not yet engaged in the decisive battle. Generals such as Weygand* still spoke of the 'last quarter of an hour', which would be decisive; of salvation, of victory in that last quarter of an hour. Let one just think of France's situation in the corresponding phase of the First World War: it was far, far more critical. And what had happened then? The miracle of the Marne.

On every such occasion, since Joan of Arc, France had been granted a miracle in her hour of need. It followed – according to the logic of the exponents of this theory – that a miracle could not possibly fail to occur on this occasion too. And the more desperate the situation, the greater the certainty with which this coming miracle was to be relied upon in the strategic analysis. Eventually this miracle actually lost its miraculous character altogether, as the unknowable acquired the status of an infallible secret weapon, manufactured in some kind of metaphysical munitions factory, whose overwhelming superiority would, at the very last moment, magically transform disaster into a Great Victory.

But a miracle would not be a miracle if it always arrived on time. And on this occasion it was not going to be pressed. It refused to do its business. Meanwhile, the disaster ran its course – sped up, indeed, to a manic pace by the encouragement and collaboration of the traitors, great and small, who had, in spite of all warnings and entreaties on the part of isolated patriots, been left in peace until it was too late.

Which is why refugees were then put behind bars.

The full extent of the internal contribution to the débâcle of France will perhaps never be known; of all the underground acts of treachery which helped to deliver the noble land into the hands of the German cutthroats.

One of the most shattering side effects of the débâcle was the Exodus.

7

Paris, ghost of an enchanted city

You SHOULD NOT IMAGINE that the Exodus – that dreadful convulsion of massed humanity in flight – was an event which began at one particular moment. It started almost imperceptibly, then gathered momentum day by day, hour by hour, before finally breaking into a chaos of frenzied activity, which was suddenly interrupted by the arrival of the Germans in Paris.

But even in the very last days before their arrival, this furious panic of the Exodus was only visible in those streets which led, directly or indirectly, to the gateways of the city. In the areas of the city set back from those major arteries, the phenomenon manifested itself in a picture so contrasting with that panic that it seemed like a hallucination. You felt like rubbing your eyes.

A different, abnormal, unfamiliar Paris was before you. An incomprehensible Paris, even. A city wearing a relaxed, dreamy expression in the delightful June sun. The buildings, with their shops closed and their blinds down, seemed to be enjoying a lazy nap. An air of pleasant lethargy hung about the streets, the parks, the squares. In front of the door to an apartment block sat the concierge, blinking at the children who were playing in the middle of the road, undisturbed by vehicles. On the pavement you would occasionally see an isolated passer-by. Paris – Paris the mercurial, Paris overflowing with life, packed with energy and activity – now stretched itself out and lay down, giving itself up to the sweet delight of doing nothing. Walking down these streets, you felt you were in an enchanted city.

But it did not take long before your consciousness of the merciless reality returned. The spell was broken; a shiver went down the spine, even in the heat of the June day.

The enchanted peace was actually just Fear taking a breath.

The quiet was more intense than the most piercing yell; the stillness more painful than a scream of despair. It was a kind of desolation that reminded you of a room from which the body of a loved one has just been taken out. Everything is still in its place; nothing has been moved; the clock on the wall ticks on, the same as before; and yet the whole room is filled with a suffocating emptiness. Though there is no visible sign of it, death pervades the room completely.

Paris in the last days before the Germans: a pale ghost on the brightest of days, in the midsummer sun. It seemed shocking that the sun *was* still shining … the flowers still blooming … the birds still singing. This peace was more like a paralysis, creeping slowly, unstoppably over the body, freezing the blood, numbing the limbs, one by one.

Just peep round the corner and – one street further on – the illusion, this phantasm of an enchanted city, dissolves into the mad frenzy of the Exodus.

And, curiously enough, the experience of this violent contrast feels like waking up out of a nightmare. The chaos of vehicles and pedestrians is more bearable than that still, silent brooding. A raging torrent of suffering – but life, at least, in some form. The desperation was at least accompanied by a desperate response; and flight after all involves the notion of refuge. And fear, that of hope.

Whereas back there, back in the lonely, abandoned city – all you could do there was wait. Wait helplessly, powerlessly, for some monstrous, inescapable fate.

8

Paths of the Exodus

ON 12TH JUNE 1940, at six in the morning, we left our apartment with a few bags and packages, containing only the most basic necessities, and put ourselves in the hands of a friend, Mr C., who had access to a car and had offered to take us as far as Poitiers. From there we would do our best to reach Albi: there we had a friend, Kofler, who had already left Paris, at the end of May.

As we walked out of the block we were greeted by a striking sight. All around us were people looking up at the sky, seeking the explanation of a strange phenomenon.

The sun was already high in the sky. But its glow was dull and murky, like that of a funeral lantern which has been veiled in black crepe. Everything seemed to have been enveloped in a haze of smoke.

My wife looked at me, puzzled, and said: 'What have you done to your face? You've gone black!' And at the same moment I realised that her face, and Sláva's, were completely covered in small black dots. I drew my finger along my cheek: it, too, became black from the soot.

A passing soldier gave us the answer to the riddle. The Germans – already quite near Paris now – had engineered this artificial darkening of the city. Not so much for strategic reasons as to unnerve the people.

We carried on. Our amazement had given way to a kind of vagabond's indifference and fatalism. We no longer had a roof over our heads; we carried our belongings with us. We had already become a tiny particle of that vast, anonymous mass whose fate was known as the 'Exodus'. Whether our faces were clean or not had ceased to be important.

The next problem was to get into the metro: to succeed in pushing oneself forward for long enough to be pressed into a carriage by the mass of the people behind one. Our new life began with dirty faces and several torn-off buttons.

When I look back on the first stages of our Exodus, all I see is a confused series of pictures, like takes from a film which seem to have been shot in the wrong order, to be put in sequence later on.

First of all, there are roads leading out of Paris. Roads in the suburbs; roads dotted with grand houses; country roads; village roads; tracks between fields. Yet all these roads now had only one, identical, distorted face: the face of flight.

A grotesque mish-mash of vehicles: luxury limousines alongside lorries; sports cars alongside farmers' carts; removal vans, mail vans, caravans, three-wheelers, motorbikes – everything from the giant to the miniature. And all of them teeming with people using every possible available seat, standing place or indeed crouching place; all of them crammed full and piled high with the items that each person considered the most vital – from beds and ovens to chicken cages and dollhouses. Every vehicle was driven by individuals who seemed eager to set off at the greatest speed, as if in a race. The intensity of their facial expressions contrasted absurdly with the snail's pace at which the endless caravan, cluttered with bicycles and foot passengers, actually proceeded, metre by metre, constantly stopping and then stumbling on again. Those on foot actually made the quickest progress, even though they had to carry all their baggage with them. Some of them had piled their belongings on to any wheeled contraption they could lay their hands on: toy vehicles, dolls' prams, even scooters.

With the idea that it might somehow expedite our progress, we sometimes left the *route nationale* and went by minor roads. The result was that in the first two days we had managed to put a total of forty kilometres between ourselves and Paris.

Before my eyes I can still see people collapsing with exhaustion. A woman – a mother – whose knees suddenly gave way. But who still had the strength to raise the sleeping child in her arms aloft, so as not to wake it.

I can see a blanket, too, laid out in a meadow by the roadside – a brand new, white blanket. Beneath it, though, could be seen the contours of a body. A foot stuck out. It was the first death. For this man, the Exodus was over.

Early on the morning of the fourth day we stopped on the road going alongside the Loire, directly opposite Blois. It was impossible to go any further. An innumerable mass of people, sticking closely together, waiting for this particular knot to be somehow loosened; during the night there had been heavy rain.

Suddenly a number of black dots appeared high above us, and at the same time we heard a shrill whistling sound – up and down, up and down. Aeroplanes. They came lower and lower, the whistling reached a spectacular, ear-splitting level. Someone close to us shouted: 'On the ground!'

By this point the heroes of the Luftwaffe had come so close that the insignia on the aircraft could be clearly distinguished. We all threw ourselves down, some of us in the mud of the road, some on the embankment. Then: two explosions, and the rattle of machine-gun fire.

And suddenly everything was quiet again – so quiet that you could hear the distant song of a lark. We got up. The air was thick with the smell of fire and gunpowder. On the other side of the river, in Blois, great flames shot up to the sky.

The great mass of people began to set itself in motion. But after one great heave everything came to a standstill again. A few hundred metres away, a bomb had produced a crater. The machine guns had done their work, too: I cannot say how many dead, lacerated bodies lay around us – men, women and children. I do know that among the thousands on that particular road – playing out just one in the countless series of episodes of the Exodus – there was not one single combatant. Goering's noble warriors had quite calmly and deliberately carried out a massacre of unarmed refugees. And, just to add a little spice to their pleasure, these happy murderers had attached special sirens to their planes, which had produced that ghastly whistling sound, so like a mocking laugh.

A few hours later we were subjected to a second bombardment, at Tours. This time we were able to get to a cellar. A third bombardment found us again on the open road. On that occasion some Italians joined in the fun. The bizarre range of vehicles which we had encountered on the road so far might have seemed pretty well exhaustive; but in Meung-sur-Loire we came across something new. A beautiful hearse, fitted out with little black columns, ropes, wreaths and a grieving angel – the type of vehicle used for the highest-class funerals in Paris.

Taking the place of the corpse on this occasion were: a family of six, a fox terrier (yapping away happily), three hens and two rabbits.

What lay beneath the closed lid of the coffin, on the other hand, I never did find out.

In Cléry we had our first encounter with troops. The army, we gathered, had been mustered here to defend the Loire line. The small market town was overflowing with soldiers – soldiers, soldiers everywhere. The odd sergeant or cadet – perhaps even a lieutenant. But above that rank, not an officer in sight. Where were they?

In the main street of the town a very smartly dressed old man suddenly came up to me. He raised his hat politely and, rather in the manner of a local who wishes to show a foreigner the chief attractions of his home town, asked me: 'Monsieur, would you like to see an army in the process of dissolution?'

I was a little taken aback; but as I looked at him, the man took a step back and, as though he was being crucified, stretched his arms out to either side in a devastating gesture of desperation. 'Voilà.' He then greeted me again, very politely, and went on his way.

Exactly eight days after we had left Paris, we arrived finally at Poitiers. Mr C., who had taken us with him in his car, left us at this point. Our intention was to continue, via Bordeaux, to Albi.

The railway station was closed; but a rumour was going round that a train might leave at five the next morning for Bordeaux. Since Paris we had spent every night – six of us together – in a small car. A bed would have represented the pinnacle of our desires. But at Poitiers any such thought was ridiculous. We spent the night in the square in front of the station, which was finally opened at four. At five an air raid took place while we were actually on board the horribly overcrowded train. It left an hour later.

The normal journey time was six hours: it took us thirty-six. We ran out of food and drink, and there was none to be had in the stations. Whenever the train stopped at some point in the open country, everyone ran like crazy to see if they could beg anything at the nearest farm. Most of the farmers took a great deal of persuasion to part with anything, at enormously inflated prices. I remember one who charged ten francs to fill a water bottle.

Finally we reached Bordeaux. It was scorching. On the walls were posters advertising a concert by the tenor Thil.* Music – human beings – concerts … did all that still exist?

We were too exhausted to proceed. But where could we find a roof for the night? Eventually we were directed to the Centre d'Accueil, in Quai de la Patugade. This 'Centre' consisted of a few hundred straw beds in a warehouse. We were given a bowl of soup and a piece of bread, before sinking into the straw.

Four o'clock the next morning: alarm bells, explosions, an air raid. One hour later we are on the road again. Back to the station, which is now surrounded by a huge throng of people.

Two hours to fight our way into the ticket hall. A train to Toulouse? There might be one … or there might not be one. Finally (at about four in the afternoon) an empty train comes in. Uproar. Chaos. Our chief concern at this point is not to become separated from each other. We are lucky: a sudden surge pushes the three of us into the luggage van. It is nearly evening when the train finally moves. But for Bayonne, not Toulouse.

Toulouse, Bayonne – what does it matter. As long as we are free of the Germans. And as long as we get to somewhere where we don't immediately have to move on again. The possibility of a wash, maybe … even a change of shirt …

Late that evening we were taken off the train at Dax and brought in buses to the refugee camp of Basta-les-Forges, about ten kilometres away. Our dream seemed to have come true: we could stay here. The camp consisted of huts, each of them accommodating about sixty people. There were mattresses and bedclothes. There was running water. And a separate hut for meals. Not to mention covered toilet facilities with separate cubicles.

We were almost happy.

9

'Armistice'

WE WERE ALMOST HAPPY. A retired Belgian general shared our hut with us, along with his wife and daughter. This man had assured us – in a tone of authority which would not admit of the slightest doubt – that, even in the very worst case, the Germans would never be able to reach this point, almost on the border with Spain.[7]

The physical location of the camp, moreover, hidden between the spreading pine forests, gave us the sense of having said goodbye to that world. And then that lovely breeze, redolent at once of the Harz mountains and the ocean; and the calming effect of that peaceful landscape. And, of course, the knowledge that we had a roof over our head and two hot meals a day. We began to breathe again. Perhaps fate would be kind enough to forget about us, here in this secluded corner. At least for a while.

---

7. France was divided at the Armistice of 1940. Parts of the Rhineland on the border were now annexed to the Third Reich, while the main division was between the part under direct German Occupation and the so-called 'zone libre' or Unoccupied Zone, administered by the 'Vichy' régime under Pétain, although in collaboration with the German authorities. While the Occupied Zone (which constituted about three-fifths of the country) was mainly the northern part, on the western side it extended south almost as far as Spain (see map on page v); and thus the natural expectation of fugitives who had come as far as this, that they would not find themselves under direct German Occupation, was frustrated.

One day one of our comrades in the hut – an old Parisian metal-worker – went for walk to the village of Buglose, roughly three kilometres away. On his return, we learned that France had abandoned any further resistance and that Marshall Pétain* had signed the Armistice.

The old working man delivered the news in the manner of someone who knows he has a sensational piece of news, and wants to communicate that; he did not appear to think that it was of great importance to him personally. He ended his report with the words: 'At least the War is over, as far as we are concerned.' He then moved on to a different subject: his discovery, in Buglose, of an inn where one could get really first-rate bacon.

The next day, we had to put an end to our isolation: we went to Buglose ourselves.

The news – the catastrophic news – was true. That became evident to us before we even exchanged words with anyone. In the main street of the village a group of youths had gathered, who were shouting and gesticulating in excitement. Were these young people protesting at France's capitulation? Were they giving vent to their horror at the appalling fate of their native land? Of course not. There was something quite different at stake. On that day, as a sign of national mourning, the government had declared the closure of all inns and restaurants and a strict alcohol ban. These French youths were up in arms for one reason only: that they had to go one day without their apéritif.

The fact that France had fallen into Hitler's lap, like an over-ripe fruit, after a few short weeks, was a terrible disaster. But this reaction which we saw on the part of young people in the main street of Buglose brought certain truths home to us ... We hurried back to Basta.

What was to become of us?

A representative of the subPrefecture in Dax came to inspect our camp. He was in an excellent mood, and told us that the

Germans would never take possession of Dax, even though we were on the wrong side of the Demarcation Line. Then he went on for a short stroll with the general's wife.

I waited for the man, and requested a few words with him before he got back into his car. I then explained to him the special nature of our situation: we were in fact the only foreign refugees in the camp; all the others were simply people who had left Paris in the Exodus. For us three, falling into German hands would mean the greatest danger. I appealed to the fellow's humanity, and begged him to help us get a car to take us to the *zone libre*.

The officer placed his hand on my shoulder in a gesture of well-meaning condescension. 'I've already told you all,' he said, 'that the Germans want nothing here. We have our official sources. But quite apart from that, as an émigré, as a political refugee you would have nothing to fear. Don't forget that you are under France's protection.'

'But it is reported that Marshall Pétain ...'

The officer interrupted me indignantly.

'Marshall Pétain would never – no *Maréchal de France* would ever – allow the slightest infringement of the right of asylum.'

And with that he drove off.

That night it rained buckets. Around 1 a.m. I heard the sound of a car. The general's wife rose immediately and ran out of the dormitory on tiptoes. About ten minutes later she returned. Noticing that the three of us were awake, she went up to my wife.

'Swear,' she whispered secretly, 'not to say a single word of what I am about to tell you to anyone.'

'For God's sake, what has happened?'

'Do you swear? Good. Well – I have just been informed that the Germans will be here in a matter of hours. Panic must be avoided at all costs. We must receive them as politely as possible, then they will not harm us. Now – pretend to be asleep, otherwise the whole hut will know.'

Another night that we shall never forget.

At last – at last – it was day. The Germans had not come. Everything in the camp carried on as normal. Even the general's wife behaved just as before: she seemed to have forgotten the whole night-time episode. The only thing out of the ordinary was that she complained of a bad headache.

Usually we took our meals together. On this occasion the general's wife said that she was still suffering, and preferred to remain in the hut. The general and his daughter insisted on keeping the invalid company. We thought nothing of this, for although the general was an impressive fellow with a white, military moustache, it was definitely the wife who was in charge.

When we returned from our half-hour's lunch-break, however, lo and behold: all three of them had vanished without trace. A van sent by the officer had come by while we were out and discreetly picked them up. We, on the other hand – well, we were under the protection of France. We would have to rely on Marshall Pétain.

A few days later the camp of Basta-les-Forges was dissolved and its inmates split up between various places in the neighbourhood. We were taken to Thétieu, a village about eight kilometres from Dax, where we were put up in a school classroom. We were, however, also given the option of finding ourselves a place to rent in the village. In the end we took a room with a fine woman, Madame Darricau, who lived on her own, and who also allowed us to share use of her kitchen. The problem of our impermanent existence seemed to have been solved for the moment.

But the Germans were already in Dax. And, almost immediately, a number of them moved into Thétieu, too. The Swastika had caught up with us. That cursed symbol, those uniforms, those faces. For us, seeing them again was like a sudden relapse in the course of a serious illness.

And so, once again – as in Vienna – the sense that one was defenceless, that one was exposed to any outrage. Once more the helpless waiting, in a ghastly uncertainty – but at the same time also certainty – for the moment when, in spite of emigration and Exodus, the Monster would once again stretch out his claws towards us. This awareness flowed in our blood like a poison, at once paralysing us and driving us into a fever of unrest. Wherever you went, wherever you stood, whether you hid in your room or sought distraction in the forest, you were still banging your head against the bars.

For people in the neighbourhood generally things had hardly changed. For the time being, the 'Occupation' did not make much difference to them in their normal activities; they began to regard it, too, as normal.

A few people preserved their dignity to the extent of keeping apart from the Germans – of ignoring them. Most were concerned to get on good terms with them, and above all to do business with them. Thétieu is only a small village of about 300 inhabitants; it is nonetheless a characteristic example.

There was in the village a female butcher, Madame Irène, who had no time for the Germans. Not only did they not buy from her, but her husband had been captured and was a prisoner of war. There was also, in the same village – just opposite our house – a publican, Madame Rose, an enormously energetic woman, and to most people an absolute dragon. At the mere sight of a German uniform, however, she was transformed into the sweetest hostess imaginable. One day the two got into an argument. I could hear the words of the publican, as she shouted threateningly at the other: 'You should watch out, and you should shut up. And if you want to know – yes, I like the Germans. *Ces messieurs* are proper gentlemen. And they pay me thirty francs for a bottle of Mousseux; your husband never even paid me ten.'

Every afternoon at Madame Rose's a number of the villagers would gather around one German soldier who spoke very good French. He would sit with them on the terrace, offer them all an apéritif, and lecture them, in a booming voice, on the blessings of the Third Reich. In Germany there was no poverty, no distinction of class, and above all the Führer had got rid of the Jews, just as the Jews must be got rid of everywhere. Because the Jews ... the Jews were to blame for everything, to blame for the fact that France had forced war upon the peace-loving Germans. France was the victim of the Jews, etc., etc. ... The good fellows listened to him with open mouths.

At the same time, in the press and on the radio, there began a spiteful, poisonous anti-Semitic propaganda campaign. And at the same time, too – in Thétieu itself, at the town hall – a large poster was displayed. In Bordeaux, it alleged, 'the Polish Jew Mendel Langer' had raised his stick as a military band went by. He had been sentenced to death for 'threatening the German army' and executed.

One day, at the beginning of September, the mayor of Thétieu, Monsieur Laborde, issued a request for me to come and see him at the town hall. I did not have a good feeling about it.

The mayor showed me a piece of paper he had received from military headquarters at Mont-de-Marsan. It contained the following question: of what nationality are the refugees ... ? (and here followed our names). And then, underlined in red: Aryan or non-Aryan? 'What does that mean, Aryan?' asked the good Monsieur Laborde.

We realised that we could remain in Thétieu no longer. We must get out as soon as possible. But ... where to?

We finally decided to return to Paris. If we were already caught in the net – if all that we could do was wait for events to take their course – then at least we could do that in our own home.

Escape, Exodus – all for nothing. They had caught up with us. They had us.

10

Paris under the German boot

PARIS IN THE LAST DAYS before the Exodus had been the fantasy image of a bewitched city – and at the same time a Brueghel picture of hell. The Paris that I returned to in September 1940 was an inexpressibly sad, ghostly travesty.

What had happened to the city's magnificence, the grandiose pride of her traditions? Her vitality, her effervescent spirit, her love of life? A trace of it was discernible here and there; rather like a smear of make-up left on a neglected face, it only served to make the present state of dilapidation all the more shocking.

I thought back to Vienna. Here, as there, the imprint of the German boot had altered the city fundamentally. Here, too, the city's physiognomy had been trampled overnight. The external contours remained; but a kind of bleak desolation seemed to ooze from every pore. The city had let itself go, just like a person who has been humiliated or degraded.

The only cars on the streets were those of the occupying power. A few cyclists; remarkably few pedestrians. The crowds of people that used to throng the pavements of Paris, like actors on a particularly bright and ever-changing stage, had shrunk to a thin line of individuals hurrying on their way, each seeming only concerned to get back home as quickly as possible.

There were, however – even at that time – endless queues in front of any shop that sold food. People queued for hours, often without even knowing what was actually available in the shop. Just as long as it was something edible. For 'ces messieurs', of course, there was no queueing: they just walked in, ordered, and had to be served immediately.

Crude wooden posts sprung up everywhere with a veritable forest of branches indicating the direction of this or that office, service or institution, all written in that barbaric abbreviated German which was such a speciality of Nazi culture. The Swastika was everywhere. They had stamped it on the very face of Paris, positioning it in all the most sensitive places – anywhere, in fact, where there was anything which might put one in mind of the great past of the city, of the glory of France.

And then, of course, the Germans themselves. They were everywhere – absolutely everywhere. These ape-like creatures – these Teutonic monsters, with their bulging necks and mammoth bottoms; they were constantly in your head, the sound of their boots the new theme tune of Parisian life. You could hear them, feel them – you actually seemed to detect their scent even when they were not actually in front of your eyes.

And what of these 'victors'? Their attitude towards the 'negroid' French[8] smacked rather of that of certain white colonialists towards the natives. They were the all-powerful planters. Even if, occasionally, they tried to be companionable.

There were daily displays of their military might, too, especially in the centre of the city and in the Champs-Élysées. The squadrons sang as they marched. Then, suddenly, a bellowed command, at which the mechanism of the goosestep would be instantaneously activated. And with every goosestep, it seemed

---

8. In *Mein Kampf* Hitler had described France as becoming increasingly 'negroid', on the grounds of supposed racial contamination from people from its African colonies.

as if the Master Race wanted to give even the air a kicking. The French, however – who never lose their sense of the ridiculous – found these barbaric, robotic manifestations of lifeless German obedience comical rather than frightening.

It was in this Paris, then, that the Master Race took its pleasure. They saw it as a brothel, whose fabled debauchery they had often secretly dreamed of, but could now actually enjoy to their hearts' content. Back home, among his 'Comrades of the People', the German man had to produce a statistically precise return from his marriage, in accordance with figures laid down by Hitler. Here, on the other hand – well! – here he could let his hair down. And not just in secret, not in some disreputable dive, having to look over his shoulder to check if he was being watched. Quite the contrary: here the Noble German could throw himself into every pleasure of Parisian vice, grunting contentedly and without the slightest qualm, exactly as the Führer had promised him. Hitler had, indeed, himself made it clear that he wished to make Paris the brothel of the Third Reich, the mire in which his men would wallow in the pursuit of 'power-through-pleasure'.

And all for next to nothing: the exchange rate imposed was twenty francs to one mark. It was practically a gift.

Ces messieurs were thus able to conduct a total *Blitzkrieg* against all the city's supplies, too. Warehouses, small or large, were soon emptied. Ordinary soldiers were to be seen making off with dozens of pairs of silk stockings, incredible numbers of luxury shoes, silk wares, perfumes, etc. There were soon no more of these items to be had.

Only in the realm of nightclubs and places of resort – in short, in every branch, offshoot and ramification of the sex industry – was there an unmitigated boom. Here there was no shortage of raw materials or manpower; here the stocks could be perpetually replenished. The Drôle de Guerre had already brought great prosperity to this industry – a prosperity which, however, bore absolutely no comparison with that visited on it by the mass consumption of the Germans, with their famous moral purity.

Even as they piled up their booty, *ces messieurs* concerned themselves at the same time with the organisation of the black market. In this realm, too, their cynicism was surpassed only by their hypocrisy.

In all official statements of the press and the radio, you had the whole lying rhetoric – translated verbatim from the Nazi phraseology – against the plague of black marketeering. Yet it was common knowledge that all major branches of the *marché noir* were controlled by the Germans. Already the undisputed masters of legalised robbery, they now built up the black market, too, to the level of a well-organised business yielding fantastic profits to everyone from the general right down to the humblest pen-pusher.

I had an acquaintance at the time who, as director of a publishing house, had frequent contact with Germans. Every time I met him he had a story of yet another officer who had offered him cigarettes, sugar, coffee or chocolate in enormous quantities. And at a comparatively reasonable price.

'Yes,' he mused fondly on one occasion, 'anyone who had just a little capital, right now – just a few thousand francs ...' But he immediately added, with an expression of outrage fuelled by the full patriotic force of his lack of capital: 'Autorités occupantes? Autorités trafiquantes!' Occupying authorities? Racketeering authorities!

11

The French ...
and the French

WHAT WAS THE PARISIAN REACTION to the Occupation at this time?

There were many who felt the deepest pain and sorrow over this whole episode of the humiliation of the Fatherland; who did not simply accept the *défaite* as a fact of life; and who, even at this stage, pinned their hopes on de Gaulle* as on the coming Messiah. There were many who reacted to the travesty of Occupied Paris by keeping themselves to themselves and avoiding contact with the Germans as much as possible.

There were many whose high principles even led them to serious material sacrifice: poor clerks or workers who turned down well-paid positions in businesses that were working for the Germans. Civil servants who quit their jobs, because they did not want to continue their service in offices which were now under German command.

There was, too, that select band of individuals who, right from the beginning, sought other ways and means to turn their abhorrence and their anger into action. Open conflict would at that time have been pointless; it would have been an act of senseless folly. They therefore took up arms – tenaciously, fearlessly – in the hardest battle of all, that waged underground and in secret.

These were the people who formed the initial core of the movement which would gradually develop into the secret army – and, later, the open army – of the Resistance. They were the heroes who founded the civilian and military 'Maquis'.

But in those days ... in those days each and every one of them had to be entirely self-reliant; to guess who his comrades were. They had to recognise and 'contact' each other; to feel their way forward in the dark with the greatest possible caution, to find their path; to work together; to organise. Steadfast in the face of mortal danger; watched over with suspicion; surrounded by spies, traitors and *agents provocateurs*.

Such were the circumstances in which these great, yet unsung, heroes had first to learn the basic techniques of that form of active and passive resistance known as sabotage. In this process they often had to improvise with lightning speed, whether it was a case of doing something that put a spanner in the works of the German terror machine, or of failing to do something that that machine demanded.

Nor was it long before the first of them would fall. The execution squads went about their bloodthirsty business, and massacred 'guilty' and innocent alike. For the great German civilisation had reserved to itself the right to employ that gruesome measure of repression known as 'otages' – hostages. The murder of hostages would, indeed, merit its own chapter in the Bible of Bestiality that constitutes the 'Heil-Hitler' Doctrine of Salvation.

Soon the first of an endless series of red posters would appear on the walls, informing the people, in both the German and the French language, which individuals had been executed on the order of the then 'Military Commander in France', General Schaumburg.* The name was followed by age and nationality. If the victim happened to be a Jew, this most serious of all crimes did not, of course, go unmentioned.

They were like veritable lakes of blood, these lists of the murdered. Twenty or thirty, on a good day; but then it might be fifty, seventy, even a hundred. No age group was excluded. General Schaumburg,* and after him his successor, Stülpnagel,* were sticklers for symmetry. If you had a boy of seventeen you should also have an old man of seventy. And how very neatly the general signed his lists, delivered his death sentences.

These death sentences, though, were actually the last stage of a path that started with imprisonment; from there led in most cases to the torture chamber; and only after that brought one to the place of execution. One speaks simply of 'execution', but the German delight in persecution was such that it had perfected the technique of drawing out a human being's final agony to the utmost degree.

At Vincennes, on Mont Valérien, and in the Bois de Boulogne, the execution squads carried out their task with machine guns. This meant that only those particularly blessed by good fortune received an injury that resulted in immediate death. Others lay with, for example, stomach or lung injuries, often for as long as thirty-six hours before their suffering was over; before yet another life was turned into a line of print on a red poster.

Among those who died in this way was an acquaintance of mine – married with two small children, Jewish. He had failed to comply with the order compelling Jews to hand in their radios; had been arrested following a denunciation, and sentenced to three months in prison. On the day preceding his scheduled release, he was taken out and shot as a hostage.

I have spoken of those French who wished to stand out against the defeat. On the other side of the coin there were others ... people who reacted to the disaster in quite different ways.

To begin with there were the Indifferent: that amorphous mass of humanity that, in their heart of hearts, were just glad to have the whole thing behind them (as they thought). Their response to the *défaite* was that of the conventional mourner, who attends a funeral with sad demeanour, but leaves with a sense of inner relief. What cannot be changed has to be accepted; so the most sensible thing is not to waste any more time thinking about it.

Ces messieurs were in charge, after all. Their job was to command, and everyone else's job was to obey.

The next level of response was that of the Sympathisers. Without openly confessing allegiance to the Germans, this group would express the opinion that the Nazi methods had their positive side, too. There was no point skulking in a corner; rather, one should observe the Germans, and learn from them.

Besides, there was a danger that the Germans might end up with a very distorted picture of France. It was actually one's patriotic duty to maintain contact with them and show them the better side of France – to entertain them properly.

These Sympathisers did not go so far as to preach open collaboration. They did not actually lick the Nazi boot; they merely polished it clean. Without being out-and-out idolisers of Hitler, they had to admit that the Nazi Overlord was someone you could do business with, and very good business at that. They were happy not to ask too many questions about where the money that they pocketed came from. And if a tiny scruple did ever penetrate the consciousness of such a Sympathiser, he was ready with one irrefutable argument which silenced any such qualm: 'If *I* don't put my hand in, there are thousands of others out there, just waiting to do exactly that. So I *will* put my hand in.'

Nor did these Sympathisers fawn over the misdeeds of the Germans with the same frenzied servility as the Collaborators; their attitude was rather one of feigned ignorance. They saw nothing; heard nothing; talked with great interest about something else altogether. On the Day of Judgement, these fellows would be sure to have an alibi.

And then there was the third level: that of the Collaborators.

The fact that France had suffered a terrible defeat was a catastrophe, certainly, but no cause for shame; it was a humiliation, but not in itself a dreadful *self*-humiliation. The fact, too, that a large proportion of the people bent under the Nazi yoke was understandable. Even the fact that so many sought to make an accommodation with the Germans, and carried out every order without comment, was in a sense also understandable. When you come to the feeding trough, you don't find many heroes. What happened, however, under the general heading of 'Collaboration' – the degree of spiritual prostitution, treachery, worm-like crawling, and sheer abject debasement – was beyond all imagining; it is, indeed, a blot of shame far worse than any *défaite*.

At every level there were the lackeys; the fellow travellers, fellow-spivs and -thugs of the Master Race of Criminals; at every level the traffickers in the black market of malice; at every level the supporters of the *Révolution nationale*[9] (which was in reality the *Prostitution nationale*); at every level individuals who were prepared to sell themselves. And there was no depth to which these individuals would not stoop; nothing that they were not prepared to do, in every area of public and private life, in every ramification of the national, social – the National-Socialist – hierarchy.

Not least 'Le Maréchal', the venerable Philippe Pétain, the illustrious hero of Verdun, who not only accepted – but also signed his name to – every one of the Germans' lies and deceptions, every one of their outrages; who, having sent Pierre Laval* away in disgrace as if he were some pickpocket who had been caught in the act, at Hitler's command immediately clasped him to his breast again and assured him of his absolute confidence. And all this simply so as to be able to play, and carry on playing, the pitiable puppet role of 'Chef d'État' in the gilded cage of Vichy.

---

9. *Révolution nationale* – propaganda term employed by Pierre Laval to suggest that it was an opportunity for a sort of 'back-to-basics' moral rejuvenation.

And not least this same Pierre Laval, though in his case one would have expected nothing else. This was a man who had in fact remained faithful to one thing only: his vile reputation. Politics to him had always been a kind of playing of the market, whereby he exploited régimes for the benefit of his shady business deals and vice versa. His political convictions had always been based on the dividends that they might yield him; and one has to admit that he understood his market perfectly. A 'son of the people', Pierre Laval had become one of the richest men in France. In fact, if anyone could have afforded himself the luxury of one moment of moral decency, it would have been Pierre Laval; but of course a leopard cannot get rid of its spots. He offered himself to the Germans, and the Germans took him.

Laval's speciality had always been that of playing a double game, of serving two sides at once; and this characteristic, which had made people so suspicious of him in the past, might have given them some hope, after the *défaite* - the feeling being that he would support their interests as it were behind the scenes, in opposition to those of the Occupying Power. The Germans exploited this to their advantage: with every new broken promise, with every fresh violation they appeared nonetheless to be extending to the French people this vague hope: 'True, Laval has had to give in again this time; but patience! He is a crafty rogue – a clever customer who at the end of the game will turn the tables on the Germans.'

In this particular case, though, Laval's calculations had failed him. Because at a certain point the Germans went too far for even the most gullible 'man in the street' to be able to give the slightest credence to Laval's emollient assurances. For their part, too, the Germans knew the man too well to let him out of their sight. It became impossible for him to move over to the other camp. He was caught on the rod, whether he liked it or not, just as if he had been one of those idiots he despised so – the ones who actually have a political conviction.

And then there were the other rascals in the servants' quarters that was Vichy, the villains, great and small, in the realms of finance, industry, science, art, the press and the radio. It was not merely that they all rushed to obey the slightest gesture that emanated from the Nazis; they actually sang heavenly hymns of praise before the products of Hitler's hell.

These people could be pressed to any task; it was merely a question of what price they required. Although there were some who offered their services purely out of personal rancour, envy and malice; and others who did not even need this motivation: people who were content with the simple fact that they were hobnobbing with the Germans. These last counted it as the greatest moment of their lives if a Nazi hand had the condescension to pat them on the shoulder in public. These lackeys made the Master Race a gift of their abjectness, quite without thought of personal reward.

But that is not all. There were even devotees whose collaboration was carried out at some personal cost. Their greatest pride was to be able to display their intimate daily intercourse with the Victors, to be able to make house visits with the top brass of the Occupying Criminals, and to make themselves worthy of such honour by paying for glittering parties and costly gifts. Which was no small sacrifice, in that time of ever-worsening shortages, when ordinary folk had to queue for hours for the prize of a pound of swede, and the weekly meat ration had been cut to thirty grams. But – as mentioned already – the organisational genius of the Germans had developed the *marché noir* to such a degree that, for the right money, even the most discriminating culinary demands could be met. The proud victors had, moreover, in their concern for the good of the people, sanctioned the opening of certain restaurants where they themselves preferred to eat, and where they were quite open to invitations from their French admirers. In the more modest of these establishments, where the clientele was not subject to official limitations or an entry fee, it was possible to eat and drink quite acceptably for 200 francs per head. If one wished to entertain a Nazi guest in the appropriate manner, however, one had to go to a particular restaurant in the Champs-Élysées, where the *prix fixe* was 5,000 francs. Per person, of course.

It can be seen, then, that life was by no means easy for the *parvenus* and snobs of the Collaboration: they had to dig deep in their own pockets. *Collaboration oblige.*

What satisfaction, what pride, to be able to say, just in passing: 'General Schaumburg? – Oh, a charming man. We had him to dinner yesterday.' What an achievement, to be able to boast: 'Tomorrow we are dining at Headquarters.' Or: 'Frau Abetz* simply insists that I accompany her whenever she goes shopping. She phoned me again, just today. She doesn't go anywhere without me.'

In this context, pride of place in the Collaborative Hall of Fame would without doubt have to go to a particular group of women. There is a famous work by Michelet portraying a series of female characters from the French Revolution; it would need a second Michelet to do justice to these Women of the Collaboration.

I am not talking here about 'professionals'. Compared with these women, the 'professionals' behaved with a degree of reserve; they in some sense maintained the dignity of their profession. Prostitution was their job. They lived by prostitution. But these Women of the Collaboration lived *for* prostitution.

Officers and private soldiers; dignitaries and Gestapo spies – they were all simply spoiled for choice. The most hideous specimen of Nazi subhumanity was able to take on the role of a Nordic hero, to whom these ladies' hearts were in thrall. This kind of woman would run after a German; throw himself at him; sue for his noble favour – and end up in his bed.

It would be wrong to imagine that these admirers of brutality were to be found mainly among the 'people'. On the contrary, the volunteers were far more numerous – at least proportionally – in those circles normally described as 'good society'. The most appalling manifestation of this shameless courting of German favour was probably the competitive zeal with which certain patrician ladies attempted, after the invasion of France, to win over the invaders in their turn, to capture them in a *pénétration pacifique*, laying before them the best that their kitchen, their cellar and their bodies had to offer.

For this kind of woman, the tragedy of France offered a level of excitement which far exceeded all the enjoyments and luxuries of the pre-war period. Here was something really new; an opportunity one could simply not afford to miss.

The crimes and atrocities of the Germans; the horrors visited on the Jews; all the inexhaustible varieties of Nazi sadism, creating ever newer and more grisly tortures in its cold, efficient laboratories of pain; the bodily and spiritual vivisection, performed for no other reason than to satisfy their evil passions; all this was a turn-on for these women – so much more stimulating than the normal methods of killing, or than the stale old guillotine. This Nazi aphrodisiac was something quite without rival.

Many, then, were the Judiths who took a Holofernes, from the *Wehrmacht* or the Gestapo, into their bed. But they did him no harm – God forbid! They slept with him, and next morning, full of desire, begged him to return as soon as he could.

One evening – the evening of a day which had broken to the grisly spectacle of yet another hecatomb of hostages, executed on the order of General Stülpnagel – a dinner was hosted by the extremely rich wife of a well-known writer, in her magnificent private palace. It was a dinner in honour of the Military Commander in France, General Stülpnagel.

All the guests were there; only the general himself had not yet arrived.

The lady of the house was beginning to show signs of anxiety. To have at one's table the man whose name had, through the red posters, become a household name, to entertain this mass murderer was a widely sought-after distinction, one accorded to only a select few. What a disgrace if he failed to turn up after all!

At last His Excellency was announced, to great sighs of relief. A crooked, deformed, gnome of a man appeared in the doorway: the Military Commander of France, the Representative of Hitler. The signatory of the red posters.

The lady of the house rushed up to him with an enchanting smile. And what words did she find to greet her exalted guest?

'Ah, le voilà enfin, notre gracieux vainqueur!' (Ah, here he is at last, our gracious conqueror!)

Her exact words.

12

From 'The Israelites' to 'The Jew'

AMID ALL THE FLOOD OF LIES with which Hitler – the High Priest of the Lie – inundated the world, like so much sewage, one of the most pernicious of all was his assurance that he did not regard National Socialism as something to be exported.

His desire to export anti-Semitism, however – that chief article of his faith – was something that Hitler had never concealed. He boasted about it, in fact. And in the context of this anti-Semitic brutality, he did not need to subject it to the slightest modification. Here he encountered neither obstacles nor resistance; this was a completely defenceless group, against which the Aryan 'Comrades of the People' and their accomplices in all places could give free rein to their murderous and covetous desires, in the most cowardly way, without let or hindrance. Here they could turn naked robbery into persecution, and persecution into naked robbery, to their hearts' content.

Anti-Semitism offers fat profits and no losses. This was a truth that even the slowest individual would quickly master.

Before the invasion there had, in spite of all the best efforts of the Third Reich, been no significant practical anti-Semitism in France. The most one came across was the attitude of certain doctors and lawyers, who would modestly hide their professional envy behind a smokescreen of anti-Semitism. Otherwise, anti-Semitism was confined to a more or less theoretical position of purely class-based prejudice which one found in certain circles of the aristocracy or high bourgeoisie.

The ordinary people, however, were not anti-Semitic. For them a French person, or a foreigner, might happen to be 'israélite', just as he or she might happen to be Catholic or Protestant. And there was no Frenchman, however well versed in ethnographic studies, who had the vaguest notion, before Hitler, of what an 'Aryan' might be.

After their entry into Paris, chief among the concerns of the Germans was to put an end to this situation once and for all. To begin with, however, they proceeded with appropriate caution. The Frenchman is a born individualist and rebel; he doesn't like having things laid down to him – not even his anti-Semitism. The job could not be done overnight; they were going to have to progress by stages.

The first was to replace the designation 'Israelite' with 'Jewish'. This was followed shortly by propaganda pronouncements which no longer spoke of French and foreign Jews, but just of Jews. The next stage after this was the terminology 'Le Juif' – The Jew: the singular used to imply a collective denigration.

The first Commissaire aux questions juives, Xavier Vallat,* had drawn up a programme, which he laid before his Nazi superior – an expert, who expressed his severe dissatisfaction. 'What are you thinking of?' he said to Vallat. 'You are trying to move much too quickly.'

'Too quickly?' Vallat was wide-eyed with astonishment.

72

'Certainly: too quickly. We must avoid acting too fast, and so provoking sympathy for the Jews. Just don't overdo it. This way we shall end up with a result that your programme could not even have dreamed of. You can depend on it.'

And indeed you could. You could depend on it to such an extent that in the end Vallat, who must still have had some trace of a sense of shame, did not want to continue his involvement – even though, of course, things were to get a great deal worse than they were then. He went, and was replaced by the notorious figure of Darquier,* a rogue, who had more than one crime in his past, and who was prepared to stoop to anything in his compliance. Besides, none of his previous jobs had ever brought him such a great material reward.

Laval, who had not shrunk from including Darquier in his 'government', may perhaps in his quiet moments have regretted that, instead of playing the role of Prime Minister, he had not rather requested from his German employers the much more lucrative, though admittedly more modest, position of *Commissaire général aux questions juives.*

Thus, the programme of 'extermination' had begun with a devilishly graded, mind-poisoning propaganda programme: the witch-hunt in the press and on the radio, in lectures, in countless brightly coloured posters and other depictions; the word 'JUIF' stamped in red on the identity card; the yellow Star of David, bearing the word 'JUIF' in a large type, imitating the style of Hebrew letters. The fact that this Star of David was made from linen, incidentally, meant that to obtain it one had to pay the appropriate number of points from one's textile ration card at the police *commissariat.*

Then there was the ban on frequenting public bars or restaurants, and the stipulation of certain times at which one was allowed to do one's food shopping – times at which everything had long since been sold. And there were many more regulations besides.

And hand in hand with these went the other 'measures'. First of all there was the *Statut des Juifs*, which 'merely' deprived Jews of any possibility of earning money. Then there was the whole series of decrees, slowly growing to an avalanche, all of which had the effect of putting Jews outside the law – of handing them over to the mercy of any arbitrary action without any protection or possibility of redress. Worst of all, of course, was what did not appear in any *journal officiel* – the perpetration of atrocities of a kind unparalleled in the annals of barbarism.

What was the reaction of the people?

Here it is important to avoid generalisation. What can be said, however, is that – with noble, indeed quite wonderful exceptions – the Nazi seed had fallen on fruitful ground.

There were, for example, French 'Aryans', who, on meeting a stranger on the street or in the metro who was 'branded' with the mark of the Jew, made a deliberate display of doffing their hat. On the other hand, people flocked in droves to the 'Exposition Juive',* that absolute pinnacle of viciousness in anti-Semitic propaganda, which opened shortly after the Occupation was established.

The most harmless group, relatively speaking, were those who took no position at all, and simply tried to ignore the crimes being perpetrated against Jews. At least these people did not commit actual harm. Alongside them, however, was the great mass of sheep-like individuals who echoed every slogan of the anti-Semitic propaganda, obediently, without reflection. And finally there were those who had sniffed blood at the appearance of anti-Semitism; who made it their profession and, in many cases, simply competed with the German bloodhounds. Of course, these collaborators in German anti-Semitism were simply following the example set by their superiors, in particular by that gang that went under the name of 'Commissariat' – and should in reality have been called 'Banditariat' – 'aux questions juives'.

All in all, then, the Germans' gamble had paid off. From the point of view of the French people, it was not just that taking anti-Semitism on board cost them nothing; rather, it involved participation in a hugely successful business, which offered the most attractive returns for no effort at all. And it must be said that to resist this kind of draw entails an inner strength which is not granted to many.

It is no wonder that many who had no particular axe to grind against the Jews allowed themselves to be 'persuaded' to participate. Many of these accomplices in the Great Nazi Robbery – taking on the role of 'buyers', of 'enforced or temporary administrators' – beat their breasts as they pocketed their gains, justifying their actions as stemming from friendly feeling towards the Jews. They had only done it to prevent someone else who in their place would have stolen far more.

It is also no wonder that others did not even take the trouble to find such a pretext, an excuse, a self-exoneration: the plundering of Jewish possessions was not only sanctioned by law, after all, but positively encouraged by all occupying and occupied authorities: it was actually a duty. Why, then, the qualms ... ?

A separate book would be needed to do justice to the industry of human misery that sprang from the root of the Jewish persecutions; to do justice to all the exploiters of suffering, of torment, of fear of death – people who somehow or other had (or claimed to have) the power to save Jews, or at least to help them. Such power became in their hands a kind of capital, which they invested in the pursuit of what was truly the most shameless and evil of all rackets.

It is hardly even worth mentioning those who got their hands on everything that Jewish people were forced to sell, at utterly derisory prices, if they were not to starve. These villains were men of honour compared with certain other traders on the black market of Jewish misery.

There were, for example, the *passeurs*, who (as long as the Demarcation Line was still in existence) smuggled Jews from the Occupied into the Free Zone. When the line was removed, most of these philanthropic individuals were able to retire very comfortably. The harder the Germans made life in the Occupied Zone, the higher went the prices of the *passeurs*. To begin with it was 500 francs per person; by the end it had risen to 50,000 or more. Nor should we forget the profits that the authorities in 'Free France', too, pocketed on these occasions – under a quite grotesque pretext.

It should be understood that every Jew who was lucky enough to cross the *Ligne de démarcation* was then prosecuted in the Free Zone for 'Défaut de Visa' – that is to say, for failure to report to the police before the escape, or, even better, to announce the escape in advance. For failure, in other words, to put his or her own head in the noose. This legal process would entail a further cost of up to 4,000 francs per person ...

Still, these *passeurs* at least fulfilled their side of the bargain. What words can be used to describe those individuals – including police officers – who, after the German Occupation of the Free Zone, offered their services to Jews who were in fear of their lives, to take them over the Swiss border in exchange for the unconditional payment, in advance, of often enormous sums – and then simply abandoned them to their fate on the way, and in some cases actually handed them over directly to the German or French Gestapo? Here I speak from my own personal experience. A special concentration camp was built for Jews in this position, not far from the Swiss border, with a 'deportation train' that left every eight days for Germany and Poland.

Cheating; extortion; behaviour of the most unscrupulous and vicious kind. And all conducted in the confidence of total impunity.

When shall we see the 'Exposition Juive' that would show – or, indeed, that *could* show – the level of the crimes perpetrated against Jews, even in this one area?

13

Stay of execution

SO FAR IT HAD BEEN POSSIBLE for a Jew at least to remain within the four walls of his own home; he had even been able to show himself on the street, albeit at certain prescribed times of day. This situation, however, represented merely a stay of execution. An unspecified – and for that reason all the more dreadful – threat was closing in on us, like a bird of prey, circling ever nearer. Life became a waiting game – waiting for bad to turn to worse, and then finally to worst.

Each morning we would look anxiously through the paper, to see if it contained any actual new measures, alongside the usual anti-Semitic filth. In October 1940 the *Statut Juif* appeared. On the day of its proclamation, I met H.-R. Lenormand,* the well-known dramatist. Lenormand had always counted Jews among his closest friends; and indeed it was Jewish critics, more than any, who had praised and valued his plays. He was enormously indebted, among others, to Max Reinhardt.*

'What do you think of this *Statut Juif*?' Lenormand asked me. Without waiting for my reply, he continued: 'I actually think that it's fairly mild.'

So mild, in fact, did he find it that, in gratitude for this mildness on the part of the Germans towards his Jewish friends, he began to publish article after article in the most viciously anti-Semitic French Nazi papers.

Perhaps Lenormand was right. Up until now it had been possible for a Jew to hide in his own house, at least, and to sleep in a bed at night.

How long would that last? The ban on using the railways, and on changing one's address; the repeated censuses of the Jews: what was the final purpose to which all these measures pointed? We tried not to spend our entire time thinking about it.

One day an inspector from the Prefecture of Police appeared at our door. He checked our papers, and asked a series of questions. He was polite, and made a pleasant impression. It seemed, too, that he had no particular enthusiasm for the task.

As he turned to go, I asked him: 'Please tell me honestly: what was the purpose of this visit? What do they intend to do with us?'

He shrugged his shoulders. 'How would I know that? You'd have to ask the Germans. I have been given the task of checking your papers, as those of other *israélites*. Which is exactly what I have done.'

I tried again. 'We hear so much about concentration camps for Jews, at least for foreign Jews ...'

Another shrug. 'Who can tell what the Germans are planning? We may all end up in the concentration camp, all of us – me included.'

And with these words of comfort he left us.

14

'For examination of your situation'

To all outward appearance we carried on – like automata. We went about our daily tasks mechanically, talked about any subject which was actually of the greatest indifference to us; tried to read. The fears were ever-present. And yet, in a small corner of our hearts, we maintained a glimmer of hope.

This trace of hope, which actually derived from nothing except survival instinct, was the only weapon left to us in this battle – this battle with our own selves. Without it we would not have been able to put up with the constant attrition.

And so passed the first winter of the Occupation, 1940–41. The worries of everyday life; the bitter cold in an unheated apartment; the difficulties in getting food – all the things that other people made such a fuss over – seemed to us mere trifles compared with the great, menacing question mark to which the life of a Jew (especially a foreign Jew) had been reduced. At that time the French Jews seemed still to enjoy at least a vestige of personal security.

Then, late in the evening of a beautiful spring day (it was about ten o'clock on 12th May 1941), the doorbell of our apartment rang. We started; and I went to open.

Outside stood a policeman, who handed me a green sheet of paper, with the following words: 'It is absolutely essential that you come: otherwise you will be arrested.' And before I could even say a word, he had gone.

It was a formal, printed 'invitation' from the Prefecture of Police. In it I was directed to attend on 13th May – the next day – at 7 a.m., not at the Prefecture itself, but at the police station of my own *arrondissement*, in Rue Lecourbe. The same place, that is, where I had spent the night of my arrest as 'ressortissant hitlérien' ...

Added in hand, underlined in red ink, was the phrase 'Pour examen de votre situation.' For examination of your situation. Another phrase, too: 'Accompanied by a family member or friend.'

The very next day ... 7 a.m. ... examination of my situation ... accompanied by a family member or friend ... What did it all mean – what lay behind it?

I said to my wife and to Sláva: 'I don't know what they want from me, but, this time tomorrow, I can hardly imagine I will still be with you.'

The poor women of course tried to comfort me. Soon, however, the three of us were sitting there in silence. And at last we went to bed – as though we really imagined we might sleep.

And this night too went by, a night which seemed endless, like an agony of uncertainty; but then again far too short, like a leavetaking.

At 7 a.m. we presented ourselves at the police station: my wife and I.

An official demanded my identity card and noted down the details; he then returned it. Trying to sound as calm as possible – though that last glimmer of hope was making it hard to breathe normally – I asked him, 'Can we go now?' For a fraction of a second he turned to me, with a look that was half pity and half amazement. He then gestured with his pen in the direction of a door, behind his shoulder, and answered: 'Go in there.' And, turning to my wife: 'You stay here.'

I entered the room he had indicated. In front of a table were two inspectors in civilian clothes; on the other side, two individuals whom I instantly recognised as my comrades-in-destiny. One of the officials gave the order: 'Hands up!'

The other undertook a thorough body search. On the table I noticed the haul of material confiscated thus far: a small pen-knife and an even smaller nail file. Hardly deadly weapons, but still, I suppose one could probably do oneself some mischief with them. *Pas d'histoires* ...

They then gestured to me to line up with the others and not to talk. We had walked into the trap. I now understood the true significance of 'examination of my situation'.

But what did they want with my wife?

Periodically the door would open and yet another man would enter, 'for examination of his situation'. No trace of shame from the two officials ...

When at last the number had reached about a dozen, the two inspectors were relieved by a couple of armed policemen, who came and stood in front of us.

The first issued a curt instruction not to smoke; but the other said, appeasingly: 'Oh, let them – while they still *have* something to smoke.'

I addressed myself to this one – in spite of the ban on speaking – and said: 'Please can you just tell us what is going to happen to us?'

He hesitated for a moment, looked at his colleague, then said, in a half-whisper: 'They are saying that you are going to go to a concentration camp for Jews. We are still awaiting instructions. All we know is that a minibus is coming from the Prefecture to collect you.'

I asked again: 'Will I be able to see my wife again?'
'Yes. But now no more talking.'

After an hour or so we were led out into the office again. In front of the door stood a minibus.

All the family members or friends were gathered in the office – women sobbing in distress, and each holding a bundle. Now I understood also the significance of that considerate instruction, 'Accompanied by a family member or friend.'

As soon as we had walked into that despicable trap, the accompanying person had been given a piece of paper, listing the items of bedlinen and clothing which – as well as a blanket – they were to fetch from home; and which they were now to hand over to us.

The policeman who had earlier shown some human fellow-feeling came up to me discreetly and whispered: 'You may tell your wife that you are being taken to the concentration camp of Beaune-la-Rolande in the Loiret *département*.'

We took our leave. The policemen hustled us: quick, quick. The vast majority of us would never see our wives or children again. Of the twelve of us taken into captivity at Rue Lecourbe, I may well have been the only one to survive.

Now the women were required to leave. They tried to stay outside, near the door, so as to be able to see us one more time. They were pushed away. We were then taken by the arm, each by one police officer, and led to the bus. We drove off, accompanied by four men.

In the doorway of a house, pressed into the corner, stood my wife. I drove past her. Once more she gazed at me, with a look ... a look ...

I shall never forget that look.

We were taken to a concealed side entrance at the Gare d'Austerlitz, where other vehicles were already unloading their cargo: adolescent boys, exhausted old men, deaf mutes, cripples, the sick and the blind. Jews.

Quick! Quick! was the command; it was not always followed. Many were scarcely able to carry their bundles.

The delightful spectacle was observed from a window on the first floor by two female German officers in smart uniform. The look on the faces of these two women is another which I shall never forget; a look of inhuman pleasure. How incredibly entertaining it was, the silent anguish of these Jews.

On the platform we were taken in charge by a unit of *Wehrmacht* commanded by an elegant officer. They were wearing combat helmets, these great heroes, and were armed not only with rifles but also with machine guns.

The officer began to roar at us; all I could make out was the refrain with which he ended each command: ' ... will be shot ... will be shot.'

We were then loaded on. In front of each of the locked cars were posted two soldiers with a machine gun. They were safe now, the brave Germans – safe from all possible Jewish assault.

We drove off.

At three in the afternoon we arrive at Beaune-la-Rolande, a small town about twelve kilometres from Orléans. The camp was about three kilometres from the town itself; so at least we were spared the experience of being paraded through the streets of Beaune.

Once again our escort consisted of German soldiers.

Two rows ahead of me a diminutive, emaciated old man was gasping for breath. One of the soldiers suddenly barked at him: 'Get lost!'

I confess that in his place I would have had just as little idea as he had as to the meaning of 'Get lost.' He looked about him in confusion.

The next moment the Aryan superhero had inflicted a terrible kick on the frail little man – a kick in the middle of the face. The victim collapsed. And before we could even attempt to help him up again, his tormentor had leapt upon him and was belabouring him with his boots, rhythmically, and with a rhythmic vocal accompaniment: 'Jewish pig, dirty yid, Jewish pig, dirty yid … ' The heels of his boots were red with blood.

We finally managed to raise him up again and helped him on his way. A few days later he died.

The other soldiers in the escort had watched the whole scene with enjoyment, as if it had been a particularly successful practical joke.

We had reached the front of the camp, and stood facing rows of high barbed-wire fences. A division of the *gardes mobiles* with their captain awaited us.

The Germans left us.

There was a definite sense of relief when they did so, and we saw the French uniforms. These *gardes mobiles* were not exactly soulmates, to be sure – but to be free of the sight of the Germans was some comfort in itself.

We staggered through the gate with our bundles. Now the barbed-wire fence was behind us. It was as if a heavy gate had fallen shut. We were now worse off than the worst common criminal: he at least has some rights enshrined in the law. For us there were no rights, and no law. We were only Jews.

We stood in the forecourt in front of the reception building housing the office of the camp commandant and the accommodation of the *gardes mobiles* until ten at night.

We were finally allocated to different huts, behind a further barbed-wire fence. There were 180 men to each hut. During the journey I had already made the acquaintance of an Austrian, Ernst Friedezky, and through him of his friend Alois Stern, a Czech who had lived for a long time in Vienna. We managed to stay together, and were allocated to Hut 8. We groped our way into it in the darkness. That first night there was no light, and no straw.

I had thought that I was too tired to feel anything. But in the darkness I suddenly saw my wife's face clearly in front of me, as it had looked as she stood in the doorway of that house on the Rue Lecourbe, gazing at me as I drove past.

15

Hut 8

ON AVENUE DES CHAMPS-ÉLYSÉES in Paris, there used to be a shop window displaying a wonderful sort of miniature kennel designed for the lapdogs of the upper classes. It consisted of three storeys of dainty, beautifully upholstered bunk beds, in which the precious creatures could live a life of undisturbed pleasure.

Of course, our existence was very far from that of the spoiled lapdog. And yet somehow that window in the Champs-Élysées, with its cosy kennel and the exclamations of delight from the genteel ladies admiring it, kept coming back to me. We too had been put into a structure consisting of three storeys of beds, with one man to a bed and each bed measuring 160 centimetres in length by 60 centimetres in height. You had to crawl into the straw on all fours, and then undress – if you could still be bothered to undress – lying down. If you attempted to sit up straight, you would bang your head on the planks of the bed above. Only those on the third storey were lucky enough to be able to sit up in comfort; on the other hand, they had to be skilled climbers in order to get there in the first place. I preferred to stay on *terra firma*.

The day after the glorious episode of the 'Examination of Our Situation', an article appeared on the first page of *Paris-Midi* under a headline which proclaimed in massive letters: 'La France se libère du joug juif': France is freed from the Jewish yoke. In this article – which a *garde mobile* actually showed us – the people were given the comforting reassurance that the France had finally roused herself to shake off the Jewish yoke. A start had been made, with the arrest of 5,000 foreign Jews between the ages of 18 and 45, and their removal to the concentration camps of Pithiviers and Beaune-la-Rolande. All these Jews, without exception, were dangerous, active 'trafiquants du marché noir', illegal traffickers on the black market, who had become incredibly rich overnight – parasites, who had finally received the proper (though far too lenient) punishment for their crimes against the long-suffering Aryan people.

Well, at least I knew, now – as far as my own case was concerned – what profession I had been practising, and what crime I was now paying for. The fact, which I mention only in passing, that I was already 55 at the time, was of course irrelevant. When one is talking about criminals who constitute a public menace, one cannot afford to be so particular.

But what of the others? If we take the inmates of Hut 8 as an example, the overwhelming majority were manual labourers or factory workers; in addition to these there were a few tradesmen; an ex-bank clerk; an engineer; a language teacher.

There were two deaf mutes; one mentally retarded person; one man with a wooden leg; a large number of serious invalids. As for age, the youngest amongst us was 14, the oldest 67.

Most of the younger inmates had fought for France – as volunteers – during the War; a number had been seriously injured; two had received the Croix de Guerre.

Such, then, was the band of desperadoes from whose yoke France had finally begun to free herself.

The manifestations of hunger can be quite diverse. Apathy verging on paralysis; dizziness that causes one to stagger as if drunk; trembling similar to a violent shaking fit. I also saw youngsters who suddenly went for each other like mad dogs and bit each other till they bled. Two of the very youngest crouched down on the ground behind the hut, held each other's hands and sobbed with tears.

I can also see myself, standing outside one day in the pouring rain, leaning against the hut wall. The clayey soil had turned into thick mud. In my hand I held a small piece of bread, but my fingers were shivering so violently that I dropped it. Without hesitation I retrieved the delicacy from the slime and gobbled it down.

The daily bread ration was 175 grams; but sometimes this was reduced, by way of 'punishment', by 25 or even 50 grams. As, for example, on the occasion when the prisoners in the camp of Pithiviers, thirty kilometres from ours, 'mutinied' – which is to say that they had thrown out the totally inedible bits of man-gelwurzel that had been given to them in their soup.

Every week a German officer from Orléans came to inspect us, accompanied by an official of the Gestapo in civilian clothes. The camp commandant, who the rest of the time vaunted himself like an all-powerful god, shrank to the status of a miserable worm in the presence of the two Germans.

On one such inspection the German officer discovered that at 6 a.m. we were given a black liquid which was described as coffee. He flew into a rage. 'What? Coffee – for these Jews?' He then turned to the commandant: 'Captain, these Jews are here to perish, not to fatten themselves. Is that understood?'

After this we were given water with our breakfast for several days – quite genuine water. To be completely fair it should be added that the water was heated. It wasn't that our captain was malicious. He did what he could.

In the hut next to mine was a Czech by the name of Prihoda, an 'Aryan' without blemish. He had apparently been arrested by mistake, although it is true that he had the misfortune to have been married for more than twenty years to a Jewess. In any case, the camp commandant had promised to try to have representations made to the military command through the Prefecture at Orléans. In the meantime Prihoda would have to wait. He had been caught with us, and he was stuck with us. His every conversation began with the prefatory question: 'So, what has this all got to do with *me*?'

During an inspection Prihoda had the bright idea of appealing directly to the German officer regarding the miscarriage of justice which he had suffered. He went up to the lieutenant, stood stiffly to attention and explained his case. When, however, further questioning elicited from him the fact of the 'non-Aryan' wife, the Nazi superior screamed at him: 'And yet you still have the nerve to complain? Concentration camp is the very least you deserve for your crime of racial impurity.'

Once the prefect came from Orléans on an inspection. Each hut had had a 'hut chief' appointed within it, who was responsible for seeing to it that all orders were carried out. In our hut, the holder of this thankless office was Ernst Friedezky.

The prefect did no more than gather together the 'hut chiefs' and make a short speech to them. Above all he demanded of them the strictest discipline. Finally he added, in a sort of attempt at consolation: 'There are French prisoners of war who are not much better off than you.'

At this point Friedezky stepped forward. 'Monsieur Préfect,' he said, 'to be a French prisoner of war – that is an honour. We, on the other hand ... we are completely dishonoured – reviled. May I please ask you: why? Why are we here?'

For a moment the prefect was taken aback, and said nothing. Then, with a gesture of embarrassment, in a muffled voice: 'You are here because you were unlucky.'

It also fell to the hut chiefs to divide people into groups for the various *corvées*, or work assignments. There was one *corvée* which was regarded by many as a special privilege, and this was the so-called *corvée extérieure*. What this meant was that particularly strong prisoners were sent with a barrow to a depot outside the camp, to bring back materials for the building of several more huts which were under construction. (The camp was being enlarged: we 1,800 were just the beginning.)

It was very strenuous work; and naturally those on the *corvée extérieure* were escorted and guarded by *gardes mobiles*. But, at least for a few hours, they did not have that barbed wire in front of their eyes.

In my hut there was a young Polish tailor, who continually pestered Friedezky to choose him once more for the *corvée extérieure*. Our hut chief, however, being a stickler for fairness, had a number of other candidates to consider, who had already been put down for the task.

The tailor had noticed that I seemed to be on particularly friendly terms with Friedezky; and on one occasion he tried to get me to intervene on his behalf.

I tried to mollify him. 'Why are you so keen on the *extérieure*, in any case?' I asked him. 'All those heavy loads – you'll only end up even hungrier.'

He looked at me, and in his look was all the pity and contempt of youth for age. He then stretched out his arms in a gesture of ecstasy. 'What does that matter?' he said, 'What does it matter if I end up hungrier? You have a chance to see a woman, at least in the distance – a woman: don't you understand?!'

There was also a young man in the camp whose appearance was much closer to that of a girl than to the masculine type. Platinum-blond, wavy hair, languorous eyes, swaying hips. He appeared to belong in one of those bars in Montmartre or Montparnasse that cater to a very particular clientele. He would certainly not have felt drawn to the *corvée extérieure* in the hope of seeing a woman, at least in the distance.

It was curious how most of the Poles seemed to have no idea of the existence of homosexuality; in this respect Paris had not broadened their horizons.

One day I was standing in front of the hut when the platinum-blond boy wafted past me. Two Poles were walking behind him. One of them pointed to the boy and said to his companion: 'What on earth *is* he – what do you reckon?' I was also able to hear the response, delivered in a tone of real admiration: 'A female impersonator. A really good female impersonator.'

The Germans had thought of everything – truly everything – that might bring our humiliation home to us with exceptional clarity, as well as functioning, from the physical point of view, as 'increased punishment'.

Originally there had been one covered privy for every two huts. But before our arrival these privies had been carefully sealed off, and a row of holes put in place a few paces from the front of our hut, which were for the use of the whole camp. These holes, and the queue of people needing to using them, constituted the view we had constantly before us. (In view of the small number of holes, and the consequent need to wait one's turn, there was always a queue.)

But this was not all. I have mentioned that these holes were not far from the front of Hut 8 and the neighbouring huts. This would clearly have made life much too easy for us. The Germans had therefore had the great foresight to put an extra barbed-wire fence around it, which could only be penetrated at a point a long way from our hut. Once one had reached this point, one had to turn round and cover the whole distance again, this time on the other side of the fence.

The strip of land in front of the excrement holes was the only place where we were able to be outside for a few moments, and get a breath of air – and what fresh air it was! And yet, in a second article that appeared in *Paris-Midi* on the subject of the concentration camps, a report described with indignation how the Jews of Beaune-la-Rolande had virtually had a country retreat built for them.

The German sense of humour even came up with a highly entertaining scheme whereby their own bodily functions could be employed to help us Jews behind the barbed wire feel the full force of Aryan contempt.

Not far from the camp was a large country estate in which a section of the *Wehrmacht* had been billeted. Life was good there. They were all very well looked after – positively bursting with good food and high spirits. This was made very clear to us on a number of occasions. What happened was that on particularly fine evenings they would take a post-prandial stroll as far as the camp to have a look at the hungry Jews behind the barbed wire. Contentedly puffing their cigars, they would draw each other's attention to particularly comical figures such as deaf mutes or cripples.

And without fail, before leaving, they took up position and vied with each other in the sport of pissing at us through the barbed-wire fence. A true German greeting from the fearless Nordic warriors – who then proceeded on their way, cackling with delight at their tremendous joke.

There came a time, though, when they left and did not return again. This was shortly after their Führer had declared war on Russia. They had been sent eastwards, these piss-heroes – sent to bring the great Swastika of German culture to the Bolshevik barbarians.

Life in a concentration camp is rather like some kind of chemical reaction, which has the effect of bringing both the good and the bad in a human being to the surface, undisguised by the mask of conventional lies. We had been reduced to the most basic form of animal existence; and in this context the fundamental character of each individual became clearly visible. This complete laying bare of the person revealed riches of inner beauty – at the same time, naturally enough, as quite a lot that was not beautiful. When all sense of bodily shame is gone, many men lose all sense of spiritual shame, too.

Behind the barbed wire you can get to know a person better in the course of a few days than you would outside in a whole life. You can find a sense of community that binds people together more closely, and leads them to a much greater commitment to each other, than 'friendships' that go on for years on the basis of mutual interest and social obligation. You learn the true nature – and the genuine, incredible value – of the word 'comradeship', this relationship whereby one human being is brought together with another human being, and not just with a business partner in the everyday business of life. And this comradeship, in the impoverishment of the concentration camp, is at the same time also a protection against that impoverishment: the only protection that one has.

On the other hand life behind barbed wire can also teach one how truly incorrigible the incorrigible truly are.

The concentration camp is not just a bitter school of humiliation, but also of humility. Yes: it really does teach the lesson of humility. It teaches you how meaningless are all the barriers erected between and against men by money, conceit, envy or prejudice. Suffering brings with it, to some extent, the brotherly bond that unites people in death. Besides, in this cage you can also see great men become very small and small men acquire a greatness that demands respect.

In this state of humility you also learn gratitude. Not the gratitude of a troublesome debt; but that other gratitude, which for those bound by it becomes a deep inner necessity – even, a comfort.

And in this state of humility you also learn to examine your conscience. You learn remorse. How many people did you pass by, in your previous existence, without a second thought; how much did you simply take for granted – or indeed take as your due; how much did you neglect, and how much wrong did you do, consciously or unconsciously. How often should you have helped, but did not, either because you had apparently more important things to do, or else simply out of emotional laziness.

You think of all these things now. With remorse and with shame.

Individuals such as Ernst Friedezky, Alois Stern, Dr Otto Seligman, the young Georg Pollak, gave me more than I can say. But many others, too, took the trouble to 'spoil' me, often in the most touching ways. Such behaviour does not come easily, even in normal life. What an extraordinarily great-hearted act to 'spoil' someone in a concentration camp.

There were times when I said to myself that I was actually better off than my wife and Sláva, who were dying of anxiety over me, and who were so alone in that heartless, bestial Paris ...

For the first five weeks we could neither write nor receive any letters. Letters that had been sent to us on spec were destroyed on the orders of the Germans. We decided to try and find a way round this.

Among those working on the building site of the unfinished huts were also some men who lived in the town. They were of course searched on both arrival and departure; but we nonetheless succeeded in smuggling letters out with them.

It was not long before the Germans got wind of the scheme, and set up their own watch at the post office of Beaune. Our only solution now was to find messengers prepared to go to Orléans to post our mail. This, however, carried a price tag of 50 francs per letter. Every such messenger would take several hundred letters per trip – a nice little earner.

We were finally given permission to send and receive one letter each per month – subject, of course, to the censorship of the camp commandant. It was a very small allowance; but in any case, the going rate for illegal letters fell to thirty francs.

Even in the smuggled letters, discussion of war, politics and the Germans was carried on only by the vaguest paraphrases. One could not be too careful.

One day Helfand, a splendid young Russian lad, rushed into the hut in a state of high excitement and showed us an illegal letter that he had just received from his wife. This is what she had written: 'Uncle Joseph – the one with the moustache – has fallen out with the painter.'

This is how we found out that Hitler had declared war on Russia. This, of course, did not change our situation in any way; but we did sleep better that night.

In a camp it is a complete impossibility, by day or by night, to have even a moment to oneself. Nor is there ever a moment's silence. There are times when this perpetual presence of other people just feels like a more extreme form of loneliness.

Even the night – when one would just like to cover oneself up, to disappear – even the night brings no respite. The fortunate among you, who have found sleep, snore, groan, sigh, or mumble. Others, who are still awake, put their heads together and whisper excitedly as though they had had no time to do so all day. And then there are many who lie motionless, with open eyes or with closed eyes; but one can still feel their sleeplessness like a tangible object. A nightly symphony of misery and sorrow, with the rustling of straw running through it like a pedal note on the organ. The air is thick with the vapour of neglected bodies and with the restlessness of unquiet souls.

Everything here is played out in front of everyone's eyes. Each, of course, bears his own secret, his own inner loneliness; but as far as the external world is concerned, nothing is secret.

If, then, you try to remove yourself from this unchosen life of exhibitionism even for the shortest possible time, this is seen by many as a lack of solidarity, or even as arrogance.

When I finally received the first sign of life from my wife, I wanted to read those few, precious lines undisturbed. I went behind the hut, waited a moment to make sure that there was no one in sight, and then began to read. Suddenly I became aware that I was no longer alone. I turned around and, sure enough, there were two Poles, reading the letter over my shoulder with the greatest interest. This time my patience snapped, and I shouted: 'Is this letter addressed to you or to me?'

The two men exchanged a look which was as much astonishment as disapproval. They turned to go. Before they did, though, one of them muttered a couple of words – a couple of words which for our Polish inmates represented the ultimate condemnation: 'Grober jung!' ['Rude boy']. This signifies the peak of tactlessness and bad behaviour. The word 'jung' has nothing to do with the actual age of the person; you might be as old as Methuselah, but you could still be a 'grober jung'.

Every day, even at first light, a group of women could be seen in the distance, gathered in a field adjoining the back of the camp, making desperate attempts to get nearer. At the same time the cries and whistles could be heard from the *gardes*, who had orders to keep them back.

These women had travelled from Paris on the previous evening and spent the night in the open air. They had come in the hope of being able to exchange a few words through the barbed wire with their husbands, brothers or sons; to be able to throw them a little pack of provisions. Or to be able to see them, at least from far off ... They made pitiable gestures to us, as though we might have been able to help them.

The very thought that my wife might be among these persecuted creatures was unbearable to me.

I later found out that she in fact had been – on two occasions.

The same wretched pantomime was performed daily over a period of weeks. These *gardes mobiles* were, to be sure, not exactly imbued with the finer feelings; still, many of them at least showed a lack of enthusiasm for the task. One of them said once to a comrade: 'You certainly have amazing wives, you Jews. I don't know how many of our women would do the same for us.'

Several of my co-mates in the hut had heard that I had the title of 'doctor', a fact which brought me the flattering nickname 'Quartier Latin', after the university area in Paris. It also, once we had been given the permission to write letters, brought me the post of secretary to those who could not write French, as it was stipulated that letters could only be written in that language.

It was an activity that brought me an extraordinary glimpse into the souls, and the families, of so many. How shattering – and sometimes how entertaining! – were the things that I had to put down on paper. Although the last thing on my mind in those days was 'literature', it often struck me that these letters would constitute a book whose variety and originality were far beyond what any creative writer could hope to achieve.

I remember one letter which began with the following graded form of address: 'My dearest child, my beloved wife, and you too, mother-in-law!'

Another letter ran as follows: 'When will God finally grant that we may see each other again, my darling wife? I think of all my favourite dishes that you ever cooked for me. But right now not even a stuffed carp or a goose breast would taste as good as you.' I can still see before me the eyes of the poor fellow who dictated that to me – eyes blazing with hunger and longing, with longing and hunger.

One other letter comes to mind, though I could not swear that the censor would have let it through. It ended with the following words: 'And now stay healthy and be patient. You will see that with God's help France will once more be a great country, and we will again be able to be Jews.'

Perhaps the most shattering of all the letters, though, was one which was never written.

I have already mentioned that among the inmates of our hut was a mentally retarded man, 'little Herschel'. Before the attack of encephalitis which had robbed him of his intelligence and also, almost completely, his ability to speak, the man had been a perfectly competent leather-worker. He would proudly show us his letters of reference. This pride, however, was as nothing to the light that came into his otherwise lifeless eyes when he brought out the photograph of a boy of about six. His whole being was transformed, and he would babble the words: 'My child, my child.' All of us were called upon to admire the photograph.

Once, when I was in the middle of writing letters for comrades, Herschel came and stood in front of me, brought out his treasure and gestured to me excitedly, indicating the act of 'writing'.

'Herschel,' I asked him, 'do you want us to write to your child?'

He nodded eagerly.

'Very well,' I said. 'Let's start now.'

Holding the photograph in front of him with both hands, he seemed to be thinking very hard. His ears burned. Suddenly he started to sob in despair, and ran away.

After that, whenever I had to write letters, Herschel was nowhere to be seen.

At the beginning of July we heard that a number of invalids above the age of 55, who had already been examined three times by the doctor from the Prefecture, were to be released. It was not the first such rumour that had circulated, and I gave it little credence. One evening, however, after his report to the camp commandant, Friedezky said to me, with great happiness: 'I believe that you will be able to go home tomorrow.' I remained sceptical, if only to avoid too great a letdown.

But the next morning the Adjutant-Chef called for me and said, without any explanation, 'One o'clock in front of the camp command, with your *paquetage*.'

Now I *did* believe – with the result was that I was completely unable to pack my bundle. Everything fell out of my hands. Friedezky and Pollak saw to the *paquetage* for me. It was a last act of friendship, and one performed quite without envy.

I was indescribably happy; at the same time I would have dearly loved to hide my face from the others, whom I had to leave.

After even a few days in a concentration camp you begin to look like a tramp, a *clochard*. Or, indeed, like a convict. Neglected, unwashed, ragged. You often hear people say: 'He looks like a criminal.' Such phrases are bandied about by the fortunate – those on the outside – and they are bandied about quite thoughtlessly and irresponsibly. After eight days, each and every one of them, too, would 'look like a criminal'.

On the day of the 'Examination of My Situation' I had been wearing a tie; this, of course, was long since in ribbons.

Just before I left the hut, a young fellow inmate called Anton Bilder came up to me, a labourer, whom I know only very slightly. 'Quartier Latin,' he said, addressing me with some embarrassment, 'if you are going home now, you can't turn up in front of your wife without a tie on. Here,' and he pulled a brand new tie out of his pocket, 'I have brought something for you.'

Once more the thought went through my mind, with burning remorse: how much we neglected – before the great persecution came upon us – how much human goodness we simply passed by, careless, arrogant ...

At 1 p.m. we were lined up in front of the camp command: twenty out of 1,800. We and our *paquetage* were subjected to a meticulous examination. The captain then appeared and made a short speech, in which he emphasised that we had had an extraordinary favour bestowed upon us, and warned us that we must show ourselves worthy of it.

In other words: we were offenders who had been granted a pardon, and we were being warned not to offend again. But what was this offence that we must not commit again? The offence of being Jewish?

Friedezky, Stern and Pollak had got permission to accompany me as far as the camp command. I took my leave of them.

We then marched, in rows of four, with two *gardes* at our head, on past the last barbed-wire fence, and out of the gate.

In the street were a couple of children who smiled at us and shouted, 'Bonne chance!'

Our escort took us to the central square in Beaune, and then turned back. We were free. We nonetheless did not dare to sit down in a café. The 'look of a criminal' was still with us – it was inside us.

One hour later the bus from Orléans to Paris came by. It seemed quite possible that I might not survive the journey in this overcrowded vehicle.

At eight in the evening we were in Paris, at the Place Denfert-Rochereau. Half an hour later I rang the bell of our apartment.

It was my wife who opened. She cried out loud.

After which it was quite a while before any of us – she, Sláva or I – could utter a word.

16

Another stay of execution

IN THE PERIOD IMMEDIATELY AFTER my release, I experienced a kind of second childhood. Ordinary things were wonderful to me – things like a bed, an armchair, a plate, clean laundry, warm water, a lavatory. I had to get used to these pleasures all over again. But I may say that since that time I have not got *so* used to any of them that I take it for granted. The concentration camp's School of Humility taught me that lesson, too.

And yet I could not be completely happy in my 'freedom'. A criminal who has completed his sentence is free. A Jew under the Swastika has never completed his sentence; it has been at best suspended. True, they had given me a document of release at Beaune; but this was just a piece of paper.

One fine day in September the entire 11th arrondissement was sealed off by police, and a furious hunt for Jews commenced on the streets and in the houses. Anyone who could not provide proof of his Aryan status was taken to the concentration camp of Drancy, which had already acquired appalling notoriety. It was there that the two German monsters, Brunner and Bruckner, competed with each other in torture.

By a great stroke of luck I happened not to be in the 11th arrondissement on that particular day. But the raids became more and more frequent, now in one place, now in another. Metro stations, too, were sealed off with increasing frequency while searches for Jews took place. It soon reached a point where no Jew leaving his house could be certain that he would return to it in the evening. And of course home was not safe either. Nowhere was safe.

I thought sometimes of my comrades in Beaune, and said to myself: at least they have it all behind them; nothing more can happen to them.

Alas – we shall see what could still happen to them.

What were we to do? I was so tired, so worn down, that left to myself I would have resigned myself to my fate, and let events take their course. Let what will be be. My wife, however, was not going to give up, and she insisted that we try to reach the Unoccupied Zone. In the end I agreed. A relative of ours, Mrs Rosa Ornstein, and two couples of our acquaintance, named Ciprut and Dreyfus, decided to join us in the adventure.

An adventure which began in Paris itself: Jews were strictly forbidden to leave their place of residence, or to use the railways. There were almost daily police checks on travellers at the railway stations. Any Jews caught there went straight to Drancy. And, compared with Drancy, Beaune appeared to have been a paradise ...

We decided to try our luck on 10th November 1941. A *passeur*, 'Monsieur Pierre', had agreed to smuggle us over the Demarcation Line at a cost of 3,000 francs per person. His 'mission', though, began only at the Line itself. That far we had to get on our own.

With one small piece of hand luggage each, we once again abandoned our 'home'. Once again we did not know where we would spend the next night. In Drancy? In a prison on the Demarcation Line? In the Free Zone?

I will confine myself to a brief summary of these events. At the Gare d'Austerlitz we were fortunate enough to board the train for Bordeaux. There was indeed a police squad hunting for Jews that morning, but fortunately they were on another train. We had been told to get out at Coutras, about an hour before Bordeaux: there the *passeur* would be waiting for us. We could, of course, have encountered another police check at any point on the way, and the shortest stop at a station seemed to us to last for ever. Finally, however, we arrived at Coutras in one piece, where we were met – after going through every imaginable precaution – by Monsieur Pierre. There were a number of Germans hanging around on the platform.

17

'Zone libre'

AND SO THE EXPEDITION BEGAN. First, several kilometres in a car to the edge of a forest. Then three hours on foot by secret paths, through thick undergrowth and woods. This area was known to be patrolled by police with dogs.

During a short rest the noble Monsieur Pierre requested that we make a small extra payment, of 200 francs per person, for the car that would take us from the Line to the small town of Mussidan, about ten kilometres away. We paid. The *passeur* had thus taken almost 2,600 francs from our group alone.

We finally arrived at a street, which we crossed at a run. Monsieur Pierre came to a halt, and announced solemnly: 'You are now on the soil of Free France!' There was at least no additional charge for this brief announcement. A car was waiting for us in front of a farmhouse, and at nine in the evening we were in Mussidan.

Next morning we had to report to the police. We had incurred a penalty, because we had not acquired a *visa de départ*; which is to say that we had not in advance advised the Germans, from whom we were fleeing, of our flight.... At the end of our hearing the official smiled as he asked us: 'Who was the *passeur* – Monsieur Pierre?' I assented. 'How much?' he then asked; '3,000?' – 'No, 3,200.' – 'I see.' He noted down the amount. It was obvious that the police were silent participants in this business.

We had been asked to which *département* we intended to go. We wanted to get to the Koflers', who lived in Voiron, in the Isère. It was explained to us that we would have to stay provisionally in the Dordogne, since the permission of the Prefecture of Isère would have to be granted first. A *gendarme* would now accompany us to Ribérac, and hand us over to the court with the relevant jurisdiction, which would decide the punishment for our lack of visa. From Ribérac we would then be brought to Périgueux, and there the police would assign us to a compulsory temporary residence within the *département* ...

This, then, was the Free Zone. Still, at least we could breathe again; and to be spared the sight of Germans was in itself a release.

We had sent a telegram to Pierre Vorms, who had settled in Guiraud, near Belvès in the Dordogne, informing him of our arrival in Mussidan; and on the very same day we had the joy of meeting our old friend and his wife. They came with us to Ribérac.

Here we were brought before the *procureur* in the court-house, who began by giving us a fearful dressing-down, and talked of the need for appropriate punishment. If this exodus of Jews to the Free Zone doesn't stop soon, he said in conclusion, completely different measures will have to be adopted. We then had to pay bail of 3,000 francs per person, as the case against us would not be heard for at least a month. Finally, we had to pay for an 'advocate': another 500 francs each.

We then drove, still accompanied by *gendarmes*, to Périgueux. There we were received at the Commissariat Spécial by a *commissaire*, an Alsatian by the name of Mincker, who made it abundantly clear by every word and look that he bestowed upon us, how much it pained him to have to deal with these Jews. He nonetheless refrained from open insult, and even, on Pierre Vorms' request, condescended to give us Belvès as our compulsory temporary residence. (Belvès is a small town on the train line from Périgueux to Agen.)

The next day, then, we were able to travel – this time without *gendarmes*! – to Belvès, where we rented a room in the Hotel Sarthou.

We no longer had a home; and our only possessions at the moment were the most basic necessities in terms of clothes and linen. But what of that: we were in the Free Zone! We had escaped from the Swastika – or so we believed.

What a fond illusion.

Belvès is a small, cosy, old-world town picturesquely situated on a hill, seeming to cling on to its steep slopes. From whichever direction you approach, it presents an enchanting prospect, reminding one of certain hill top towns in Tuscany. The surrounding country is enchanting, too; it is a part of the Périgord that casts its own peculiar spell, one that never seems to wear off. The landscape, with its wooded hills and slender, elegant rows of poplars in the valleys, has a lovely, though somewhat harsh, attraction. The air is mild, but strong; the light clear, but full of subtle shades. You are not quite in the South, and yet you already sense its presence. 'Midi moins le quart'[10] – 'a quarter to the South' – is the local expression. A little bit of the earth that you can't help falling in love with.

We had nowhere to call home any more; but within a short space of time we began to feel almost at home in Belvès.

Of course we could never have guessed, then, all that we still had to go through. And we certainly could never have guessed that, here in Belvès, human beings would come into our lives of a kind that we had never before encountered.

---

10. The pun is of course untranslatable: the same French word means 'the South' and 'midday'.

Human beings to whom, in the final reckoning, we owe the fact that we are still alive. Without them we would have perished a long time ago.

And yet it is not just our physical survival that we owe to them. If there had *not* been human beings like this, too, along our path, I believe that I would not have been able to endure the misery, the depression produced by the horrors of Hitler's world. How well I could understand Stefan Zweig,* whom I was bound to by long, long years of friendship. I learned of his death one day in Belvès, through a newspaper report, which consisted of a single line: 'The Jewish author Stefan Zweig has committed suicide in Brazil.'

True, he was living far, far away, in Brazil. True, he was fêted and honoured in his exile. True, too, that he was at the peak of his fame and his creative powers. And yet, one day, he could not carry on any longer, and departed voluntarily from this life. Incomprehensible? No. The Age of Hitler had finally ground the 'Jewish author' down. The Brazilian authorities gave Stefan Zweig a state funeral. But before that he had gone to the grave in the deepest despair, and taken his deepest convictions into that grave with him.

Belvès is a small place, and we didn't go out much. We were nonetheless able to form a picture of the mentality of the 'Free Zone' at this time; in fact, life in a hotel was in a way rather informative. In addition to the long-term residents there was a constant flow of people passing through; and the conversations one would hear in the dining room were quite revealing in this respect.

Those in the *zone libre* had not been made to feel the consequences of the War very acutely; even food shortages were much less significant here than in the occupied territory. There was also, of course, the fact that the population was spared the physical sight of Germans in uniform.

The result was a fairly widespread feeling of indifference. People had adjusted to the *défaite*; it was an accident of nature; no one could be blamed for it. Pétain's propaganda dressed up the humiliation in the high-sounding slogans of the 'Révolution Nationale', all of which ended with the same refrain: 'Give Marshall Pétain your support, and everything will be all right!' Whatever went on in the rest of the world, even in that very nearby part of it, the Occupied Zone, was of little concern to people. Their attitude was one of accommo- dating themselves to the *défaite* as comfortably as possible, rather in the way that one accommodates oneself to an apart- ment which is undeniably smaller, but nevertheless quite acceptable.

Nor should it be forgotten that the *zone libre*, too, bristled with all varieties of collaborative fauna – all prepared to make common cause, and common business, with the German Rep- tile. Nor, indeed, that Vichy, capital city of treachery, was in the *zone libre* too.

About a month after our arrival we were sitting down one eve- ning at dinner in the hotel dining room. Someone had turned on the radio, on which Vichy was broadcasting the 'Radio- Journal de France'. Suddenly we heard the report: 'In Paris there has been another attack on a German solider. The occu- pying powers have arrested twenty-five hostages, Jews and communists, who will be executed tomorrow, if the guilty party does not come forward.' The speaker then carried on: 'The French government has furthermore decided to place all foreign Jews who entered France after 1936 in concentration camps, irrespective of whether they are in the Occupied or in the Free Zone.'

Our fellow diners paid no attention at all and continued their meals calmly. What concern was that of theirs? For us, though, the breathing space was over – yet again. This one had lasted just a month.

So, then: this was it. The release from Beaune-la-Rolande ... the flight across the Demarcation Line ... all for this. This was the freedom of 'France Libre'.

Once again, we had simply exchanged one trap for another. And once again we began to live from one day to the next, from one hour to the next. Again the constant expectation of the moment when they would come to get us. Whenever we saw a policeman, a shiver went down the spine: 'Now – *this* time this is it!' The *gendarme* would pass by; we would breathe again. It had *not* been this time – it had been put off a little longer.

And so the days went by, and the days turned into weeks. Christmas ... New Year 1942. We were still in our room; we still had a bed to go to at night. But the uncertainty allowed us not one moment of peace.

In the main street of Belvès there is a hairdresser's by the name of Tabart. One of the assistants who sometimes served me there seemed rather to stand out – a handsome lad of about eighteen, with strikingly fine, delicate features and deep brown eyes.

One time we started talking. The young man was called Jacques Rispal;* his father was a decorator, and his mother ran a hardware store in Rue du Fort. I spoke to Pierre Vorms, who had previously set up an amateur theatre in Belvès with some of the youth, and he described 'Jacquot' Rispal as the most gifted member of his troupe. 'That boy could really amount to something,' was his opinion.

I began to be interested in the young man. On a couple of occasions he visited me in the hotel in the evening, and we talked about everything under the sun. I was struck by his intelligence, his interest in cultural matters, his open outlook. But above all I sensed in the boy a truly fine human being. Here was sensitivity, idealism, an unerring – often furious – sense of justice, not to be deceived by any propaganda. There was, too, a profound goodness of heart, and a remarkable capacity for empathy with

109

others – all the more extraordinary in one so young, one who had not yet experienced any real suffering. He hated the Germans, hated anti-Semitism; and he expressed these sentiments openly, not only in the presence of Jews and refugees.

One day he invited me to visit him at his parents' house; and after this visit the boy's character seemed to me less inexplicable. His mother was an attractive, elegant woman, who combined the most heartfelt generosity with the greatest tact and sensitivity; his father a true revolutionary at heart, and had for many years been a militant communist.

The injustice and violence that these three saw happening all around them did not, as in the case of so many others, have the effect of deadening their feelings; rather, they provoked in them an even stronger sympathy and desire to resist. As for their reaction to anti-Semitism, the whole propaganda of the persecution had only served to turn them into committed *anti*-anti-Semites. We would ourselves, one day, receive the most overwhelming proof of this fact.

After our first visit, which was to be followed by only one more, I could only regret that we had met this family so late – although at this stage I could not know how soon our separation was to be.

The case against us was heard at the court in Ribérac in January, and the result was a fine of 2,460 francs per person.

Our request for permission to reside in the Isère had not yet been considered; we learned that it had simply been filed away, and were quite happy about that. Except for the fact of having arrived in France after 1936, and the Sword of Damocles that therefore hung over our heads in the form of a concentration camp, we felt relatively at ease in Belvès, and desired nothing more than to be allowed to stay there.

But then, one day just before Easter of 1942, we received an invitation to the Commissariat Spécial in Périgueux. With no positive expectations, we made our way there.

In Périgueux we were met by Monsieur Mincker, the same gentleman who had made his antipathy to us so clear on our first arrival in the *zone libre*. He pulled out a document and asked us curtly if we still intended to go to Voiron.

The question seemed to me to imply that a choice might still be open to us. I therefore replied: 'If it were possible, we would prefer to stay in Belvès.'

We knew Monsieur Mincker already, of course; still, we could hardly have expected what now followed. He leapt to his feet with clenched fists, threatening. 'J'en ai marre de vous youpins,' he screamed: I'm sick of you yids, sick of your *youpineries*. '*Youpins, youpineries*' – the words went on ringing in our ears. He ended with the words: 'You will hear from me again!'

We went to the Prefecture, to see if we might there obtain some clear information, rather than simply a stream of vulgar insults. There we spoke to a very polite lady official, from whom we learned that our request, submitted more than five months previously, had been granted by the Prefecture of Isère. This meant that we now *had* to leave Belvès: we had no choice in the matter. She also communicated to us that, as foreign Jews who had entered the country after 1936, we had only been spared 'internment' as an extraordinary act of leniency. We should not, in fact, have been at liberty at all. She showed us a piece of paper. 'All I would have to do is present this to the prefect for signature ...'

There was, then, no question of our remaining in Belvès or in the Dordogne. But we were given four weeks' grace before our departure.

And so, on 25th April, we were on the road again: we would travel via Lyon to Voiron. Yet another farewell.

Shortly before our departure Gabriel Rispal,* the father of my young friend, came to us in the hotel and brought with him a bottle of vintage Burgundy, something which even in those days was a valuable rarity.

'Why do you rob yourself like this?' I said to him, in an attempt to hide my true feelings. He stood there, in his white painter's smock, with tears in his eyes. I had previously spoken with the man twice – three times at the most.

He took my hand and replied: 'You can't rob yourself, for a friend.'

The words had an especially strong effect; for I still had Monsieur Mincker's '*youpins, youpineries*' in my ears.

18

Voiron

EMIL KOFLER HAD NOT SUCCEEDED in finding us a place to live in Voiron. He therefore offered us hospitality in Criel, a small place in the country outside Voiron, in the house where he lived with his wife, son and stepdaughter.

The only positive side of this arrangement was the company of our old friends; Voiron, a dull industrial town of some 16,000 inhabitants, was not a place where we could feel at home; it seemed too fundamentally different from 'our' Belvès.

Physically, the Isère region with its Alpine scenery is undeniably very attractive; but it is a kind of scenery that grabs the eye without warming the heart. Here are dramatic effects of nature which provoke admiration, certainly, but not affection.

The type of person one meets here is different, too – a fact which is even reflected in certain of the region's traditional sayings. One quip has it, 'If you want to drink a good bottle of wine with a good friend in the Isère, make sure you bring the good bottle and the good friend with you.' There is, perhaps, some truth in that.

Even though we had no home anywhere, we felt a sort of homesickness for Belvès. There we had begun to feel a little bit 'at home'; here we felt constantly the status of the *résidence*

113

forcée – the compulsory residence. Indeed, just in case we forgot that status, we had to report to the police every Saturday. And this applied even to Miss Kolářová, whose Aryan credentials were now suspect as a result of her association with us Jews – a suspicion, indeed, which was to have very serious consequences for her, in spite of her 'innocence'.

After about three weeks we finally had the good fortune to find an empty house in Criel, not far from the Koflers'; and my wife and Sláva, using a bare minimum of furniture – borrowed or rented from one place or another – succeeded in turning our little billet into a liveable home.

The cottage even had a small bit of land attached to it. The two women set to work on it with incredible gusto, transforming the bare ground into a model miniature vegetable garden which provoked the admiration of all our neighbours.

In the midst of all these wonderful arrangements, though, I found myself beset by anxiety, especially on Saturdays, when we had to report to the police. In our *dossier*, which the official brought out at each visit, the first word that appeared – in large letters of red ink, and doubly underlined – was: JUIFS. Jews.

In the middle of July we were surprised by the appearance one day of Mrs Mila Friedezky, the wife of my fellow inmate and hut chief in the concentration camp. Her demeanour as she entered our house was superficially calm – too calm. It was that frozen calm which is more disturbing than the most violent expression of despair.

What had happened?

In answer she handed us a letter – a letter of farewell from her husband. It was one of the most shattering human documents that the cursed Age of Hitler ever gave rise to. What human nobility in this letter, what love, what suppressed agony. And what a silent indictment.

After fourteen months of incarceration in Beaune my fellow inmates had been awoken one day at first light by the whistles of the *gardes*. 'Within one hour,' was the command, 'everything packed and ready to decamp.'

To decamp – into freedom, at last?

No. Packed and ready for deportation to one of those living hells in Germany or Poland which were designated, with typical German matter-of-factness, as 'Extermination Camps'.

Lublin or Dachau; Auschwitz or Buchenwald; it made no difference. It was equivalent to a death sentence – a death sentence which is carried out in tiny stages, in instalments. Death divided into a hundred deaths; extinction prolonged into a hundred agonies.

'Within one hour, packed and ready to decamp.' Within this hour, Friedezky had somehow found the strength to write his last words of comfort to his wife.

Let us try for just one moment to imagine that actual experience: the husband, as he rushes desperately to get down on paper his testament of love; the wife, as she takes that letter in her hand.

Mrs Friedezky had not been able to remain in Paris any longer. The round-ups had begun again – this time over a very wide area, and without distinction of age or sex. The German police had now joined in the activity with the French, who apparently had not been sufficiently meticulous.

When the thugs entered their flats, some mothers had thrown their small children from windows, before jumping themselves. And yet the broken bodies on the pavements had as little effect on the Germans as a pile of rubbish; there would be another lot along soon. Terminally ill patients, as well as those who had just had operations, were thrown out of the hospitals. When my friend, the wonderful Dr Elbim, who was chief surgeon in one hospital, had dared to protest, the reply he received from the heroes of the Wehrmacht was a terrible blow in the face with a rubber truncheon.

In front of the dwellings of Jews who had been captured in this way, furniture vans would appear punctually, on the same day. Everything that was not actually nailed down was loaded up in a trice, in a highly expert criminal operation, and then taken to special warehouses. The admirable efficiency, and attention to detail, of the German theft machine were undeniable.

Mrs Friedezky had spent the last days before her flight hiding in a friend's house. Three times the Germans had arrived at her apartment looking for her. At last the moment came when the *passeur* who was to take her over the Line (along with several others in a similar situation) gave them the signal for departure. This public benefactor contented himself with 30,000 francs per head. The Germans had further tightened security along the Line. They were now even using aeroplanes to assist in the hunt for Jewish game.

It was, on the other hand, an open secret that one could obtain official permission to cross for 60,000 francs through helpful suppliers at the *Commissariat Juif.* The 'normal' cost for such a document was ten francs. And for half a million you could even get an absolutely watertight Aryan passport. The noble French fakers shared the booty with the Germans: the blond people of the north and the 'negroid' French found a shared interest here.

It was remarkable that Mrs Friedezky had been given permission, just a few days after her arrival in the *zone libre*, to travel to the Isère. What seemed even more striking, though, was something recounted by an acquaintance of hers, who had escaped from Paris shortly after her, and also come to Voiron.

(There were now twelve of us in all – twelve foreign Jews in Voiron. I mention this incidentally, only because the mayor of

Voiron had made a statement to the effect that the huge influx of foreign Jews into the town was responsible for the shortage of food: they were eating the indigenous population out of house and home.)

But let us return to Mrs Friedezky's acquaintance. This person had had a quite extraordinary encounter with the French police: he had been allowed to travel directly to Voiron, from the 'Line of Demarcation', without any provisional stay anywhere else.

But ... but the police commissioner had explained to him: 'As far as *I'm* concerned, travel where you wish. It is all the same to me where you are picked up.'

What did this mean? Nothing good, certainly.

We now had a 'home'. And the wife of our neighbour, Madame Pellat, even persuaded my wife to lay in a small supply of fruit and vegetable conserves for the coming winter. Madame Pellat, of course, was in the fortunate position of being able to plan for the coming winter as for any other new season, without any other complications ...

19

Nine gendarmes versus five Jews

MEANWHILE, EVEN IN THE 'FREE ZONE', the anti-Semitic fervour of both press and radio had been growing by the day. There could be no doubt of it: if the Germans decided that they wanted to act against the Jews in the *zone libre* too, their Vichy lackeys, with the Maréchal at their head, would happily do their bidding.

In a speech at the beginning of August 1942 Hitler had once more heralded the eradication of all Jews in the lands occupied by him. In *this* context, at least, his word could be relied upon. It could also be relied upon that no one would attempt to stop him from carrying out his programme.

We were compelled to report weekly to the police station; but evidently that was not enough. One day – it was 25th August – I went into town in the afternoon, for a consultation with Dr Ferrier in connection with my heart condition. Dr Ferrier gave me strict instructions to avoid any kind of excitement. (I unfortunately neglected to ask him exactly how I was to follow this régime.)

On my return I learned that two *gendarmes* had paid a visit during my absence. They had been friendly enough; they had explicitly assured us that the visit had no particular aim in view. They had just dropped in; they happened to be passing. No doubt they were anxious to find out how we were getting on. Purely as an afterthought, they had asked about me; they had then quite politely taken their leave.

In the evening we went as usual to Kofler's house. There we heard the French transmission of the BBC from London. Among other things, the announcer read out an urgent warning addressed to all foreign Jews resident in Lyon. According to reliable sources, a preliminary number of 600 would be arrested that night, and handed over to the Germans for deportation.

At that moment Emil Kofler returned from Grenoble – a journey he had made at our request in the attempt to get some kind of reliable information as to what measures were being planned. He spoke to an acquaintance of his who enjoyed good relations with the Prefecture there. The acquaintance was not able to give him any concrete information, but he did tell him this: 'All foreign Jews now would be best advised to hide.'

To hide ... *where?*

We set off for home. 'See you tomorrow,' I said to our friends, 'if we are not taken before then.'

Back at home, we looked at each other helplessly. Rosa Ornstein, who lived with us, was extremely agitated. She was adamant that she should pack her things. We dissuaded her – more out of superstition than anything else. Besides, perhaps our fears were exaggerated. So far the English radio station had only spoken of Jews in Lyon, and then only of 600; so this could not be any kind of general policy. We did our best to pretend, both to each other and ourselves.

We said goodnight and went to bed. There was, of course, no question of sleep. Each of us lay there awake, silent, the same thoughts going round, endlessly, in all our minds. Whatever we had said to each other had just been putting a brave face on it. And so we stayed silent – heartbeat after heartbeat, hour after hour. From time to time we looked at the clock. If only this night would end …

Around four in the morning we heard a dog bark. My wife and I both leapt out of bed instantly and rushed to the window. In the pale light just before dawn, we could see a number of figures moving slowly, gingerly towards our door. *Gendarmes.* Seven of them, walking one behind the other, like Indians on the warpath, and with shouldered rifles. At their head was the brigadier himself.

A contingent of seven heavily armed men, against three women and myself.

A few moments later the bell rang. I pulled back my wife, who was already at the door, and hustled her into the room. I then opened the door. Two men remained in front of the door, presumably to prevent any attempt at escape; the others entered.

The brigadier followed me into our bedroom, accompanied by two of his men. The two others (the same two who had 'visited' us the day before) knocked on the bedroom doors of Sláva and of Rosa Ornstein.

'Get dressed,' ordered the brigadier, 'and pack some clothes and linen. But quickly, quickly! We haven't got any time: we still have other Jews to pick up.'

At this point my wife fainted; and it took several minutes for her to regain consciousness. As soon as she opened her eyes again the brigadier snapped at her roughly: 'No more play-acting, now! It won't help you.'

We had no way of defending ourselves; but this brutality was too much for me. 'Can't you at least be silent?' I shouted at the man. 'This is a job you should be ashamed of.'

An unpleasant smile spread over the brigadier's face. 'Calm yourself, monsieur. I am a gentleman: no one can take that away from me. I've even arranged for a nice, comfortable bus to take you to Grenoble. I do my best for the ladies.'

I now knew what was in store for us: deportation.

My poor wife was desperate to try to save me, at least. She begged them to phone Dr Ferrier. 'My husband saw him only yesterday,' she said. 'Dr Ferrier will certify that my husband is not fit to travel. Our neighbour, Pellat, has a telephone.'

One of the *gendarmes* stepped forward and asked if he should make the call.

'Don't interfere!' hissed the brigadier to his subordinates. 'My task is to send these Jews to Grenoble, and that is what I am going to do. Nothing else concerns me.'

'You have that noble task,' I said, 'to arrest these Jews and send them to Grenoble. But what business have you with Miss Kolářová? You know very well that she is not Jewish.'

'She may not be Jewish,' was the reply; 'but in any case she has crossed the Demarcation Line with a group of Jews. That is sufficient. She goes with you.'

Miss Kolářová had by now joined us in the room and had heard everything. Normally, the woman was shyness itself; now she turned on the brigadier with blazing eyes. 'Of course I will go with them,' she shouted at the wretch, 'and I would go with them even if you wanted to leave me behind. I would rather stay with Jews, a thousand times, than with Christians of your sort!'

We exchanged no further words after that, apart from my asking the brigadier to inform Emil Kofler, which he graciously agreed to do. He refused, however, to leave the room – he and his men – while my wife got dressed.

And so we got dressed. We packed our bags. What to take with us, what to leave behind? Everything seemed so necessary to take – and at the same time so pointless. Poor Rosa could not pick anything up without dropping it. She could do little more than sob silently. One of the *gendarmes* helped her.

By now Emil Kofler had arrived. We said our farewells. Then the *gendarmes* escorted us out and we left 'our' house, which was then immediately sealed by the brigadier.

In the Pellats' house, everyone was asleep. Our neighbour opposite, on the other hand, Madame Regnier, was already in her garden. Seeing us sandwiched between the *gendarmes*, she began to cry. 'How awful,' she sobbed. 'How awful!'

'Awful?' the brigadier responded cheerfully as he walked past her. 'Everything that these Jews leave behind goes to the *Secours national*.'

On the other side of the road there is still a bed and breakfast, which belongs to a Madame Marquet. This Madame Marquet had now positioned herself in front of her door and, as we were led past, she clapped delightedly, as if she had just watched a particularly well-performed scene in a play. And the brigadier smiled at her, flattered – just like the actor acknowledging his applause.

The next stop was the house where Frau Friedezky lived. She was already waiting on the street, flanked by two *gendarmes*. It was not even six weeks since her flight from Paris.

So: five prisoners, now – escorted by nine *gendarmes*. We were taken – by a roundabout route, to avoid attracting attention – to the courtyard of the police barracks, some way outside the town centre. There we waited for the remaining seven Jews to be delivered. The process was finally completed about eight in the morning. Twelve persons. The brigadier rubbed his hands together.

Just before we got into the bus, Monsieur and Madame Pellat came up on their bicycles: Madame Regnier had told them the news. At first the brigadier refused to let them in, but the determined Madame Pellat started to make such a scene that he thought better of it, and gave in. We were thus able to say farewell to our neighbours.

And so, on the radiantly beautiful morning of 26th August 1942, in a genuinely comfortable tourist bus, we began our journey to Grenoble.

20

Caserne Bizanet, Grenoble

IF I TRY, NOW, to put into words what we went through on that day, and what we had to witness, then every word I use seems to me terribly inadequate – and at the same time, not simple enough. One has a duty to bear witness. But if it were not for that, it would be best to say nothing.

The tragedy was being played out almost silently, almost unnoticed. In the middle of a large, carefree town which carried on its business as usual. On a glorious summer day. No thunder, no lightning, no sign of divine rage descended from the cloudless, feelingless sky. There was no outward sign of the pain and the human goodness; the fear and the prayers; the persecution and the heroism that Caserne Bizanet held within its walls. Even amongst us, inside – even amongst the damned – there were no great scenes, no pathos, no emotional outbursts; there were barely a few, quiet tears. And yet language is quite inadequate to the attempt to make clear our deathly sense of desolation; inadequate to give voice to the silent groan of agony that we all had locked inside us.

There were perhaps no more than a thousand of us in this barracks. What happened to us there would constitute a tiny, invisible particle in the monstrous body of misdeeds perpetrated by the Germans against defenceless Jews. The series of crimes is endless; so is the number of the victims. And yet, what punishment could there be that could ever be an atonement, even for what was done here – done to the relatively small number of Jews in the Caserne Bizanet in Grenoble?

And what small comfort from the silence, the indifference of the world in the face of Jewish suffering.

At the time of my committing these notes to paper – December 1943 – there has been much discussion of the deportation of 1,500 Norwegian students, priests and teachers to Germany. Sweden, Finland and Switzerland have lodged an official protest against it. Sweden has even put her money where her mouth is and, under the pressure of public opinion, significantly reduced her trade with Germany.

All this is extremely welcome and gratifying. The magnificent people of Norway deserve this and so much more. But it is surely understandable if I cannot get out of my head the thought: what official voice was raised in response to the fact that every conceivable atrocity has been – and is being – inflicted on millions and millions of Jewish men, women and children? Which neutral régime thought our sufferings worth the loss of a single contract? Which country converted indignation over our ordeal into actual, concrete measures?

Even the Allies ... well, they at least have done something. But they neglected the issue to a monstrous degree, when there might still have been time. Their official outrage, in any case, was largely confined to words; and there were times when one could not help thinking that crimes against Jews were regarded by them mainly as fuel for the propaganda machine.

Let us return to Grenoble.

After a journey of about one hour our bus stopped in front of a barracks, the Caserne Bizanet, which was now serving as a prison for all the Jews arrested in the Isère region.

Other coaches were arriving at the same time as ours, each with its own cargo. A thick wall of people had gathered in the road by the front gate, curious to know what was happening. Most of them at least had the decency to watch in silence; others regaled their companions with a jokey commentary on events, as if they were having a particularly enjoyable time at the cinema. Nowhere a cry of indignation, nowhere a protest.

How many of them are still alive – this consignment of Jews, led into the barracks yard in front of all those gawping eyes?

We were received by soldiers: French soldiers in helmets, with bayonets at the shoulder. Helmets and bayonets, to herd this miserable flock into the grip of the German Beast.

A flock, incidentally, that consisted to a large extent of women, children, invalids and cripples. There was no distinction of age or gender. There was only one gender here: Jews – Jews to be eradicated. There were men and women in extreme old age. And then there were the children.

I do not wish to be guilty of any exaggeration here. Children under the age of two were left 'in freedom'. They had been snatched away from father, mother and siblings; but they were themselves 'free' – the freedom of a domestic animal deprived of its master. One day over your second birthday, however, and you joined your parents in captivity.

At least, then, these children over the age of two were not separated from their parents; at least they were allowed to die together? To allow oneself such sentimental fantasies would be to betray a poor understanding of the Germans. We shall see what became of these children above the age of two – what was allowed to become of them, without the protest of a single régime.

Anyway – this was the nature of the army that these helmets and bayonets had been called out to deal with. A few months later, when the Germans decided – flying in the face of all their previous undertakings – to occupy the *zone libre* too, then, of course, all the helmets and bayonets were meekly handed in to them. The campaign against Jewish women, children and old men had been glory enough for the great Pétain, Maréchal de France.

We were first taken to an office, where our names were entered in a register. There followed the separation into groups, each of which was allotted to a room with the appropriate number of sleeping spaces.

Anyone who had to perform a bodily function had first to report to a guard appointed for this purpose, and to wait. Once the number of candidates reached twenty, they were led by this heavily armed warrior across the yard to the toilet. After the performance of the function, they were carefully counted and escorted back. The next division followed in its turn. In this particular case, French organisation left nothing to be desired.

In comparison with Beaune-la-Rolande the accommodation here was very comfortable. Moreover, this time I was together with my loved ones. And yet, I now looked on the concentration camp with something akin to nostalgia. It was a place where there had at least been some approximation to hope; some approximation to life. Here, on the faces all around me, I constantly had before me that final, indifferent expression which is in fact the face of death. An expression that makes you instinctively want to whisper, to go around on tiptoes.

The reason for this was that most of us (I mean here the adults) had made the calculation that it was over. We were already in a sort of No-Man's-Land – a Second Realm – between life and death. But on the other side of the Demarcation Line, the Germans awaited us. There would begin the Third Realm – *das Dritte Reich* – which was a realm of agony. Nor would we be given the small comfort of being allowed to die together. They would tear us apart – we knew that. Not a voice, not a look, would be allowed to reach us there. Nothing but the mocking laughter of our executioners.

That is why so many – though still alive, though still unscathed – were already wearing their own death-masks.

Others, meanwhile, were curiously composed, simply because they lacked the imagination to grasp what lay before us. We had heard that our stay in the barracks would last three or four days. These people clung to this notion of three or four days: they escaped into each individual minute as if it were a hiding place.

Others again, especially the young, wanted to spite their fate by not showing any reaction at all. Inwardly, youth coursed through their veins with all youth's torrent of emotions; but they smiled at it all. That smile was more terrible than any grimace.

Any such expressions will seem false and empty; and yet, one cannot put it in any other way: there was, in this prison of people condemned to 'liquidation' a kind of nameless heroism which commanded awe, even reverence. There was no complaint voiced, among all these unfortunates. Each, in his or her own way, and all collectively, bore their pain with a dignity which was quite without show – a fact that made it all the more shattering. They were, all of them, no more than a little morsel to feed the Master Race's delight in torture. They were Jews. But they should have been immensely proud, these Jews: proud of their nobility, their greatness.

There could only be *one* punishment for the Germans, that would be a sufficient atonement – only one punishment that would be just. That would be if they had to suffer, eye for eye and tooth for tooth, what they made us suffer. And I should like to see how they behaved then.

For the rest of my life I shall have before me the small children, playing together in between the sleeping spaces, happy,

carefree, without malice. And for the rest of my life I shall see
the look of inexpressible sorrow on the faces of their mothers
– following them, watching over them, pressing them to their
hearts.

From a back window in the room you could look down on
to a narrow street. There, too, children were playing, and out
of the house opposite mothers were looking out at them, too.
Happy children, happy mothers.

Here, children playing, with their mothers. Over there,
children playing, with their mothers. No more than a narrow
street between us – no more than a couple of steps. Only, what
was happening there was a beginning, and what was happening here was the end. That is all.

In the course of the morning, my heart had already started to
play up. You will understand that I had had some difficulty following the instructions that Dr Ferrier had given me in Voiron
the previous day, when he strictly forbade me any kind of emotional disturbance.

In a room on the ground floor a kind of sickbay had been set
up, with a doctor and a nurse. Shortly after our arrival we had
seen a woman – a mother – taken away on a stretcher; she had
suddenly gone mad. Her small child remained behind.

At my wife's insistence I asked the guard in front of our door
to be allowed to see the doctor – but he would not hear of it.
The problem unresolved, I returned and lay back on my mat-
tress. Towards evening my condition rapidly worsened. With a
superhuman display of energy my wife succeeded in dragging
me down to the sickbay. Hardly had I got there when I suffered
an attack of greater severity than I had ever previously experienced. The nurse put something between my teeth, while the
doctor prepared an injection, which was followed by a second.

He was a human being, this doctor. He was not German. I
wish that I knew his name.

When I had come to myself sufficiently, he said to me: 'Stay here and lie quietly for the moment. The Prefect is in the barracks now. I shall give him my certification of your illness, and present you to him personally, once you are in a condition to walk again.' Glancing at my wife, he added: 'Madame will accompany you.' He then dictated something softly to the nurse and went away with the piece of paper.

When he returned, he was followed by a man who walked with difficulty on two crutches, with a child of about eight years. The man was whimpering in pain. He was a Polish Jew, who understood not a word of German; the boy – who spoke French like a native – acted as interpreter. 'Help my father, monsieur,' he implored. 'Help my father.'

The man was given an injection, but the pain continued. The boy began to weep inconsolably and covered his father in kisses. 'You'll see,' he reassured him, speaking in Yiddish, 'it'll be better soon.' Then, to the doctor, in French: 'That's right, isn't it, monsieur: we'll soon be able to go back home?' The doctor was unable to speak. Then, in Yiddish again: 'You see, father – better already!' The father gave no response; but bestowed on the child a look of indescribable pain and tenderness.

They left the room.

At last my condition improved to the point where the doctor and my wife could accompany me to the Prefect.

The Prefect said to me: 'You can go back home.' And then he added, with a peculiar emphasis. '*Immediately.*' He then gave me a document stating that I had permission to return *provisionally* (the word was underlined) to my residence, accompanied by my wife.

I thanked him. My wife also begged the Prefect to see the two other persons who belonged with us, Miss Kolářová and Mrs Ornstein. He agreed.

We returned to the second floor. On the way my wife said simply: 'A miracle, a miracle.' Dazed, I stretched myself out on the bed again. I had only a sort of numb awareness of our salvation. And then, what would the Prefect decide about Sláva and Mrs Ornstein? Sláva had stubbornly and consistently refused to appeal to her 'Aryan' status. She was determined to share our fate to the end. Now, for the first time, she declared her readiness to approach the Prefect, together with Mrs Ornstein.

While the two women were down below, a soldier came and took my wife to one side: 'I hear that you are free to go,' he whispered to her. 'Leave the barracks without delay.'

'My husband is still too weak,' she objected. 'We must wait a few hours, at least.'

'Let me say one thing to you,' the soldier insisted, 'just one thing. Get out of here, even if you have to carry your husband on your back!'

We recalled the Prefect's emphatic '*Immediately*'.

Just after that the two women returned. Sláva had the same document that we had. The Prefect had been satisfied with her certificate of baptism, although he had added: 'You will still have to present proof of your Aryan status before the *Commissariat général aux questions juives*.'

Mrs Ornstein? One glance at the unhappy woman was enough to show that she had not received mercy at the hands of the Prefect. This white-haired lady, who suffered from such bad *arthritis deformans* that she found it hard to dress herself, had had the temerity to request a medical examination on her own account.

The Prefect cut her off indignantly: 'Who decides that – you or me?'

He then sealed her fate with a simple: 'Vous pouvez disposer.' That will be all.

We had to leave her behind. Her and Mila Friedezky. And so many others. Of course, if we had stayed, we would not have been able to alter her fate in the slightest. It would not have helped any of us. In any case, we would have been separated.

We knew all that: reason told us that. And yet we felt almost ashamed of ourselves. We wanted to ask her pardon.

Finally we crept away, like guilty things. It was one in the morning. The whole building was silent. But this was a sleepless, agonised silence. A silence to choke you.

In the courtyard a soldier came up to us. It was the same one who had warned us. He said: 'I am glad that you are free. May God protect you.'

As the sentry at the gate checked our documents, he muttered under his breath to my wife: 'You have one last chance, now, to get away.'

We were on the street – back on the street. An unimaginable miracle. My wife and Sláva, already laden with our baggage, carried me more than they led me; and at last we reached a hotel. There was no room free; but they allowed us to spend the rest of the night in the foyer.

From one of the bedrooms we could hear the sound of breathing – the deep breathing of peaceful, contented sleep. We thought of those in the barracks.

At six in the morning we took the first tram to the station; and two hours later we were back in Voiron.

The same time yesterday ...

The same time yesterday, we were on the way to Grenoble. Now we are back here. Twenty-four hours between the two. Twenty-four hours which seemed more than a whole lifetime. And between them, too, a miracle; the miracle of a resurrection. But one of us was gone.

21

A toast

AT THE POLICE STATION, where we went to get back the key to our house, they were very surprised to see us. The brigadier even pretended to be pleased.

On the door of our house there was already a notice: 'Confiscated by order of the prefect of Isère.' Fortunately, though, they had not yet had time to remove our possessions.

From the Koflers we learned that buses full of prisoners from the Caserne Bizanet had already been seen driving through Voiron in the direction of Lyon. In one of these buses – one which was full of women and children – Rosa had been among the passengers. Kofler had even managed to speak with the poor woman for a couple of minutes.

We had gathered that the transportation was to take place in three or four days' time; in fact, the whole camp, entirely without exception, had been evacuated at five that morning. The *gendarmes* who accompanied them had been ordered to deliver them to the camp of Vényssieux near Lyon. There the deportees would apparently remain for several days, before being taken to the Demarcation Line and there handed over to the Germans.

We had to try everything possible to save Mrs Ornstein. Young Edgar Kofler,* our friend's son, had already gone to

Lyon on the first train. Two days later he returned empty-handed – all his efforts in vain.

In Lyon, the admirable Cardinal Gerlier* had set up a kind of rescue service, which was conducted by one Abbé Glasberg.* Rumour had it that this tireless and fearless priest had already helped a number of the camp inmates at Vényssieux to get away. Edgar Kofler had, besides, been in contact with a friend of Rosa's in Lyon, Madame Danon. This woman knew a distinguished advocate, who had influential contacts at the Prefecture. As long as Rosa was not yet in the clutches of the Germans, perhaps all was not yet lost. The crucial thing was to get there before the executioners.

But chance, or fate, wished otherwise. Through a disastrous chain of circumstances, all efforts came to nought: Abbé Glasberg was away; and the advocate was busy pleading a case in the court.

It was nearly evening when Edgar Kofler finally succeeded in making contact with the Abbé, who had in fact been at Vényssieux all day and had succeeded in getting a number of women and children to safety. The Abbé promised to go the very next morning and do his best for Rosa. And the advocate agreed to use his contacts at the Prefecture. For an appropriate fee ...

But when Abbé Glasberg arrived at Vényssieux the next morning, he found the camp empty. The Germans had learned that prisoners were being saved and had given the order that the victims be brought immediately to the Demarcation Line. They had also threatened Cardinal Gerlier with arrest.

As early as 2 a.m. the prisoners were removed, at great speed, from Vényssieux, in three separate groups: men, women and children. All that we were able to gather was that they were to be taken first to the camp of Drancy near Paris, in order to be deported onward from there. Madame Danon immediately sent a man to Paris on her behalf; but all his attempts to reach them at Drancy were fruitless. The prisoners had remained there a total of two days.

In Voiron we received a devastating couple of lines that Rosa had been able to write from Vényssieux. And that was the last we heard of her, or of Mrs Friedezky.

Much later we were to learn that the children – those children we had seen playing in Caserne Bizanet – had remained in France. They had been spared, then, you are perhaps thinking. Any such notion would show a poor understanding of the Germans.

Along with thousands of other children – 5,000 in all – these children had been packed into 'my' camp, Beaune-la-Rolande. And had then been 'liquidated' by lethal injection administered by Nazi women sent there for that specific purpose.

Among these Nazi women there were, without doubt, mothers – mothers who sat down calmly at the end of a day's work to write the most affectionate letters to their children.

At the beginning of September 1942 an issue of the mass-circulation paper *Gringoire* appeared with a massive headline on the front page: 'Le bobard des enfants séparés de leurs mères' ('Children separated from their mothers – the myth'). Below which an article spluttered indignantly about how people even had the audacity to give currency to such gruesome fabrications. Of course children had never been separated from their mothers.

And so we were again 'back home' in Voiron. Here we received many tokens of sympathy. From Belvès, too, we received a letter from Jacquot Rispal, blazing with fury and revulsion. If this letter had fallen into the hands of the censor, it might have had the severest consequences for our young friend. And Pierre wrote announcing a visit.

This was all very comforting. At the same time, we felt that our miraculous escape was again only temporary.

Two days after our return, two *gendarmes* appeared at our house. 'Purely out of sympathy', as they both assured us –

simply to enquire about my condition. They sat by my bed, smoked a cigarette, and drank a toast to my full recovery. Nor did they fail to condemn this entire action of the Germans in appropriate terms – 'completely between ourselves', of course. We parted like old friends.

Not long after that I was honoured by a visit from two more *gendarmes* – again, to drink a toast, from no other motive than that of respect. Anyone who had seen us sitting together there, chatting so intimately, would have taken the good *gendarmes* for my guardian angels.

Eight days later: yet another visit. But the closer we got to the bottom of the liqueur bottle, the clearer it became to us that this touching concern was of a similar nature to that of the cat for the mouse.

Our neighbour, Monsieur Pellat, had taken soundings at the Prefecture in Grenoble. 'Until further notice,' they had told him, 'they have nothing to fear.'

Until further notice.

True, the noose around our necks had not – by a miracle – been tightened. It was, however, still around our necks. All it needed was a little tug, and the cord that had been twisted out of my Jewishness would do its work. The task of the brave *gendarmes* was that of periodically checking whether our heads were still sitting nicely in the noose. Until further notice.

And then there were other events, other symptoms. Jews who had been spared up till now were arrested and taken to the concentration camp of Rivesaltes. The protests of such church leaders as Cardinal Gerlier and Monsignor Saliège,* which had become well-known even in neutral countries abroad, now only had the consequence that the French authorities refrained, for the moment, from operating on a large scale. They delivered their victims to the Germans in small groups. This was much less visible, and allowed Vichy to utter the most bare-faced denials.

Pierre Vorms, who had come to us in the meantime, insisted that we must do something. A miracle like that of Grenoble would not happen a second time. We understood that perfectly; but what were we to do? In our situation there was – at most – one path of salvation: escape to Switzerland.

22

Escape to Switzerland

But how to get to Switzerland ... ? Two obstacles presented themselves, like gigantic prison walls: one was the difficulty of getting out of France, and the other was the difficulty of then getting into Switzerland.

The Vichy régime was a match for the Germans in another field, too – that of despicable mendacity. On the one hand, Laval had explicitly stated to foreign press representatives that 'nothing would prevent him from getting rid of all foreign Jews'. But on the other hand he removed from these Jews any possibility of leaving the country. There was a strict ban on the use of railways. There had been an enormous tightening of security on the Swiss border. Anyone caught trying to escape to Switzerland ended up a prisoner at Rivesaltes.

As for entry into Switzerland: every Jew who had the great fortune actually to succeed in crossing the border risked being *refoulé*; in other words, handed back to the French; in other words, delivered – with even greater certainty than before – to the German knife. Switzerland had, however, at least declared that it would investigate each case individually and would not deny entry to Jews (such as Austrians and Czechs) who were in immediate fear of their lives.

Bearing in mind that we belonged to this category, Vorms continued his efforts. Over a period of weeks he went back and forth between Voiron and Grenoble, in search of a possible solution.

Some refugees had managed to make their way on foot through Savoie and then over the Alpine passes into Switzerland; but in view of my condition, this possibility could of course not be entertained.

Vorms continued his efforts unstintingly. One day, at the beginning of October, he returned from Grenoble and declared: 'This time I believe I have finally found the answer. But you must decide at once.' And he proceeded to outline the plan.

A lawyer in Grenoble had – reluctantly, after much hesitation, and 'from purely humanitarian motives' – given him the address of one Monsieur Roland, at the same time remarking, in a significant tone of voice: 'If he really wants to, he can do anything.'

After many failed attempts Vorms finally managed to find Monsieur Roland, who lived in a hotel, and to get a meeting with him. A young woman whom Roland introduced as his representative was also present at the discussion.

In brief: Monsieur Roland eventually identified himself as a police inspector of the Sûreté in Grenoble, assigned to the border brigade at Annecy. In other words, he was one of those special tracker dogs that Vichy set upon Jews who wanted to flee to Switzerland. It was, therefore, scarcely necessary to explain our situation to him; he grasped it immediately.

After some consideration he finally declared his willingness to take on our case, and to get us across the border.

But how could we get to the border? We had no papers except for those identity cards with the word 'JEW' stamped on them prominently in large letters. The police officer's only response to this concern on the part of my friend was a dismissive wave of the hand. Anyone who was under his protection would need no papers, and need have no fear of police checks or anything else. Such obstacles existed only for common or garden *passeurs*, not for a police inspector.

In short, it would be child's play. All that our high-minded benefactor required, for this child's play, was 20,000 francs per person, which is to say, 60,000 francs all told, payable in advance.

Vorms had the audacity to suggest that such a bill – payable in advance – was excessive. At this Monsieur Roland very nearly showed him the door. He gave him the stark choice: either accept my terms unconditionally or stop wasting my precious time. He added, purely in passing: 'If your friends don't mind ending up in Rivesaltes within the next fortnight, then they don't have to spend a centime. Because that is where all foreign Jews will be within a fortnight – I can give you my word on that.'

We discussed it over and over. Finally, we decided to sacrifice the last of our money; to convert everything we could into cash; and to accept Roland's conditions.

Vorms summed up his impression of Roland as follows: a gangster, certainly, but a gangster who sticks to an agreement once he's made it. He then went to make the telephone call. (He had agreed with Roland that he would ring him in his office at the Sûreté in Grenoble.) On his return, he had these instructions for us: we must travel on the last train to Grenoble the day after tomorrow. This train arrives at midnight. A young lady – Roland's representative – will meet us there and tell us the rest. We must take no luggage – at most one small suitcase or briefcase.

And so the appointed day came, and we crept away in the night, like criminals, accompanied by Vorms and using roundabout routes so as not to risk running into one of our friends from the *gendarmerie*. At the station we huddled in a dark corner. Then there was the journey to Grenoble, in constant fear of a police check. We were lucky. At the station the young woman was waiting for us, in accordance with the agreement.

Only a few weeks had passed since the experience of Caserne Bizanet. Once again, we faced a leap into the unknown – a leap which might very well lead to the same disaster that only a last-minute miracle had averted on that occasion. The young woman made a sign to us to follow her.

She stood for a quarter of an hour in front of a house in Rue Thiers, then opened the gate and let us in. We groped our way after her in the darkness, following her right up to the fifth floor. There, at the end of a long corridor, was a dirty, stuffy attic room. A bed (just the one), with no sheets on it; a table; three chairs.

The young woman explained that she would pick us up at six the next morning. Monsieur Roland would be waiting for us in a café opposite the station. We should not make ourselves known, but simply follow him inconspicuously into the station. He would board the fast train to Annemasse, in a first-class compartment; we should get into the same carriage. In the event of a police check, we would simply direct the officials to the inspector, and not worry about anything else. At Annemasse Roland would see to everything else, and take us over the border, to the electric tram which would take us the five kilometres to Geneva.

Before she left us, at 1 a.m., the young woman demanded that we hand over the 60,000 francs, saying that she had to go to the Sûreté now to inform the inspector of our arrival and to give him the money.

6 a.m. We sat and waited. No sign of the young woman. Six-thirty ... Seven. No one. By now the train that we were supposed to be on had already left Grenoble.

Finally, at 8 a.m., she appeared, pleading 'last-minute technical problems'. We should understand that Monsieur Roland wanted to proceed with absolute security and not allow us to be exposed to the slightest risk. He therefore recommended that we now travel by the evening train. She would come for us at six in the evening – six on the dot.

At seven she finally arrived – to tell us that our departure had been put off until the next day.

To cut a long story short: we did not depart the following morning; nor the following evening. The four of us had now been in the attic room for two whole days. At mealtimes we stole out to grab something quickly in a restaurant; at every moment we had to be on the lookout for patrols looking for Jews. Our nerves were shot to pieces; we had reached the point where we wanted an end to the terror, rather than this terror without end. We wanted to have our money back and return to Voiron, come what might; and Vorms had arranged to meet Roland late in the evening for this purpose.

Towards midnight he finally returned and begged us earnestly not to lose our nerve at the last moment. He had been at the Sûreté in person, and had been able to see for himself the sort of power that the inspector wielded; his word was absolute law there. And Roland had been able to produce a wholly plausible explanation for the repeated delay. He offered us the option of taking the money back or travelling with him the next morning; and this time, he guaranteed that everything would go according to plan.

The previous night, another group of Jews had been taken in Grenoble. We finally decided to go with Roland ...

This time the young woman collected us punctually. In the café opposite the station I had my first sight of Roland: a man of obvious self-confidence, and the demeanour that knows that all doors open in front of him. With him were a huge man with a vicious bulldog face and a stocky young fellow of extremely dubious appearance. Both these individuals, the young woman explained, were also members of the police, and would be accompanying us as far as Annemasse.

Before Roland boarded the train with his entourage, he signalled to the young woman to go to him, and exchanged a few words with her. She returned with the message: 'I am to inform you from Monsieur Roland that your arrival over the border is as guaranteed as that of a parcel sent by special delivery. You can have a quiet nap until Annemasse.'

We took our leave of Vorms, who said he would wait in Voiron for a telegram from us before returning to Belvès.

We were due to arrive in Annemasse at 10.30.

Our 'escort' in the neighbouring compartment was in splendid form: we could hear them laughing and joking. In the end they began a game of cards.

As we approached Aix-les-Bains, the young boy entered our compartment and gestured to my wife to follow him into the corridor, where he whispered something to her. I could see her shocked reaction, and the vehemence of her response.

I stood up and went out. 'What's going on?' I asked.

The boy looked me straight in the eye, quite without shame; his voice was calmly insolent. 'I have already told Madame: you must get out. A police check will take place after Aix. If you do not get out, all three of you will be arrested. Is that clear?'

By now the train had reached the station. On the platform was a whole platoon of *gardes mobiles*, preparing to get on.

We had to get off: what other possibility was there? My wife had grabbed the boy by the arm and pulled him with her on to the platform. 'We insist that Monsieur Roland at least remain with us and accompany us back to Grenoble. Otherwise we will make a scene: tell him that!'

The train would only stop in Aix for a few minutes. The man made as if he was going to return to Roland in the compartment; but on the step he stopped and gave my wife such a hefty shove that she fell over backwards. He then pulled himself into the carriage and closed the door. The train started.

To this day I find it hard to believe that this whole scene did not arouse the suspicion of one of the policemen ... hard to believe, in fact, that we were able to control ourselves to such an extent that our rage and despair – not to mention the indescribable feeling of exhaustion – were not clear for everyone to see. Here we suddenly were, thrown out on to the station platform – which might just as well have been the middle of enemy territory. A casual demand to see our papers from any *garde* that we now encountered would have meant the end.

What were we to do? How could we get out of the station? How could we get back to Voiron? And – in the event of our being forced to spend a night in Aix – how could we possibly find a place to stay where they would not ask to see our papers? We knew no one at all here.

These were the questions that immediately raced through our minds as we stood helplessly on the platform – and on top of it all had to behave casually, as though we were tourists who had decided to take advantage of the fine autumn day for a casual outing.

We decided to go first to the station buffet, and to wait there in the hope that those *gardes mobiles* who had not boarded the train might leave the station. On entering the buffet I noticed that the back door, which gave on to the street, was wide open. A door to freedom ...? I crept towards it, virtually hypnotised by this possible path of escape. In no time at all, though, a bad-tempered waitress had planted herself in front of it. 'What do you want here?' she barked at me. 'This isn't an exit.'

I muttered some kind of excuse, and ordered a drink. The waitress had obviously not taken to us, and kept her eyes on us constantly. Our stress was doubled by the need to give the appearance of carrying on a perfectly casual conversation. We were entirely at the mercy of this simple waitress. We were Jews: there was no one whom we were *not* entirely at the mercy of.

After a quarter of an hour we decided to go. Fortunately there were now no *gardes* on the platforms. We could proceed to the street without hindrance. But what next?

We began to wander the streets of the town without direction. We remarked on people going for a walk, people here for the spa. We stared with enormous interest at the display windows of the shops (even though these were practically empty). Finally we went into a café. Here I gathered the information that there was no train to Grenoble until the next morning. There was, however, a bus at four in the afternoon.

We began to stroll about once more, even though we were fit to collapse with exhaustion after all we had been through. We went to another café. At the next table someone was recounting the local news, which included the fact that a group of Jews had been taken through Aix under guard yesterday – Jews who had attempted to flee to Switzerland and who had been handed over to the police by their *passeurs*.

We had actually been *lucky* with our Monsieur Roland, it seemed ...

Finally – finally – it was three o'clock. We walked to the bus stop, which was in the main square. Quite a few people were already waiting, and new people kept arriving. It was a good thing we had arrived so early.

Suddenly I saw a *gendarme* making his way, slowly and showily, across the square to our group. 'Oh – *another* police check!' growled a woman next to us angrily, and she began to look for her papers in her handbag.

The bus was already in sight. For us, though, there was only one thing to do: get away, as quickly and unobtrusively as possible. As everyone else surged forward, we pushed our way backwards. I could already hear the *gendarme*'s voice: 'Vos papiers!'

Then, suddenly, exactly like a *deus ex machina*, a man came out of a garage, ran up to the *gendarme* in a state of excitement and started to tell him something ... and the two disappeared together in a hurry.

Would the *gendarme* return? Should we stay where we were – or try to get away? We grabbed our chance, went back to the bus; and, as soon as we had jammed ourselves on to the crammed vehicle, it started moving. We breathed again. How we breathed again.

The relief was almost as great, in fact, as though we had actually managed to cross the Swiss border. For a moment we almost forgot what had actually happened to us. We drove on, and as we drove on we knew that we were out of the reach of that *gendarme*. At that moment, that was all that we were conscious of.

The bus stopped for a half-hour break in Chambéry, which for us was a half-hour of anxiety. There are *gendarmes* in Chambéry too, after all. But the stop passed without incident. Grenoble: we rushed to the station and just made the evening train. At nine in the evening we were back in Voiron.

Our Swiss Expedition was at an end. So was our strength.

I should briefly mention the sequel to the Roland episode. We ourselves could do nothing, of course: any complaint on our part would have had the direst consequences for us, as of course the police bandit knew perfectly well. However, Vorms, together with our neighbour Pellat, did go in pursuit of Roland, to see if they could at least get back the 60,000 francs. They finally managed to find the rogue – who condescended to return 20,000 francs, promising to pay the rest within eight days. When Pellat returned to Grenoble on the agreed day, however, Roland had vanished without trace. From what Pellat was able to find out, it seemed that the police inspector had practised similar deceptions on a number of individuals who did not happen to be Jews, and who had therefore been able to denounce him. Roland had, however, managed to make himself scarce in time; there were other police officers implicated in his schemes, and it had been more convenient not to be able to find him.

Fortunately, our friends from the *gendarmerie* in Voiron had not looked for us during our absence; and so our attempted escape had not been noticed. We had lost 40,000 francs – but, apart from that, nothing had changed.

There was no point in banging our heads against the wall any longer: all we would achieve would be to injure ourselves still further. We were tired; indescribably tired.

23

A telegram

A COUPLE OF WEEKS WENT BY. Among the letters that we received was one from Jacquot Rispal, in which he wrote that he was looking forward to seeing us again, soon, in the Dordogne. The Dordogne? I had no idea what the young man meant, and attached no significance to it. Wishful thinking, I said to my wife – just something he had written to cheer us up.

Meanwhile, our beloved *gendarmes* had honoured us with yet another visit. We had chatted away like old friends, and they had given us a solemn assurance that under their protection in Voiron we were as safe as in Abraham's bosom. Naturally, I gave this no credence whatsoever. But it made no difference to us any more; we had become utterly passive.

Then, one day at the beginning of November, an urgent telegram arrived announcing Jacquot's arrival for that very evening. The journey from Belvès to Voiron took a full twenty-four hours. Why, we asked ourselves, would our young friend undertake such a long and difficult journey?

Once the greetings were out of the way, and once young Jacquot had unpacked the wonderful gifts that his mother had given him for us, he explained, shortly and succinctly, that he had come to fetch us. The position of Jews was becoming worse and worse. We must travel with him immediately – the very next day. Everything had been taken care of, planned down to the last detail. All we had to do was get on to the train with him. We must leave everything else to him and to his parents.

We stared uncomprehendingly at the boy; and he decided to give us a little further explanation.

After our disastrous attempt at flight, his mother had sworn to herself that she would save us. But how? She lay awake at night, grappling with the question. Then, one night, as she lay there, it came to her – a flash of inspiration. A few kilometres from Belvès, in a quite isolated position on the top of a hill, is a Franciscan convent, with a hospital for female patients with epilepsy and mental disorders, run by the Sisters. Its name is the Convent of Labarde.

Gabriel Rispal, Jacquot's father, had done odd jobs at the convent from time to time over a period of years. He was on very good terms with the Mother Superior, Mère Saint-Antoine.

Hélène Rispal* had woken her husband in the middle of the night and said to him: 'First thing tomorrow you must go to Labarde. We must persuade Mère Saint-Antoine to hide the Scheyers in the convent. I could be sure they were safe there.'

Next morning, sure enough, Rispal paid the Mother Superior a first visit. Like a good diplomat, he didn't come out with it straight; he needed to test out the ground first.

He returned full of confidence: when he had come on to the subject of the persecutions of the Jews, the Mother Superior had shown her sense of outrage at what had been happening. On a second visit he told her the whole story, describing our situation and at the same time explaining how deeply he and his wife cared about us. He then made the request.

The Mother Superior was by no means hostile; but there was one major obstacle. Labarde is a convent for nuns, with an institution for female patients attached to it. Mère St-Antoine

148

was happy to take my wife and Sláva; but some other hiding place would have to be found for me – perhaps with one of the farmers in the surrounding area.

Now, Rispal was not so easily deterred. He went over our experiences once more; talked of my terrible state of health; pointed out that there was a room with a separate entrance in a side wing of the institution; offered to undertake all the necessary work himself; in short, he won the day and was able to return to his wife with an unconditional yes from the Mother Superior. And on the evening of the very same day Hélène Rispal had dispatched her son to Voiron to collect us. All we had to do was get on to the train.

'But,' I objected, 'we can't get on to a train at all. If we are found, with our papers ...'

'Naturally we have thought of that too,' Jacquot interrupted with a smile. 'Here!' And with a triumphant gesture he pulled three identity cards out of his breast pocket. 'A nephew of my parents, René Mathieu,* is mayor of St-Cernin-de-l'Herm. With his help we have got false identity papers; they just need to have your photographs added.'

I stared at him, this fresh-faced nineteen-year-old, who sat talking to us so earnestly. We were speechless – speechless with amazement and emotion.

These were people who scarcely knew us – or, as in the case of this René Mathieu, did not know us at all. These were people who were not themselves in danger; were not Jews; had not personally experienced any of our sufferings. They could at best only imagine what our existence was like. And they had done all this for us. They had not only disrupted their own lives when they could have carried on in peace; they had not only taken upon themselves all this trouble; they had also voluntarily placed themselves in danger in order to help us. Here was a mother who, without hesitating, had risked her only son's safety for our sake. Such things still happened.

And, at the same time, I could not avoid asking a question of my own conscience: 'Would I have behaved in the same way, if the positions were reversed?' I do not know the answer.

Even though we had decided to make no further attempts ourselves, we could hardly refuse, after everything that these people had undertaken on our behalf. There was, then, nothing to discuss.

The only problem – which we explained to our young friend – was that we needed to delay our departure for a few days, so that this time we could bring at least *some* of our possessions with us, and store the rest safely. Jacquot was against this, but eventually agreed. We fixed on the date of 16th November, and he spontaneously volunteered to return to fetch us on that day. Early next morning he set off back to Belvès.

We accompanied him to the station, where we happened to bump into one of our friends from the *gendarmerie*. 'Not leaving us, are you?' he asked me anxiously. 'The idea!' I replied. 'We are simply seeing someone off at the station.' 'Oh, I see.' And he shook my hand in relief.

This time, we resolved, this time, at least, there would be no rush. But events decreed otherwise.

Almost immediately after Jacquot's departure came the Allied landing in Algeria,[11] which was used by the Germans as a pretext to occupy the *zone libre*. 'France Libre' had just ceased to exist.

The consequence of this event for us was that now we had no time to lose. The Swastika might arrive in Voiron at any moment. We decided to leave the town the next day; sent a telegram to Jacques Rispal; and on 11th November we managed to board a train for Lyon without being noticed by our *gendarmes*. There our young friend was waiting for us: he had received our telegram just in time to make the journey in the opposite direction as far as Lyon.

---

11. 'Operation Torch', the British-American amphibious invasion of North Africa, which started on 8th November 1942.

We arrived in Belvès on the morning of the 12th, but remained on the train: it had been agreed that we would get out at the next station, Le Got, to avoid the risk of being recognised in Belvès. Jacquot left the train and his father got on in his place. As Gabriel Rispal happened to be with an acquaintance of his, he pretended not to know us. He nonetheless managed, with a conjuror's sleight of hand, to slip a packet of cigarettes into my pocket.

In Le Got he got out; so did we. He walked towards a car which stood in front of the station; so did we. Pointing to the driver, he said: 'You can trust this man.'

Once in the car, we threw our arms round each other. All four of us wept.

After a journey of about half an hour, the car stopped. There was a turn-off from the main road: a country lane leading fairly steeply up to a hilltop. By the turning was a sign which read, 'Asile de Labarde'.

We took this lane. After a further quarter of an hour, we had reached the top. On the left was a huge statue of Christ which dominated the landscape; in front of us a wide lane, which led past some farm buildings to a rambling old house.

We had arrived.

24

Labarde

WHEN I THINK BACK TO 12th November 1942, that cloudy, cold, wet late autumn day seems to me one of the most moving, and also one of the happiest, of my life. Amid the hell of Hitler's world, a snatch of the Music of the Spheres.

We were absolutely worn out with exhaustion. Everything that we had gone through dragged us down, down to the ground – like a piece of baggage that is too heavy to carry. And what did we have before us? Our new 'home', Labarde – a house for mentally retarded women, epileptics and the incurably ill. A house of sorrow.

And yet the day of our arrival in this house was one of the most beautiful days of our lives.

By our side was Gabriel Rispal, his eyes lit up with the joy of seeing his wife's plan turned into reality. What did these people know of us? That we were outcasts. Jews.

Then there was the reception we received at the hands of the Mother Superior, Mère St-Antoine. A woman of about fifty came towards us, her still beautiful face framed by the black-and-white veil of the Franciscan nuns. I had the image fixed in my mind of some strict, unapproachable abbess who had condescended to allow us the use of a corner of the convent; but who, apart from that, would probably make us feel tolerated rather than welcome – who would regard us as beggars that had to be given alms out of the duty to 'love thy neighbour'.

Instead I saw before me a woman whose title, 'Mother', represented not merely some rank in the religious hierarchy but the nature of her whole being. I felt immediately at ease and relaxed with her – as with a mother. I felt immediately, too, that this noble woman was also a guide of souls.

She received us, not as beggars to be given something out of kindness; not as outcasts in need of shelter. She received us as if it were a particular mark of honour to be able to put her house at our disposal.

And she treated us with the care and attention bestowed on patients in convalescence. Without asking questions, she encouraged us to speak; she opened the door for us; and I noticed that, as she listened, there were tears in her eyes.

She then took us to our accommodation – though not before she had laid particular emphasis on the pains that the Rispals had taken to put all this in place.

We had expected a very primitive kind of lodging, and would have been quite happy with that. All that we longed for was a little peace. To our surprise, however, we found a clean, heated room with three comfortable beds, fitted out with everything necessary and even equipped with its own lavatory.

And the Mother Superior actually apologised that she could not offer us anything better ...

On that first day we had lunch, not in our own room, but with Rispal in the *parloir* where Mère St-Antoine had received us. She had delicacies laid out for our welcome – items whose existence we had almost forgotten, such as sardines, butter, an omelette. And then she appeared in person with a tray: 'I have something more here, for your dessert,' she announced, and placed a dish of *compôte* in front of us. 'You must eat properly, and get your strength back; that's the first thing. Let me worry about everything else.'

In the afternoon Pierre Vorms came, staying with us until evening. And we were promised a visit from Hélène Rispal and Jacquot for the next day.

We felt positively intoxicated by all this care and warmth. We almost forgot that we were not in some holiday home, but in a clandestine location – in a hiding hole. I sometimes wondered if it was actually happening. We felt like human beings among other human beings, not like wild animals being hunted.

A suite in the most luxurious hotel could not have seemed more comfortable than this simple room in which we sat with our friends. And when our friends had left, on that first night under the roof – under the protection – of Labarde, we fell into a deep, peaceful sleep, after which, for the first time for ages, waking up was something other than fear and anxiety in the face of the new day.

I hope that I may have succeeded in explaining why I look back on that day –12th November 1942 – as one of the happiest of my life.

And on the day after that we had the joy of seeing Hélène Rispal and her son.

If, even then, we felt the profoundest gratitude towards this woman, the emotion has since been replaced by one of boundless affection. With every day that has passed, and that we have got to know her better, we have fallen in love with her more. She is like a sister to us now. And her child is like our own child.

This quiet woman is simplicity personified. Modesty personified. She gives no thought to herself; on the contrary, she is positively surprised at any expression of affection, and does not understand that others may not find it so natural to take or receive as she finds it to give – to give of herself.

In the final reckoning, she saved our lives – she, with her husband and her son. And we shall see how she took care of us later, too. And yet we have long since ceased to be 'grateful'. For only if you can describe gratitude as love, and love as gratitude – only then do we three feel what we owe to Hélène Rispal.

The state of euphoria into which we were plunged by the first days of our sojourn in Labarde could not, of course, last for ever. But it was certainly not replaced by any sort of terrible disillusionment.

We realised, of course, that we were by no means out of danger; we were only hidden from it. It was true, too, that we could not afford any false sense of security, and had to avoid the slightest lack of caution. We were hidden, not safe. And we were living among the mentally ill and the retarded.

From the very beginning, however, we felt surrounded by an atmosphere of goodwill and sympathy, and had the sense that Mère St-Antoine here in Labarde, as well as our friends in Belvès, stood before us as protectors; and this knowledge buoyed us up and gave us hope. It seemed that in shedding our identity (which was known only to the Mother Superior and to our friends), we had also somehow shed the consequences of that identity – at least the immediate and terrible consequences.

Life in an institution for fools and epileptics is no holiday. A convent, in itself, is not the most entertaining of places. Moreover, we could not risk straying beyond the confines of the house. The crucified Christ at the end of the lane represented the limit to our freedom of movement; and even within this limit we had to be careful.

Yet none of this was able to impair our contentment. The smallest complaint would have seemed a sinful act of pride – a tempting of Fate. Never before did we appreciate the value of a roof over our heads, of a warm oven, and of every single bit of bread, as here in Labarde. Never before had my wife and Sláva gone about their work with such zeal as they did here, where from early morning until late at night they carried out the most varied and most demanding jobs for the house happily, as though it were an offering of thanksgiving.

The three of us were brought closer together. Every day that we were able to live without fear was something that we experienced each time as another blessing – a gift. At the end of the day we went to bed with one wish: that this great fortune might be granted to us on the next day, too. We did not take it for granted for one moment. After all, we only had to think what was being done to others, who had not found any Rispals, or any Labarde.

We do not know whether it will be granted to us to remain in Labarde and to survive. I write these lines at the end of December 1943. Germany is a very long way from being defeated. It may be that our sojourn here is merely a final stay of execution that has been granted by destiny. But even if that were the case, we will have been fully conscious of, and thankful for, every half-peaceful day that we have lived here: we regard them as gifts.

25

Blessed are the poor in spirit

OUR SOCIAL ENVIRONMENT HERE consists of two elements. On the one hand, the inmates of the hospital – the *enfants*, about eighty in number.

'Enfants', children: the word is here used to express a concept of neighbourly love. All the patients here are referred to by this term, from the youngest, five-year-old Monique, to the oldest, the nearly-eighty-year-old Marie Mass, who was brought here as a ten-year-old orphan by the *Assistance Publique*. Marie Mass has lived within these walls for nearly seven decades: many thousands of identical days and nights. Were it not for her terrible fear of death, however (for she is mentally 'normal'), Marie Mass would be completely happy.

On the other hand we have the convent, the *communauté* of fifteen Sisters, under the guidance of the Mother Superior. It is a microcosm in which worldly values and standards have no place. The microcosm is, however, no less full of work and trouble, of dramas great and small. But all these are borne in the belief that our days on earth are no more than a fleeting, trivial pathway to another life, the life eternal. This belief gives the Sisters the strength to do without any earthly thanks or reward; and this applies to the twenty-year-old Soeur St-Félix just as much as to the eighty-five-year-old Soeur Marthe, who still works in spite of her age.

And these two little worlds – the mentally ill, the 'abnormals', and those who look after them with so much dedication – intertwine to form a whole, in a way which has taught me to be less ready with a number of received ideas that one tends to go about with.

'Blessed are the poor in spirit, for theirs is the kingdom of Heaven.'

The kingdom of Heaven? Provided that they are not suffering from some painful bodily affliction, the 'poor in spirit' are already blessed on earth. They live without having to fight, and death has no terror for them; they have no conception of it. Marie Mass is 'rational'; that is why she has such a terrible fear of dying. The others, on the other hand, in their 'irrationality', are possessed of that highest form of wisdom, which protects them from suffering.

A number of them are subject to delusions of one kind or another. This delusion, however, in its every logical ramification, will be more real to them than our realities.

One of our *enfants* is an old woman, Mémé, who once, many years ago, was a telephone operator. Every day she conducts highly animated conversations, for hours at a time, on an imaginary telephone with imaginary partners. Once, in the middle of such a conversation, one of the Sisters came into the room suddenly. 'Excuse me,' Mémé said to her interlocutor, 'I must ring off now. Soeur de l'Annonciation has come in, and what we are talking about does not concern her. I shall ring you again later.'

Others, who seem to exist in a semi-conscious state of lethargy, are periodically subject to violent emotional outbursts, which appear like some kind of earthquake of the subconscious. In these cases, though, nothing is allowed to inhibit their behaviour, which takes its course without restraint or punishment. The most that is done is to separate them from the others for the duration of the crisis. In the worst case, where they threaten others with violence, they may be placed in a straitjacket. The punishments that our own consciousness of reality would cause to us 'normal' people, if we allowed our emotions free rein, are not something that they have to contend with – never mind severer punishments than separation or a straitjacket.

Then we have Germaine, a shy, peaceful, to all appearances completely harmless individual. Germaine had formed a particular attachment to Soeur Benigna; she would follow the Sister everywhere and obeyed her slightest gesture. One day Soeur Benigna was moved, and in her place came one Soeur Marie-Bernard. Germaine could not abide the new Sister, and simply ignored her. But when Soeur Marie-Bernard once insisted on the performance of a task, Germaine – who was normally completely quiet and submissive – leapt upon the Sister, pulled off her wimple and showered her with the filthiest words of abuse. Germaine did not lose her 'position' as a consequence: she is 'simple'. What would happen to a 'normal' person in a similar case?

Moreover, these people are able to lose themselves in their dreams without any sort of hindrance. Most of them slip from waking to sleep, and from sleep to waking, until they finally slip into death. Neither in waking nor in sleep has life been a source of fear to them.

I think very often of Minou. I never heard her utter a word, and could easily have concluded that she was mute.

One of the patient bedrooms shares a wall with our room. When it is quiet, every movement, every sound from next door can be heard through the thin wall. And night after night, always at the same time, ever so softly, a delicate, ghostly melody would start up in the dark. It was like a sweet, forgotten song of childhood – a secret caress. A fragment of a dream – a dream turned into sound. It was Minou who was singing to herself like this, for a minute, or for two minutes, night after night. No one told her not to; she was simple.

One night she was singing; but suddenly stopped in mid-song. In the morning she was found dead.

Irrespective of age, our *enfants* are also children to the extent that they have remained in an original state of nature.

Take their self-centredness, for example. They live in a house guided by the principle 'love thy neighbour'; but most of them have absolutely no conception of their neighbours. There is a sort of herd instinct which makes them tend to stick together; but if one of their number disappears, many of them do not even notice.

Since our arrival at Labarde several of the patients have died, young as well as old. But since the word 'dying' has no significance for the mentally retarded, a death makes not the slightest impression on them. And the funeral procession, led by the Mother Superior and a priest, which goes from the chapel to the small cemetery behind the convent, is to them just a welcome change to the routine. They do not feel the obligation to put on a sad expression, to interrupt what they are doing, or to engage in insincere, unnecessary eulogies. 'Elle est partie' – She's gone away – is the most response you will get if you ask about the deceased. She's gone away. What more needs to be said?

At night-time there is an empty bed in the bedroom. But not for long: soon a new patient will come in and the bed will be occupied again. Nothing has changed: one face is replaced by another. No one was expecting an inheritance from the departed; no sought-after post has become available at her death – nothing that would initiate a competition among the others. Whether she is alive or dead, the soup still arrives on the table at the usual hour for everyone else.

This is, after all, a home for the simple.

Another aspect of this 'original state of nature' among the poor in spirit is their openness. They can allow themselves to give their thoughts honest, unadorned expression. When they talk, they do not make speeches, and they have no use for white lies.

One day I was walking past the cowshed with Jacquot Rispal. Louisette, whose animal greed knows no bounds, was about to chew on a huge mangelwurzel, still covered in dirt. 'Can I have a little bit, Louisette?' I ask her. In answer she presses her index finger to her left eye, which means: 'You'll have to wait a long time for that.' I nudge Jacquot. 'What about me?' he asks. 'Won't you give me some, either?' 'Oh, yes,' she coos happily, in her rough bass voice, offering him the root, 'oh, yes, I'll definitely give *you* some, because you are young and handsome, Monsieur Jacquot.'

One day the Mother Superior received an instruction, via the mayor of our municipality, to the effect that all those patients who might be encountered outside the institution must be provided with an identity card. There were about fifteen who were employed in agricultural work and needed this document, and therefore first of all a photograph. My wife, who had managed to get hold of a Kodak, undertook the role of photographer.

Huge excitement for all those chosen. Each one of them tries hastily to pretty herself a little; even among the most pitiable specimens of humanity there remains a trace of feminine coquettishness. All the others are severely disappointed. (They have no idea how wonderful it is simply not to need an identity card; they cannot imagine that there are countless individuals right now who would give anything to be beyond the Good and Evil of the identity paper.) They are unhappy; but the one who takes it worst is Madeleine.

Of all our *enfants*, Madeleine is perhaps the ugliest. Barely twenty, she looks like a shrivelled, crooked old woman – or perhaps like an embryo. Her appearance is something that takes some getting used to, even though God knows we are hardened to such things here in Labarde.

Madeleine's sobs are heartbreaking; she wants to have her photograph and her *cartité*, just like the others. No words are of any use whatever. She carries on crying and begging until finally my wife promises her: 'All right, Madeleine, you shall have your *cartité*. Just calm down, and I will take your picture.'

Beaming, Madeleine takes up her pose; and my wife takes the snap. Job done. Only, Madeleine wants to have her *cartité* right there and then. It is not so easy to explain to her that she has to wait for a while.

'You didn't have any film left in the camera,' I say to my wife, once we are back in our room. 'Of course I didn't,' she replies, 'but don't worry. She'll get her *cartité*.'

My wife proceeds to cut the portrait of a film star out of an old magazine – a beauty with perfect waves, languorous eyelashes, a tremendous low-cut dress, diamond earrings and three pearl necklaces. She takes a piece of pink card, and sticks the picture on to it. She adds the word 'MADELEINE' in calligraphic writing, at the bottom. The fact that Madeleine can neither read nor write is of no importance whatever. This is the way it is done.

I go and fetch Madeleine. 'You see,' says my wife, 'because you were good, your *cartité* is already ready. Here you are!'

Madeleine takes the piece of card, examines the picture and falls into a veritable ecstasy of joy. She then runs to the Mother Superior: '*Ma mère*, I've got it, I've got my *cartité*, and look! What a good picture of me it is!' The Mother Superior, the Sisters – the entire house – are called upon to admire the picture. And each time Madeleine repeats with delight: 'What a good picture of me, what a good picture of me!'

I don't know why I ever entertained the smallest doubt about the procedure. Madeleine has never looked in a mirror; she is unshakably convinced that this picture of a film star, complete with the perfect waves, the pearls and the jewels, is *her* picture; and therefore it *is* her picture. Truth is what we believe.

(Among 'normal' people, too, most of us would rather see, on the *cartité* of our life, not the picture of the person we really are but a fiction: how we would like to appear. And while many may succeed in deceiving the world around them, to how many is it given to deceive themselves too – and to go on doing so right to the end?)

The 'weak-minded' Madeleine has no conception of all this. Her mirror is this picture of the beautiful film star; her illusion is truer than our pretended realities; and therefore her *cartité* is more accurate than so many genuine identity cards.

This episode with the identity cards brought to my attention the superiority of our *enfants* from another point of view, too. For there is not one 'non-Aryan' amongst them.

They are at home here, and that is the end of the story. Even the most mentally incapable of them is still a citizen, and stands under the protection of the law. They have nothing to fear, and do not need to hide. We, on the other hand ... we are hunted animals. If Einstein were here, he would be a hunted animal. Louisette, with her mangelwurzel between the teeth; Madeleine with her *cartité* – they would never understand it, but, in terms of human rights, they should feel enormously superior to an Einstein ... a Bruno Walter* ... a Franz Werfel.

Blessed are the poor in spirit. For theirs is – already – the earth. Just as long as they are 'Aryans'.

26

Nuns

BEFORE DESTINY BROUGHT ME to Labarde, I had a superficial, conventional – and therefore almost wholly false – notion of the world inhabited by women in a convent.

Nuns ... The word strikes certain chords; it brings with it a series of associations connected with strictness and solemnity, and also with something idyllic and lovely. Mortification and meditation; the playing of organs; bright voices from an unseen choir of angels; prayer; walking silently amid the flowers of the convent garden, behind high, protective walls.

What else did I believe I knew about the women of a convent? That they had renounced everything that most women look to for fulfilment in life; that they look after the sick and the poor; that they instruct and educate children, and also that they have incomparable skills when it comes to capturing the souls of the young. I have a cousin who spent her youthful years in a convent. Decades later, long married and with a grown-up daughter, she would undertake long and difficult journeys just in order to see one of her former teachers for one or two days. I used to smile indulgently, seeing this as some kind of prolonged adolescent attachment. How well I can understand it now.

Mère St-Antoine may herself serve as an example of what a nun can actually be – although this remarkable manifestation could hardly be taken as the norm.

For Mère St-Antoine, her office represents not just an aim, namely that of being worthy of eternal life, but also a means, namely that of mastering life here on earth. The faith of this woman – who is by no means young, and who, besides, has some quite serious health problems – instils in her a truly remarkable energy and physical strength. Her noble heart may be a heaven; but her sound understanding of human nature is very firmly planted on the earth. I have seen her smile as she embraced a child covered in scabies; and I have seen her carry out the most menial tasks with the same smile. I have seen her control a woman in the grip of a frenzy by the sheer power of a look; and I have seen her guide her great institution with the far-sightedness and organisational ability of a seasoned businesswoman. She has had a small stage constructed, on which she allows her charges to perform theatrical pieces on special occasions; and she has also installed a laundry at Labarde, as well as a number of pieces of agricultural equipment, which would be desirable items for many an ordinary, secular business.

That, then, is Mère St-Antoine. An exceptional character, to be sure. But even the normal, 'average' nun leads a quite different sort of life from that commonly imagined.

'They have renounced worldly things.' It is such an easy thing to say – without thinking what it really means. 'Still,' people will say, 'in compensation for that, they don't have the struggles of life; the fight for daily survival; the anxieties about old age. They may spend their whole lives within the walls of the convent; but these walls protect them from the storms and devastations, from the disappointments and sorrows of life on the outside. Actually, their position is rather enviable.'

Let us look at things a little more closely.

Well, yes – they are enviable. They are enviable for the inner strength that has enabled them to sacrifice everything by which they might have achieved peace, both inwardly and externally. Most of these women were still very young when they took the veil; life lay enticingly before them; many were very attractive and had no shortage of admirers.

They made a renunciation. More than that: they killed, with their own hands, everything that Nature demands, everything that life holds out as a promise to other women. It is this inner power of resistance that is enviable in them; so too their balance, their cheerful resignation; their silent, unshakeable patience; their ruthless severity towards themselves, which leads them to undertake the most menial and thankless tasks without any other satisfaction or reward than that which their faith promises them: the reward of God. Also to be envied is the unwavering spirit of humility in which they follow the law of obedience. They submit to every command as to the dispensation of Providence, regarding the decisions of their superiors, too, as nothing other than instruments of God's will.

I once expressed to one of the Sisters my admiration for this practice of renunciation which is involved in life in the convent. 'But we knew about that beforehand,' she replied, with a gesture that seemed to say: none of that is terribly important.

This same Sister was transferred to another house within the Order. Which meant that after eighteen years of service in Labarde, one fine day she received the order to leave next morning for her newly appointed location. Eighteen years – eighteen years of familiarity, of attachments, with people and things. She did not find the leavetaking easy; what human being would have done? But not for one second did it enter her head to enquire as to the reason for her transfer, let alone to oppose it. Her duty was to obey; and she obeyed. That is enviable.

Most enviable of all is their unshakable certainty that the short span of our earthly existence is no more than a preparation, a transition to eternal life.

In other respects, though, their life is very far from being enviable. They lead an existence whose rigours are difficult for someone on the outside to imagine. Let us take these Franciscan nuns here as an example.

We have here a group of Sisters who tirelessly look after patients none of whom can ever be cured; even that satisfaction is denied them. Their task is not merely that of caring for the sick, but also that of tending to the insane. Here in Labarde, moreover, we have quite a number of patients who soil their bed on a nightly basis, and who therefore have to be cleaned and have their bed changed, not once, but several times a night. And there is hardly a night that passes without some kind of attack or crisis.

Well, one may say, these are all things, after all, which are part of the duties of carers in the outside world, too. And that is true. But in the world outside a nurse will have a day shift or a night shift, and will then be relieved; they will also have days off; days away from the workplace; holidays. Here in Labarde, our Sisters are on duty constantly. For everyone the day begins at five in the morning and ends at eight-thirty in the evening. Between eight-thirty and five is the time to sleep – or should be. But for those Sisters who are in direct contact with the patients, there is no such thing as undisturbed sleep. Their patience and gentleness in these conditions are, frankly, beyond words.

Or consider another example: Soeur Scolastique, the cook. At the age of sixty-two, she has the task of preparing meals for about a hundred people. For decades she has stood at her stove, seven days a week, every month of the year, starting at five in the morning. She is hard of hearing, and by no stretch of the imagination could she be called robust. 'If I can't carry on any longer,' she says, 'they'll replace me. But as long as I still can, I must.'

What, then, of the other Sisters? Each has her own 'emploi', her own particular area of activity for which she is responsible: the grounds, the cows, the laundry, the tailoring, etc. Each of them has a workload that, in the world outside, would not be imposed on any worker, or on any farmhand – not even on the most humble servant. And no normal workforce would accept the other aspects of their living conditions here, either. Very few of the Sisters have their own – tiny, unheated – cell; the others live in a communal dormitory. As for nourishment, even in normal times it is barely sufficient to keep the Sisters healthy. They eat in order to be able to carry out their work. In the fiercest midsummer heat they must go about dressed in exactly the same way as in winter. Non-serious illnesses – even quite painful ones – are only acknowledged when they develop into serious ones.

There is no retirement age. Most of the Sisters only cease to work when they cease to live.

Should one then begrudge these women a little bit of peace and quiet – begrudge them the fact that the walls of the convent, which exclude them from all the pleasures of the world, at least also protect them from its noise and ugliness?

But even within the refuge of these four walls it is not always easy to maintain a sense of inner peace.

It should not be forgotten, after all, that these women, for all their self-denial, remain creatures of flesh and blood, that they still have human responses and reactions. Even the strictest rule of an Order, with all the homogeneity it imposes, cannot destroy completely all the differences and oppositions of character and replace them with a perfect unity or uniformity.

Even within the walls of a convent human nature remains what it is, and human beings are still imperfect. Everyday concerns have their effects here, too, and even those who have dedicated themselves to Heaven find that they cannot always keep themselves in that elevated state of grace; there are relapses into worldliness. And then not all those nuns who believed themselves to be called are also chosen. Not all of them are saints. But for those who are not, it is all the harder, and more meritorious, to lead the life of a saint. They are even less to be envied than those who are never troubled by temptations.

I do not know if there is such a thing as Heaven. But I do know that, of the nuns that I have met, there is not one who would not deserve to enter it.

27

A glimpse through a peephole

Convent; hospital; hospital; convent ... It was like living in a bubble. We had no radio, and only occasionally had sight of a newspaper – which would be one of those disgusting rags whose nauseating love of Hitler made them look like a French translation of the *Völkischer Beobachter*. My wife and Sláva went from one task to another – which is, after all, the best way of keeping oneself occupied, and of not thinking too much.

We were almost totally cut off from 'outside'. Nonetheless, there were people who came to visit us in our den, and through them we met others, too; and we got to hear this or that piece of news. In a way we were better able to observe and judge events on the outside, seeing them from this hiding place, than if we had been outside ourselves.

Some books were even brought to me in my retreat – the works of Eugène le Roy,* for example, which would otherwise certainly have been unknown to me.

The Rispals visited us as often as they could. They would come singly or together; they would come in all weathers, sometimes even on the darkest and most icy winter evenings. Between visits Hélène Rispal would write to us, too, addressing the letters to Madame Marguerite or Monsieur Maurice. Our family names were known to no one apart from the Mother Superior.

Here I must jump ahead for a moment. I want to quote from just one of these letters, a letter that she wrote to us one day, when she had sensed, from afar, that we were beset with new worries and anxieties.

In February 1943, scarcely three months after our arrival, Mère St-Antoine was called away from Labarde to be Mother Superior in La Trène near Bordeaux – to our great sorrow and distress. Her successor was to be one Mère Espérance. We wondered whether the new Mother Superior would be amenable. If we were not able to remain at Labarde, what then? Where would we find another refuge? Our peace was shattered once more.

At this point we received the following letter from Hélène Rispal, delivered to us by her husband:

My dear, good friends,

If circumstances should prevent you from remaining where you are, you must not suffer even a moment's anxiety on that account. You have put your trust in us, and we will keep you safe – and keep you safe to the end.

Please do not worry, my dear, dear friends. You have overcome far greater obstacles in the past than the one which rises before you now. You belong to us, you are under our protection, we will not let anything stop us: we will protect you.

My husband will explain to you what I decided earlier tonight. I embrace you as I love you.

Hélène

I cannot add anything to this testament of fidelity and devotion.

I cannot go into the details of Hélène Rispal's plan to keep us safe in the event of the new Mother Superior's refusal to let us stay in Labarde. I can, however, say this: that the execution of the plan would, once again, have entailed enormous trouble as well as personal risk for the Rispals.

Fortunately, none of that was necessary. Mère Espérance agreed to our continued stay in Labarde.

The seventy-two-year-old Mère Espérance is an outstanding person in her own way, although very different from her predecessor. On a first impression she seems rather unapproachable; but once you get past that, you find a heart full of human kindness. What may be mistaken for coldness and distance is really just a kind of shyness and loneliness. Mère Espérance is not an outgoing personality, but she responds gratefully if one makes the first approach. Naturally there was something of a period of transition, while we got to know each other better. I believe that I may now say that we enjoy her total sympathy.

A short time before her transfer, Mère St-Antoine had given asylum to another individual, whom she lodged in an farm building near the institution. A 'colleague' of ours, if you like – another fugitive, although one who had not, fortunately, gone through what we had. His case is, nonetheless, worth recounting.

Monsieur Fanchtein was a French Jew, resident in Paris, baptised many years previously and married to a 'one-hundred-percent Aryan', with whom he had three young children. He had been called up at the beginning of war, and after the débâcle was demobilised at Belvès, which is how he came to make the acquaintance of Mère St-Antoine. He later returned to Paris, where he worked as a clerk in a factory.

When the *décrets juifs* were issued, Monsieur Fanchtein neglected to report himself as a 'non-Aryan'. No one imagined that he was Jewish. His wife is a devout Catholic, and his children attend a convent school. He could carry on his life as normal.

But, as ill luck would have it, he had to renew his identity card. The official at the Préfecture de Police, who had learned his lessons well from the Germans, was suspicious. Fanchtein? Fanchtein? You are clearly Jewish. Why did you not report?

Monsieur Fanchtein denied it, protested his 'innocence' – but to no avail. As he was unable to produced the required 'proof of Aryan status', he was indicted. The next stage was the investigating judge – another Frenchman who turned out to be an able pupil of the Germans.

'You are not Jewish?' he began politely. 'Then I am sure that you will have no objection to undergoing a small procedure involving the court doctor. A pure formality.'

And the court doctor – who also knew what he owed the Germans – certified that Monsieur Fanchtein was circumcised. He certified it with sincere regret; but duty is duty.

Prosecution. Indignant speech from the state prosecutor. Spiteful observations from the presiding judge. Judgement from the French court: six months' imprisonment.

Fortunately, Monsieur Fanchtein had been provisionally released: the criminal was allowed twenty-four hours' grace before beginning his punishment. He used these twenty-four hours to remove himself from the appointed expiation of his crime by running away. He knocked on Mère St-Antoine's door; and she did not close it to him.

Monsieur Fanchtein is one of those French Jews who would previously have thought that 'something like this' could never happen in France. He admitted as much to me himself. In the course of time we became good friends.

Labarde is on a hilltop. In the valley below, as well as on the slopes opposite, there are a large number of scattered farms. I gradually came not just to know who owned each of these farms; I also got to know these owners quite well by reputation. Gabriel Rispal knows nearly all of them, and sometimes he would tell us stories about his farmers. So too would Vorms, who lived in Guiraud, on the other side of Belvès, in close proximity with farmers. The Sisters of the Convent had contact with the farmers, too. It was thus possible for me to form a picture of the rural mentality.

From a political point of view the attitude of the farmers in most cases left nothing to be desired. Many of them were later to play an active role in the uprising of their country, in the Resistance and fighting in the Maquis. Among the casualties of the Resistance movement there are a large number of farmers.

The Dordogne, moreover, was regarded even as early as 1943 as a particularly suspect *département*, and was to suffer ever harsher persecutions in the form of the terror of the German 'reprisals'.

As regards the social attitude of the rural folk, on the other hand, and their attitude to the privations suffered in the cities, it cannot exactly be claimed that they were imbued with a particularly strong fellow feeling. If one listened to the farmers talking, one would hear expressions of great sympathy for the poor devils in the city – for all those, that is, who could not keep up with the inexorable inflation of prices on the black market. But expressions – with a few noble, but isolated exceptions – was all.

Let me mention one small, but very typical experience, which Rispal related. He had asked a very well-to-do farmer to let him have two kilos of ham at a halfway affordable price, because he wanted to send it to friends in Paris – working-class friends. The farmer didn't want to know. Rispal appealed to his conscience, painting a vivid picture of everything that a family with many children in the capital was having to go without. The farmer listened attentively, thought it over for a moment and finally declared with a furrowed brow: 'Poor people! But if I were you I wouldn't send them anything. You see, your friends in Paris have been used to hunger for a long time now. A food parcel like that – how long does it last? A matter of days. And after that your friends will find it all the more difficult when the hunger starts – like beginning all over again. No: trust me. You would do much better *not* to send them anything at all, even if I were to *give* you the ham.'

Not long after our arrival the Rispals brought their nephew, René Mathieu, a teacher and the mayor of St-Cernin-de-l'Herm, a small market town in the Dordogne. It had been Mathieu who, without even knowing us personally, had arranged our false identity papers. We also made the acquaintance of his delightful wife, Henriette,* also a teacher, and later of her sister, Madame Rousset, who taught at the École St-Esprit in Bergerac and was the wife of a prisoner of war (another teacher). Later all of them were to play an important part in the Resistance.

Through the Mathieus and Madame Rousset I gained an insight into the admirable clandestine activity that a large number of teachers were involved in, both inside and outside their schools. In school, these brave men and women had found a way of telling their children the truth about the Germans within the framework of their lessons. An indication of the challenge that this kind of teaching entailed may be taken from the fact that the Minister for Education, Abel Bonnard, for example, had not balked at actually removing unpalatable things like the French Revolution and the Napoleonic victories from the curriculum. It was, however, incumbent on teachers to emphasise the disastrous errors committed by France since time immemorial in her relations with the peace-loving Germany, as well as to highlight the glory and greatness of the Third Reich in the most vivid manner.

But while these men and women were endangering their livelihoods and their freedom daily by their activity within the school, outside it they did not hesitate to risk their very lives. In addition to the spiritual sabotage, the work they undertook later in the active Resistance and in the Maquis should never be forgotten.

For someone like René Mathieu it has gradually become his main job to give assistance and food to *réfractaires*;[12] to conceal weapons; to take care of persecuted Jews, to transmit secret messages to the Resistance, to issue false identity papers and ration cards. The fact that he is so far still at liberty, indeed that he is still alive, is pretty much a miracle.

Even before the War, in a quite other context, Mathieu accomplished some quite extraordinary things.

He succeeded in introducing sewerage in his district, and in having his school fitted with warm and cold showers, lockers and other such conveniences. Revolutionary acts, when one considers the living conditions of the rural population of the Périgord. Under the pretext of tradition, of following the customs of one's forefathers, there is a backwardness, even among the well-to-do farmers – a lack of cleanliness, in fact an illiteracy in matters of hygiene which one would hardly believe possible in Western Europe. If one tries to enlighten people, to teach them a better way, one always comes up against the same blinkered, irrefutable argument: 'C'est comme ça' – 'That's just the way it is.'

One may well believe that Mathieu had to overcome very considerable resistance, indeed hostility. Now, of course, everyone in the district is very proud of their teacher and mayor.

A visit from the Mathieus was something like light relief for us. It was not just that they would come bearing all kinds of delicacies, for after these generous gifts had been shared out, Mathieu would begin to give free rein to his irrepressible optimism, which would brook no contradiction. He is a magician – an alchemist of interpretation: even the most depressing news is changed in a moment into the gold of confidence.

---

12. *Réfractaires*: the term refers to people who went into hiding – and often also into some form of resistance – in response to the *Service du Travail Obligatoire* of 1942, whereby French men of military-service age were sent to Germany to provide labour.

His optimism can be contagious. In the autumn of 1943 we allowed ourselves to be persuaded by him to a great act of recklessness – leaving our hiding place and spending a day with him at his house in St-Cernin. He picked us up with a car and brought us back in the evening. All went well and Mathieu was triumphant; he had been right yet again.

It was a day that we looked back on for a long time. A celebration of hospitality, which had a most unusual effect on us – at the same time intoxicating and also exciting. It was a little like a fine vintage wine, at once bringing forgetfulness and arousing ghosts.

We sat at a beautifully laid table. In a home – a family home with its atmosphere of permanence and calm, surrounded by hundreds of objects that had been assembled over a period of decades, which had been handed down from generation to generation. They are only things, of course; you can do without them if you have to; but still, you become attached to them.

We, too, once had a home like this, with its hundreds of superfluous things that we had become attached to. Was it really only five years ago that we had been turned out of it? Not five decades – five centuries? However indifferent you may feel you are, standing by the grave of your former self ... there are moments when, all of a sudden, you cannot resist its power. The grave suddenly opens up.

It was not that I was ungrateful; it was not that I would ever forget that it was only a miracle that had brought us our room at Labarde. Nor did I fail to appreciate the warmth and friendship that surrounded us: I drank them in to the full. But I could not help suddenly looking upon myself – ourselves – as though we were people long dead. And it was not the present, but rather the past that appeared to me as ghostly, impossible to grasp.

Another wonderful person that I have got to know in Labarde is Monsieur Maisonneuve, the mayor of Ste-Foy, which is our own district. He had been let into the secret of our situation by

Mère St-Antoine. For a long time now he has been issuing false ration cards for us.

He too looks us up from time to time, either on his own or in the company of his aged mother, a very robust, red-faced lady, whose eyes sparkled with good nature. Hers is a spirit which is still very much alive. The son's love for his mother is incredibly touching; she did not merely bring him into the world; she *is* his whole world. One senses this from every word, and every look that the two exchange. And this love is the stimulus for the good that these two individuals do, too; it prevents them from becoming dulled.

A short time after the departure of Mère St-Antoine there was an inspection of Labarde by the chief Mother Superior, Mère Sainte-Anne, from the chief house of the Order, at Devèze. I had quite a long talk with this distinguished woman. Rather than attempting a character sketch, let me confine myself to recording a few of the things that she said to me.

For example: 'I have two Jewish families hidden in a house belonging to our Order, in Rolleville near Le Havre, under the very eyes of the Germans; and I stake my entire honour on saving them for a better future. For a number of months I have also been putting up English soldiers.'

Or again: 'We in the convent should not concern ourselves with politics. But that does not mean that we must not know what is going on, if only so that we are aware where our duty as human beings – and as French people – lies.'

And lastly: 'Those of us who do not want to see the present as a model for the future must keep our eyes open – but at the same time we must often keep our ears closed.'

As I listened to the words of Mère Ste-Anne, I considered, with admiration, how the greatness of the Catholic Church consists not least in its capacity for putting the right person in the right position. It may one day be reduced to ashes by the Germans, but Rome will still remain the Eternal City.

28

Music

ONE, DAY, IN THE AUTUMN OF 1943, Gabriel Rispal brought us a substantial package. When we opened it, we could hardly believe our eyes: what appeared was a radio.

It was the Rispals' own radio. They had felt that we could not remain on our own any longer without a radio. And since it was not possible to get hold of another one, they lent us their own ... And so we had a radio. This was something quite magical: it meant not just that we could listen to London, New York, Algiers, but also that we rediscovered something that had long been denied to us: music.

Concerts; operas; song. In Labarde. The very anticipation of this pleasure was something wonderful. As soon as we had installed the radio, we began to go from one station to the next, eager to get a taste of everything.

There was some music which brought me a complete escape – not just from the present, but from time itself. If I listened to Mozart, then I ceased to suffer from the present, ceased to drag the past along with me as a burden; ceased to feel the threat of the days to come. I felt my dark destiny fall away from me. It was like a blessed release of the self – a death, a dying.

Beethoven, on the other hand, made me forget the *present*. It brought the message that above and beyond the vile blasphemy that constitutes our times there is, still, such a thing as God's kingdom among human beings. The message that is proclaimed in the Third Leonore Overture by the offstage trumpet: it seems to come from Heaven. Beethoven was shattering, but not depressing; he brought tears which were the tears of release, not of despair; a bursting-open of the heart; a torrent of rain after a long, dreadful drought. Behind this ghastly grimace, a different life was made manifest – a life full of tragedy and beauty.

But something else was made manifest, too. While Mozart transformed everything into his unique realm of enchantment, Beethoven was capable of giving rise to something like a scream – a scream which cannot be suppressed.

It is not the case that beautiful memories are necessarily a solace. They may be so, when there still exists some point of connection between them and the present. Otherwise such memories may be a source of pain; like those moments of truth that finally dawn during a sleepless night of anxiety, such memories may simply have the effect of throwing a particularly relentless light on the present – of increasing your awareness of what you have become. They are a reminder of the many deaths that you have died since then, a reminder of all that has died within you.

Vienna. Vienna before March 1938. The Great Hall of the Musikverein.* The festive, elevated atmosphere of the Philharmonic Concerts. That apparent confusion of sound which is the tuning of the instruments – in itself a symphony of enticing promises. The familiar faces in the orchestra. The conductor's rostrum. Franz Schalk, Felix Weingartner, Bruno Walter.

The Vienna Opera. *Fidelio*. And then, suddenly, after all these decades, I see Gustav Mahler* before me again – that noble, illuminated face of the ascetic; the face of a master, a devotee at the altar of genius; I suddenly feel again, with every nerve in my body, the excitement, the sense of solemnity, of consecration inherent in the moment when he raises his baton in the darkened house. From the concertmaster's rostrum Arnold Rosé has his gaze fixed on him intently, his bow poised. Among the cellos sits Friedrich Buxbaum. Mildenburg sings Leonore, Schmedes Florestan, Hesch Rocco, Demuth the Governor. I see them now; I hear them now.

Then, my last performance of *Fidelio*, as late as the beginning of 1938. And the *Lied von der Erde* – that song of *another* earth. Bruno Walter, the great disciple and inheritor of Mahler, conducted on both those occasions.

After the invasion of Austria, Bruno Walter had gone to France and there taken French citizenship. Herriot* brought him his decree of naturalisation in person.

On the occasion of a visit which I made to him in Paris, François Mauriac* told me how proud he was of this new compatriot. Mauriac had attended some of Bruno Walter's performances in the Salzburger Festspielhaus. Later, he had heard Walter's revival of *Carmen* at the Vienna State Opera. 'I actually had the impression that I was hearing the opera for the first time,' said Mauriac. 'No Frenchman has ever succeeded in revealing Bizet's work in this way.'

Bruno Walter was able to save himself in time. Pétain's France would not have hesitated for a moment before handing the *juif* Walter over to the Germans.

Gustav Mahler is long dead. And Bruno Walter, fortunately, is in America, beyond the reach of the Swastika-Reptile. Otherwise, they would both have perished miserably in a concentration camp. Gustav Mahler and Bruno Walter – two 'Jewish pests' to be exterminated.

How many pests of this sort were among the countless number of Jewish children done to death by the German people – the nation of Hitlers and butchers? How many pests of this sort – geniuses, who would have been called to do great things in all the different realms of art and of science – have already been nipped in the bud in the 'Extermination Camps'?

29

Eugène le Roy

ANOTHER EXPERIENCE THAT I OWE to my time in Labarde is that of making the acquaintance of Eugène le Roy.* In spite of having exerted myself since my youth to gain a reasonable knowledge of French literature, I must admit that I did not even know the name of this great epic writer. In mitigation I may mention that it is a sin of omission which I share with a large number of very well-read French people. Le Roy cannot disappear into oblivion, but from the point of view of the wider public he has yet to be discovered.

He died many years ago – in 1907. It is a good thing that he belonged to a completely different generation; his noble heart would have found this world of ours difficult to bear. It is over-whelmingly likely that this great Frenchman would have ended up in a concentration camp.

In terms of style as well as the time of their writing the works of Eugène le Roy seem to belong to a world far, far from any kind of 'contemporary reality'. Far, too, from any sense of fashion. But this is precisely the source of their universal value, their ageless beauty. In their simplicity, their breadth, their sense of peace and of harmony, they seem to stand above any particular time – like Nature itself. They seem to have sprung – without art and without effort – from the soil of the Périgord, like a delicious fruit. But in fact they are the creation of a great writer and a genuine man.

The stories of Eugène le Roy seem all to confine themselves to the land and people of the Périgord, this unique region in the south-west of France. In reality, though, their scope is the whole world: their charming local colour and their characteristic folk themes are a reflection of life in general. Here is the deep, quiet wisdom of a heart whose beat may be slow, but which never ceased to take the part of the weak and the oppressed, never tired of taking a stand against injustice, deceit and hypocrisy, even when these evils are sanctioned by the written and unwritten laws of the bourgeois order. This was the cause of the hostility that le Roy encountered in certain reactionary, or even simply conservative, circles, in spite of the fact that he abhorred politics and never belonged to a party.

In his personal life, too, Eugène le Roy followed those unim-peachable ethical standards which are implied by his work. He scorned honours and profit, despised all public acclaim, had no pride or vanity, and would not make any kind of concession or compromise. He was not interested in career or in social acceptance. He merely desired to continue straight along his own path.

There is a certain internal logic to the fact that he was nearly sixty years old when he was, purely by chance, 'discovered'.

The senator Alcide Dusolier was waiting for the train to Périgueux one day at a small railway station in the Périgord; and he bought a copy of a local newspaper, *L'Écho de la Dor-dogne*. Purely out of boredom, he even read the *feuilleton*, an instalment of the novel *Le Moulin du Frau*, by one Eugène le Roy. Dusolier was so enchanted with it that he went to the offices of the newspaper in Périgueux in order to find out something about the work and its author.

Eugène le Roy? Oh, they said, he's an old eccentric; a modest official in the tax office in Montignac, who writes in his spare time. The senator went to Montignac, looked up Eugène le Roy and eventually, almost by force, obtained his permission to show his *Moulin du Frau* to the publisher Dreyfus in Paris – who immediately published it. Dusolier's confidence was not misplaced: the book was a great success. Émile Zola and Alphonse Daudet both expressed their admiration to the author. People tried to persuade him to move to Paris.

But right up until the end of his life, Eugène le Roy refused to leave the Périgord. He even declined the *Légion d'honneur*, not wanting to be or become anything other than the modest tax official in Montignac. A wonderful individualist. As for the idea that after his death they would one day erect a monument in his honour in Montignac – he would simply have smiled.

It is certainly not my purpose here to give a description of the life and work of Eugène le Roy. All I wish to do is to point him out; people of goodwill – people who suffer – will perhaps find a friend in him. Today, more than ever, we need books which are not just 'literature'; which offer something other than pretentious artistic games – dazzling, but ultimately empty and pointless. More than ever we need books that come from the feelings of the heart, not the deliberations of the intellect. Books that take us by the hand, and guide us. Books that help.

To all those who may be in need of such help, I can only say: read the works of Eugène le Roy – at least *Le Moulin du Frau* and *Jacquou le Croquant*. But above all *Le Moulin du Frau*. Read this wonderful book and, if you have children, give it to them to read. At some point in the future it may make it a little easier for them to fulfil that very difficult task: to remain a decent human being. It may also keep their hearts from drying up in indifference and idleness.

Notions which are called into question nowadays, obviously – notions which evince a superior smirk. For that very reason, though, it may be that they are more important than ever. And for that very reason, too, the work of Eugène le Roy is called upon to outlast this age, too, just as, in its proud modesty and single-mindedness, it has survived many names that were trumpeted everywhere yesterday and are today forgotten.

30

Informers

A BOY OF ABOUT TWELVE goes into the Gestapo building in Bergerac. 'What do you want here?' they ask him. 'I am from Belvès,' the boy explains. 'I need money and I have come here to denounce a Jew.'

He is immediately taken to a friendly official, to whom he gives the name and address of an Alsatian Jew who is in hiding in Belvès: Salomon, Rue Pelevade. He then receives his payment of 500 francs, and departs.

The boy does not leave it there, though. He catches the next train home, and goes straight to Monsieur Salomon – stricken by remorse, you are no doubt thinking. That would be a fundamental misunderstanding of this enterprising character. Rather, he has hatched a plan to catch two birds with one stone. He is hoping for a double reward for his labours.

'Don't be afraid,' he says to Monsieur Salomon by way of introduction. 'The reason I am here is that you are in a very serious situation. Don't ask me how, but I happen to know with complete certainty that you were denounced to the Gestapo in Bergerac today. For this information I require a fee of 2,500 francs. It is a very small fee – but my main concern was to be of service to you.'

Monsieur Salomon seized his benefactor by the collar and threw him out. He then went to Gabriel Rispal and told him the whole story. Rispal sought out the boy and interrogated him until he became exhausted and admitted everything. He then took the little informer to the brigadier of the *gendarmerie*, Monsieur Dubeau, a fine man, who even then was already working secretly for the Resistance. Dubeau locked the boy up. This, however, did not alter the fact that Salomon and his family had to disappear from Belvès that very evening. They fled to Mathieu's in St-Cernin. And indeed Salomon had not left a moment too early: just after midnight four Gestapo men came in a car from Bergerac, to pick up the Jew. On this occasion they had to content themselves with looting his dwelling thoroughly.

'I need money and I come to make a denunciation.' There you have the business of the informer, reduced to its most brutal, cynical essentials. The Germans guessed right, when they promised themselves great successes with this trade in human misery and human life. As for the reward offered, they were more than generous: it started at a few hundred francs and could go as high as hundreds of thousands, even millions. A person who kept his eyes and ears open could be assured of the most wonderful returns for almost no effort at all. There was money available for other kinds of collaborator too, of course: it was lying there in the street. All they had to do was bend down – bend low before the Germans – and pick it up. But these informers did not even have to bend down: all they had to do was open their mouths and spit out a name. No more than that.

And yet the Germans were able to make substantial savings to the budget of their Judas money, for alongside these professional informers there were also many keen amateurs, who would do the job by anonymous letter, without any hope of reward. For this last category of informer, whether male or female, the knowledge that they had sent their fellow human beings to torture and death was the really important thing.

For all their sophisticated developments in the creation of terror, the Germans would still not have managed to do so much evil in France had they not so often had informers to act as their guides in villainy. Every successful catch, every vile deed that they perpetrated, required particular itcms of local and personal information which they could only get from informers. Such French citizens as these frequently showed them the way to things which, left to themselves, they simply would not have found. The most malicious, dangerous enemy of the Resistance was this invisible, inaudible work of denunciation.

Quite truthfully, the German Gestapo would have been enough on its own. But side by side with that *official* Gestapo we had also the *officious* one – the private, French Gestapo.

The attitude of some French people towards those informers who were discovered and dealt with by the Resistance was quite remarkable, too. To listen to them, you would have imagined that we were talking not about villains who had finally received their just reward, but about innocent individuals who had been randomly slaughtered by the 'terrorists'. Friends and relatives clasped their hands together above their heads – look, they cried, these were harmless, law-abiding citizens who wouldn't hurt a flea; and then one day they were treacherously ambushed and shot. Where will it end? Is nobody safe now?

It was a waste of time trying to point out to these people the connection between cause – the deed carried out in the darkness – and effect.

The laments of these sensitive souls were, of course, most welcome to the Germans and their French accomplices. They served, in a melodramatic way, to underscore their propaganda against the 'terrorists', the 'bandits', the 'communists'. (I mention here only the commonest of the descriptions that were constantly applied to the Resistance in the press and on the radio.) Indeed, the Germans even hit upon the idea of having genuinely innocent people murdered by French *assassins provocateurs*. One need think only of the murder of the ex-Prime Minister Sarraut, among others. Full of outrage, the murderers then laid the crime at the door of the Resistance, rushing to the cry: 'Stop the murderers!' Thus a climate of opinion was created which could be exploited to discredit the Resistance, even among many of their sympathisers.

The Occupation brought to light the secret powers of the Resistance, as it were the discovery of a wonderful treasure; but at the same time, sadly, also the infamous activity of Denunciation – like a revolting heap of vermin.

31

In place of a chapter on the Resistance

An account of the Resistance in France would require a whole book, not a chapter; and this book will be written, in all kinds of different forms, by many different authors. Not to mention the sublimated account of the Resistance that will be found in every other realm of artistic endeavour: fiction, painting, music, sculpture, theatre.

When we speak of the Resistance, we are not just speaking of those men in the Maquis who lived a troglodyte existence and whose heroic deeds – often carried out with the most primitive materials, even with their bare hands – are worthy to live on in posterity. We are not just speaking of the partisans, *maquisards*, both foreign and French, who hid in thick woodlands, in caves, in mountain gullies, in forests and who, with for the most part only very basic equipment, carried out incredible feats against a mighty oppressor – against heavy weaponry, tanks and bombs. Nor just the *réfractaires* who, in their various hiding places in the town and in the country, exposed themselves to the most terrible dangers and deprivations rather than be compelled to do the Germans' slave labour.

We are speaking also of that other *guerrilla* organisation: a secret army, without distinction of age or sex, without weapons or badges of rank, which covered the entire land – almost infinite in their variety – like an invisible, unbreakable net of resistance. An army of millions, men and women who opposed the oppressor at every level of society, in every position and profession.

It was this army, too, that daily left its dead – and its missing – on the field of battle. They left them in the places of execution and in the torture chambers of the Gestapo, both the German Gestapo and the French one that had been provided by Vichy.

It should be mentioned purely in passing, and without the slightest sense of irony: the fact that it was possible for the Resistance to develop into such a tremendous organisation under the Germans' very nose; the fact that the German terror machine, with all its appalling techniques of repression, was not able to stamp it out; the fact that the Resistance often managed to spring up where one would least have expected it – all these facts are less astonishing than the fact that the Resistance flourished alongside a culture of thoughtless, carefree openness in conversation.

In one sense, discretion is a French national virtue. You could hardly find a country as tactful, as free of inquisitive, intrusive questioning as France. On the other hand, you could also hardly find another country where the 'seal of silence' is so casually broken – or, if not broken, at least loosened a little. The usual way of keeping a secret is to communicate it to someone else in the strictest confidence – or at least to allow it to become clear by unambiguous hints, nudges and winks. This is not done out of any sense of malice, but simply from a desire to appear interesting or important; to create an effect; to amaze – to appear better informed than ordinary mortals.

The Resistance could devote a whole volume to the dreadful consequences that often came from indiscretions of that sort.

The great beast that was the French Resistance took on countless different forms, countless faces. Within the modest scope of this book I must limit myself to mentioning a few small examples that I was able to observe from my peephole at Labarde. Here I will not even mention the clandestine activities of people like Jean Cassou or Pierre Vorms, which I was able to follow. The actions and initiatives of men of this sort may be regarded as part of what one might call the 'brains-trust', the spiritual backbone, of the Resistance. Here let us just look at a few episodes – a few snapshots.

In a girls' school the teacher explained to her charges how they could observe the movements of German troops in the town without being noticed, so that they might then communicate them to her. These observations were then passed on to a *maquis* that was encamped near Bergerac. The teacher concluded her exposition with the remark: 'Do you know that, purely because of the things that I have explained to you, I could go to prison today?' A voice from the back replied immediately: 'You can trust us, Miss. And if you *did* go to prison today, we would get you out, by tomorrow at the latest.'

The teacher in question was Madame Rousset, René Mathieu's sister-in-law.

A group of railwaymen overseeing a stretch of track near Belvès. They come to an agreement with the *maquisards*, who want to destroy the same stretch of track, that the latter will bind and gag them. They remain in this state for many hours before they are found. But they have their alibi for the Germans.

Official doctors who produce false X-rays showing stomach disorders, bone problems and so on, for young men who had been ordered to Germany for front-line service.

The *curé* in St-Cernin-de-l'Herm, who kept *réfractaires* hidden in the rectory, and weapons under the altar.

The postmaster at Belvès, Despont, who had installed a whole secret telephone exchange in his apartment.

In a village not far from Belvès the Germans drove up to a farm one night and dragged out two *maquisards* who had been hidden there for a short time. The two young men were taken to Périgueux, tortured and, finally, after every form of torture had failed to make them speak, executed. The owner of the farm was deported.

They had been victims of a denunciation. Suspicion fell upon the secretary of the borough council.

One day two men appeared at his door, introducing themselves as members of the Gestapo.

'The service you performed was such a valuable one,' said the first, 'that we have come to thank you in person.' A gratified bow from the secretary.

'One other thing,' continued the second. 'Have you already received the reward for the two bandits that you located for us?'

'Oh, yes – the money was paid immediately.'

'And were you happy with the amount?'

'Oh, absolutely – thank you very much. Always glad to help.'

'Then please be so good as to stand by the wall over there,' – at this point two revolvers appeared – 'now it is the turn of the Resistance to pay you out.'

Two shots rang out.

Jacquot Rispal was the first *réfractaire* from Belvès. Before he could reach a *maquis*, he was hidden by farmers in an abandoned farm building. One day a man whom he did not know arrived at the farm and said to him: 'You are Jacques Rispal from Belvès. I have been sent by the Resistance. I have to tell you that you must leave this place immediately; otherwise you will be arrested tomorrow.'

Jacquot followed the instruction. Going by secret pathways on a pitch-black night, he managed to reach Labarde, where he knocked on our window. We hid him in our room for three days, until his parents were able find a new hiding place for him. And from there he was able to attach himself to a *maquis*.

The unknown messenger had spoken the truth: next day, at first light, the brigadier of Le Bugue, a man named Faure, had arrived with three *gendarmes*. They searched the farm and subjected the inhabitants to interrogation. No sign of the *réfractaire*. There must have been a mistake. The brigadier made a report and drove off again with his men.

It was the brigadier himself who later told Jacquot's father what had actually happened. The *gendarmerie* of Le Bugue had received a tip-off which said: 'There is a *réfractaire* hidden in the farm of Lebos. If he is not arrested within twenty-four hours, we will get you *gendarmes* a rap on the knuckles from the Germans.' Brigadier Faure could not simply ignore the tip-off. He had no option but to set off with his men. Before he did so, however, he made sure that Jacquot was informed in good time by a messenger.

Perhaps it will one day be possible to trace the anonymous informer.

When we speak of the Resistance, we should remember also the women who, in spite of all the Germans' prohibitions and threats, kept laying wreaths on the graves of executed *maquisards* – wreaths whose blue-and-white bows' bore the inscription, 'Mort pour la Liberté'. He died for Freedom.

32

They're coming –
they're not coming
– they're coming!

IN OUR ROMAN LAW CLASSES we learned the following formula:
'*Dies certa, sed incerta quando.*' A day which is certain to
come, although it is uncertain when it will come. Such a day,
such a '*dies certa, sed incerta quando*' was the date of the
'débarquements', the Allied landings in France.

We waited for this day, in an anxiety of anticipation, for
an appallingly long time. We pinned our hopes on it; it represented our only chance of survival.

That they would come – the Allies, the liberators – we were
absolutely certain. Out of survival instinct, if nothing else, we
could not afford to doubt it, however disheartened, and at times
even embittered, we might sometimes feel. Because, to be very
honest, something a little like bitterness was a possible emotional response, when we kept hearing the same words of advice
and encouragement again and again from the French channel
of the BBC in London: 'Hold out! Keep your spirits up!'

How we were to do that – to hold out, to keep our spirits up – these counsellors prudently failed to tell us; and there were sometimes moments when we felt like shouting back at them: 'It's easy for you to talk! Just change places with us; just try our existence for a bit; then you will know what those words mean: hold out, keep your spirits up!'

No reasonable person would have denied the force of the argument that the Allies needed time – a long time – to plan their landings down to the last detail. What we might sometimes criticise the propaganda machine for, however, was the sort of 'Scottish shower' that we would be subjected to – hot, then cold, then hot, then cold – which would leave us nervous wrecks.

There were so many times when the landings were mentioned as absolutely imminent, only for nothing to come of it. The effect on our nerves was as though they were a rubber band that someone had stretched almost to breaking-point, before suddenly releasing it again. 'We're coming, we're coming', was the slogan one day. 'Have patience: we shall be there some time soon', was the message the next day. And the whole game would start again. Again and again.

Even in our darkest hours we did not doubt that 'they' would come. *Dies certa*. But when – when? *Incerta quando*. And in the meantime the days became weeks, and the weeks months. So many months – months without end.

And with every day that passed, it became harder to hold out – to keep our spirits up. The terror operation of the Germans and of their French partners in crime became constantly more ferocious, more terrible. Roundups, lootings, executions, murder, arson: 'reprisals'. And add to that everything that went on behind closed doors – in the torture chambers, within prison walls, behind the barbed-wire fences of the concentration camps. How many atrocities there must be which one will never even hear of …

When it comes to cruelty – devilish cruelty, cruelty that knows no limit in its frenzied sadism – the Germans have no equal in the history of the world. No one can contest this title of honour; no one can remove it from their 'culture'. At the same time, however, they are poor psychologists. Otherwise they would have realised long ago that every one of their 'reprisals' led only to a strengthening of the Resistance. It would be truer to see the Resistance as a response to the reprisals than the reprisals as a response to the Resistance.

In the last months before the *débarquement*, however, and in the period immediately following it, the Germans did not even attempt to mask their brutality under the pretext of 'reprisals'. It was clear that their aim was no longer to destroy the Resistance, to conquer the *maquis*, nor yet to capture more slaves for the front line in Germany; to plunder the land; to rob it of its men; to reduce it to a condition of fatal weakness. Their aim now was rather to give free rein to their dehumanised instincts – for one last time, and right up to the last possible minute.

In Frayssinet, a hamlet not far from Belvès, a captain of the *Wehrmacht* hammers with his revolver on the locked door of a cottage where an extremely aged woman lives on her own. The revolver happens to go off, without, however, causing anyone the slightest harm. As a result the door is broken down, and the old woman dragged out and hanged. The brave officer shoots twelve of the male inhabitants for good measure. Finally – but only after careful, meticulous looting – the whole place is torched.

'Reprisal.'

The day will come, *dies certa*, when the master race – the masters of lying and killing – will whiningly attempt to deny their crimes. The day will come when, with abject, crawling hypocrisy, and at the same time with a brazen face, they will trundle out the myth of the 'other Germany', of the true-hearted, pure Germany, that knew nothing. Knew nothing of their 'Führer', nothing of Himmler, of Goebbels, of Goering, of the concentration hells.

The day will come when no one will have been a Nazi.

Can anyone even now imagine what the existence of Jews was like, in this year, 1944 – Jews, that is, who had somehow against all the odds managed to avoid deportation to a death camp in Germany or Poland?

As for those who did not avoid it ... Even during the transport, in sealed goods trains, before they even got out of France, men, women and children, heaped together, choked to death slowly from the gases produced by the urine and faeces laid down on floors that had been lined with lime.

Wherever the Germans arrived, their first priority was always the hunt for Jews, led by the merry 'Hoyotoho!' of the Gestapo. They no longer contented themselves, by the end, with tips, official lists or other forms of information that had been given to them by spies or informers. Anyone whose nose looked suspicious to them might have his trousers pulled down, even if his papers were in completely 'Aryan' good order. If he had the misfortune to be circumcised, his fate was sealed. In the case of women the outrage was, if anything, even greater: their lives depended on a 'blood test'!

As time passed we began to feel less secure – I could say, more insecure – in Labarde.

Convent ... hospital – if the Germans came, they would have no regard to either of those institutions. We knew that all too well. And if we were found, it would not just mean the end for us; the whole house would be subject to 'reprisals'. To the growing sense of our personal insecurity was added also the pressing awareness of our responsibility towards those who had taken it upon themselves to offer us asylum.

One day in the middle of May 1944 Gabriel Rispal arrived at our place. This time, though, he was not his usual, cheerful, confident self. He was bathed in sweat and exhausted. This time he too was a fugitive at Labarde: the Germans had raided Belvès.

After so many other places in the Dordogne, then, it was now the turn of Belvès. A special Gestapo car had stopped outside the Rispals' house. Hélène Rispal had saved her husband just in the nick of time, pushing him out of the house by a back door. She herself stayed behind; while Rispal had finally reached Labarde via the most roundabout route.

Now we sat with him in our room and waited. He had been saved in time. But Hélène Rispal – what would they do to her? She had promised to come as soon as possible. As soon as possible ... But what if the Germans arrested her in lieu of her husband? That sort of thing was not uncommon. Outside, in the courtyard, our *enfants* went about their usual jobs and pastimes, knowing nothing, caring nothing. Mémé was carrying on one of her endless imaginary telephone conversations. She was enjoying it enormously – blessed are the poor in spirit.

Finally, at about eight in the evening, Hélène Rispal arrived. We breathed again.

The Germans had come with a list of twenty-seven people whom they wanted to arrest. Gabriel Rispal was the second on the list. When they failed to find him, and his brave wife firmly insisted, in spite of all threats, that he had gone away on business, they undertook a search of the premises, in the course of which they pilfered money, jewellery and clothes. But Gabriel had got away safely. Belvès as a whole had been fortunate, too: the Germans had 'only' set fire to two houses before finally driving off with ten of the twenty-seven. The others had managed to get away in time.

At the end of it the leader of the contingent, a captain, had declared: 'We may not be locals, but we are just as well informed about everything as if we were locals. We'll be back.'

The Germans' implication that there were informers even in Belvès doubtless reflected the truth – as did their promise to return. Gabriel Rispal would remain with us until further notice.

And the Germans did indeed return, more than once. Each time they covered a wider area outside Belvès, overrunning a number of villages and farms in close proximity to Labarde. On one occasion they were below us in the valley, less than 300 metres away. I am jumping ahead, and it would not be of interest to go into details; but with each day and night that passed we were forced to take more and more seriously the probability that they would come to Labarde.

We considered what was to be done. We certainly could not remain in our room, detached as it was from any link to the main building. There we would be caught as in a mousetrap. Thinking of the women of the convent, we also had to get rid of any trace of ourselves; our room would have to look as though it were uninhabited.

And so, once more, we gathered up all our worldly possessions and put everything in the loft. Letters and photographs were burnt. The pages of my manuscript I buried.

But what next? What were we to do with ourselves? The Mother Superior had given us use of an empty bedroom on the second floor of the main building. From the window we could see quite a distance down the road. At night we organised a sort of sentry duty: we did not undress, and took turns to do three-hour stints at our lookout post by the window. If the Germans did come, we would still have time to get out of the bedroom.

To get out ... but where to? Into the open air – perhaps into the forest? Or could we find a hiding place in the house itself – in other words a hiding place within the hiding place? We racked our brains, but could not find the answer. This failure to reach a decision was a greater strain on the nerves even than anything else.

One evening we were discussing the matter again. We were whispering – going over the possibilities, back and forth, back and forth. It was already after the Angelus, and the whole house seemed as though it were submerged in the gentle peace of the May night. But a fire on the horizon provided us with a reminder of the presence of the Germans.

Suddenly two of the Sisters came over – two who were particularly attached to us, Soeur de l'Annonciation and Soeur Marie-Bernard. They smiled as they gestured to my wife, and then disappeared with her across the courtyard. It was a while before the three of them returned. Now my wife was smiling, too. She beckoned to us to follow; and we all set off.

On the other side of the courtyard, in a wing of the convent, is the chapel. Behind the chapel is a door leading to a small, narrow room: the morgue, the room for the dead. The furniture consists of a bed on which the body rests, and next to it a small table with a candlestick. The wall at the head of the bed is covered with a black cloth which reaches all the way to the ground. Above the bed is a great crucifix.

If the bed is pulled to one side and the lower part of the wallcovering is lifted, a hole becomes visible in the wall – a semi-circular opening whose existence no one would guess, just wide enough to crawl through on all fours. On the other side you find yourself in a kind of cave, large enough for several people to remain, bent over and pressed up together, for a few hours if necessary. Any longer than that, and there would be a risk of asphyxiation, since the only ventilation is from that opening into the morgue, which is in any case covered with the black cloth.

We were absolutely delighted with the good Sisters' discovery. The hiding place within the hiding place had been found. Now at least we knew what we had to do. And we organised a sort of dress rehearsal, there and then, which met with general approval.

What we and the Sisters agreed was as follows: in the case of immediate danger, we disappear into our cave. The Sisters put the cloth back as it was, push the bed back in front of the opening and then lock the morgue from the outside. Even if the Germans were to demand that the morgue be opened, and were to proceed to search it, they might perhaps, with luck, still not find our hiding place. Perhaps. But at least, now, there *was* a perhaps.

Rather than get bogged down in tedious details, let me rather proceed to the result – the provisional result.

We have been lucky. Up to the present day – 6th July 1944 – we have had to go into the cave behind the morgue twice. On both occasions the Germans turned back at the last moment. Will we continue to be lucky? The question persists, now as before. But in the meantime the *débarquement* has at last – at last – taken place. The Allies are in France. And they are moving inexorably forward.

They are still a long way away from us here. We are still not out of danger. The Germans continue to commit outrage upon outrage. Still ... it now seems a little easier for us to 'hold out, keep our spirits up'.

Whether we will ourselves live to see it, or whether we will perish before then: the liberators are approaching from all sides; the Brown Beast – One People, One Empire, One Führer – will, in the foreseeable future, be destroyed. That will be the end of Hitler's thousand-year-long Third Reich. It will have lasted not much more than a decade – barely a fleeting, transitory moment in world history. And yet, the Monster's words were true. For, measured in misdeeds, in misery – measured in evil – this fleeting, transitory moment will weigh heavier than a thousand years.

33

The morning of June 6th 1944

WHEN WE MOVED TO THE BEDROOM, we naturally also removed the radio from our room. It lay, wrapped in a blanket, in a corner of the convent's medicine room. We were now dependent on the news and rumours that reached us in various ways from outside.

At about 9 a.m. on 6th June 1944 I was alone in our bedroom. My wife and Sláva were working in the vegetable garden. Gabriel Rispal, who could still not risk returning to Belvès, was also outside. I stood by the open window. One of the Sisters, the phlegmatic Soeur Emmanuel, walked by below. After a remark on the rainy weather, she called something else to me as she went by: 'They say that there are American warships in the Seine estuary.' With that she went on her way.

American ships ... Seine estuary ... Impossible! But could it be that the *débarquement* had really, finally, taken place? I rushed downstairs like a man possessed, determined to get the radio out of the medicine room. I think that even if there had been Germans approaching the house, at that moment it would not have stopped me: I had to know. The *débarquement!* The *débarquement!* Nothing else was of any significance.

I got hold of the radio and took it up to the bedroom. Then, while I was busy trying to make it work, I suddenly heard a cry from outside. Two cries, to be exact: a female voice, letting out one cry and then another.

I instinctively stopped what I was doing. To hear people cry out is not such an unusual experience, in a madhouse. But these two cries were something different. This was the sort of cry that stays with you forever. It seemed to burst forth from the very depths of the soul. A tremendous release of pressure. A cry – an eruption – of relief. Years of pent-up agony and one great stream of joy – like a stream of blood, red, hot and steaming. A lament for the dead and a cry of resurrection.

I was shaken to the core; I had to get out; I had to see who had let out these two cries.

In the doorway I met my wife and Sláva. Behind them was Gabriel Rispal. I didn't even have to ask: his face transformed, all he was able to do was repeat the same phrase over and over again: 'Ça y est, ça y est.' It's happened. It's happened. All four of us had tears streaming down our faces.

We then listened to the first *communiqués* – Churchill's declaration, Eisenhower's manifesto. We listened to them in all the languages – in languages that we understood and in languages that we didn't understand. We knew them by heart by now, but we wanted to hear them over and over again. We were like men dying of thirst, who want to drink a river dry.

On this day my wife wanted to see only happy faces around her. She still had left one large jar of fruit conserve, which was now brought down from the attic and shared out among the *enfants*. They, of course, had no idea what the occasion was for this delectable treat. The word 'débarquement' would have been no more than a meaningless noise to any of them. Which did not, of course, make their enjoyment any the less: the 'weak-minded' are wise enough to enjoy their feasts whenever they come.

While my wife was preoccupied with the fair distribution of the jam, our dear friend Soeur de l'Annonciation arrived. She had been in the street outside. 'I didn't know anything,' she said, 'but I realised just from the faces of the passers-by that something big had happened.'

The telephone was out of order now: the Germans had immediately severed all the connections. So Hélène Rispal sent us a letter via a messenger. It consisted of one sentence: 'I embrace you with all the hope that this day brings with it.'

Our beloved friend had chosen her words well. This 6th June 1944 was not just the day of the Great Event, the realisation of which we had waited for so long and so fervently. Most important of all was the total sense of hope that shone through that day. In the hearts of millions upon millions of human beings.

We needed this sense of hope, so as to be able to hold out a little longer, so as not to go under at the last moment ...

34

Summer

ONCE UPON A TIME ... the sound of a fairy-tale – blown to the winds, long forgotten.

Once upon a time it was summer, and in those days even the word 'summer', as you said it, was alive with warmth and fragrance; it tasted like a ripe, juicy fruit. Summer meant relaxation, holidays, mountains, sea. It meant enjoying yourself – taking it easy. It meant living like a 'God in France'.

That 'God in France' – the one who, not long before the War, was held in such high esteem by the likes of Friedrich Sieburg* in his perfidious book. Only the good old French people didn't notice anything. Or those that did notice it did not wish to notice what purpose was being served by this sort of declaration of love on the part of 'friends' like Sieburg. They took everything in return for cash; felt tremendously flattered and took Herr Sieburg – and after him Herr Abetz, and the whole Fifth Column, those friends of the Nazis who visited upon the land of the French the mentality of Hitler – to their hearts, with feelings of warmth and gratitude.

They were laughing behind their hands, this whole jolly crew. Really, these gullible, 'negroid' French had fallen for it hook, line and sinker. Their naïveté exceeded even the highest expectations.

Summer 1944. The *débarquement* has come. And yet …

Over the whole land, as far as Normandy, where the inexorable advance of the Allies was putting a stop to his activities, this Swastika-God in France was scattering the blessings from his cornucopia ever more extravagantly: *Wehrmacht*, Gestapo, torture, deportation, murder, arson, looting …

Since the success of the landings it seems that the Germans are not just seeking revenge for every inch of soil that they are forced to abandon. It is as if they want to wallow, like animals, for one last time in the mud of evil; it is an orgy, a paroxysm of bestial cruelty before the Monster breathes its last.

The events of this summer – which is surely the last summer of the War – will be dealt with by countless historians. But there is another history, which should at least be mentioned, an inner history, if you like, which allows one to glimpse the desolation and devastation that were perpetrated on people's *spirits*. To glimpse the extraordinary distortions and derangements that took root in – if I may use this term – our *mental* perspective. (And we may reach a worse state yet, if this sixth summer of war extends also into a sixth winter with the Germans.)

Here we are, in the open air, enjoying God's own country, in the glorious summer of 1944. And it is not that we are indifferent to the natural world, as some might be tempted to believe; on the contrary, it arouses very strong and varied responses in us. It is just that these responses are of a very strange kind.

Here, for example, is a wood – a deep, silent forest. Our reaction to it now is not: how delightful it would be to revel in the solitude, the shade, the silence of this forest. Today, in the summer of 1944, our first thought is rather: would this forest be thick enough, dark enough, impenetrable enough to function as a hiding place in the case of pursuit?

Or again: here is a magical clearing, a true elfin meadow. Involuntarily you find yourself measuring it mentally: would this stretch of land give English planes enough space for a night-time *parachutage* – a parachute drop of weapons and ammunition for a *maquis*? In this connection our dreams take another bizarre turn, too: in Belvès after one recent *parachutage* some parachutes were cut up and the bits shared out. We were given a piece to look at. What wonderful material! Pure silk – an excellent, imperishable fabric, which can be made into the most beautiful shirts, blouses, etc.

Or again: here is a garden full of roses, jasmine and gladioli. It creates a delightful interplay of sensual experiences, of scent and colour. Now, though, the predominant reaction is one of indignation at the frivolity of having planted all this useless, inedible stuff instead of cabbage and beans!

Or: a fabulous moonlit night in July, wrapped in an unearthly shimmer of mystery. And the ultimate expression of ecstasy aroused by this midsummer night's dream of 1944 is: 'Wonderful visibility tonight for the Royal Air Force!'

Books. You find yourself reading through them at random, purely mechanically, while your thoughts are far, far away. Or you throw the book aside after a few pages. Provocative twaddle. The worries and problems of happy, high-spirited individuals, who have no idea what a real worry or problem is.

Radio. You listen to the *communiqués*, the purely factual reports: concrete facts – facts that speak for themselves – are all you are interested in. The rest is empty words – propaganda. Only what can be followed on a map is of any importance. And so too with the news that one receives by word of mouth. Nothing has the power to surprise any more. We are blunted, deadened.

Well, occasionally some new event still has the capacity to provoke anger, to make the blood boil. When, for example, you learn that, by way of 'reprisal' in a village, the Germans have crucified a baby on the church gate; that in Castelnau they poured ten litres of water into their victim through a funnel and then trampled on the swollen stomach with their boots.

You hear of these heroic deeds and you shake with powerless rage. But after a while you fall back into a kind of paralysis. What else can you do? At the end of the day, this catatonic condition is the final resort of self-defence; a sort of insulating layer. Otherwise you would simply die of despair, of disgust. If you had tears left, you would be crying for the rest of your life.

And, with the exception of the few people that we can place our absolute trust in, what, now, does our relationship with the world around us come to? Something incredibly ugly, sad and shameful.

All the time that a person is hidden and shut away in a clandestine location, he must also always be on the lookout, on the defensive. Every face that he encounters may conceal an enemy. Every chance event may lead to danger, against which he must be on his guard, must take precautions. Every stranger – and even every acquaintance – with whom he has even the most superficial contact provokes the silent question inside his head: might this person have the capacity to destroy me?

And so he weighs every word with the utmost caution, takes great care to evade every question, senses the threat of disaster behind every utterance, however harmless, becomes distrustful, suspicious, imagines the worst of everyone. All human contact is poisoned in advance.

And with every day that passes you become poorer within; the internal frost becomes sharper, the heart hardens. Yes, you are alive. But in order to stay alive – in order to have at least a chance of surviving – you allow yourself to die, bit by bit.

The radio in London reports that the old king of Sweden, Gustav, has attempted to intervene with Hitler on behalf of the Hungarian Jews, in an effort at least to save them from the gas chambers, the ovens and the other German 'Jew – perish!' policies. This gesture from the worthy monarch will certainly have had no effect, other than that of provoking the mocking laughter of the slaughterers. But the fact that at last *one* neutral head of state has at least made an attempt to raise his voice 'in the name of humanity' – in spite of the fact that it is only Jews that are at stake – this fact is something remarkable in itself, and must fill us with endless wonder and gratitude. A king, who takes a stand on behalf of innocent people who have been condemned to a gruesome death through the arbitrary acts of a raging monster: this is something that appears, not as the conscientious duty of any powerful person whose word might have some influence; not as an appalling sin of omission on the part of all those who – when there was still time – looked on in silence and indifference: no. One feels with the action of the Swedish king that one is in the presence of a miracle.

That is the extent to which we have come to take our own suffering for granted.

But, for all that, we here must still be considered the favourites of Destiny. The liberators are in France; every day brings them nearer. Will they get to us in time?

The Allies are advancing, constantly advancing. But if we here are anxiously asking ourselves 'Will they get here in time?' what of those who will necessarily have a much longer wait, in their fear, than we? What of those who may still be alive in the many death camps, the repositories of torture, in Germany itself ... How many will still be alive, when the liberators finally open the gates?

I may perhaps be forgiven, if at this point I present a small, provisional account on the domestic front: the account of one family among innumerable others. My wife has so far learned that, of those of her relatives who remained in Czechoslovakia, one brother, one brother-in-law and one sister-in-law have perished in Terezín Concentration Camp. There is no word of her other siblings, nephews, nieces – young women and small children among them. We are still in the dark about their fate.

In the dark? How I fear the day when that dark will be made light.

35

The first step into freedom

23RD AUGUST. MIDDAY. The liberation of Paris is announced on the radio. And at the same time we also learn that the Germans have retreated from our *département*, the Dordogne.

Everywhere around, from Belvès to the last abandoned hamlet, the bells begin to sound the hymn of liberation. Our own modest chapel bell must not be left out, and its bright, delicate sound joins eagerly in the general sound of jubilation. Even those of the patients who were sitting motionless and apathetic in the courtyard now feel that something extraordinary has happened; they jump up and start rushing this way and that. They are left in peace. The Sisters in charge of them are themselves too excited.

Among these 'poor in spirit' is one who has occasional lucid moments. She rushes up to me and asks: 'Is it really true that we aren't Germans any more?' When I confirm this, she turns to her companions and shouts happily: 'Today we're definitely getting a dessert!' It is the first immediate consequence of the great event.

It is not over yet. There will be more horror to come. But Paris is liberated and the Dordogne is liberated. The last Germans have left Périgueux and they had to do so very quickly indeed. They nonetheless found time, at the very last moment, to slaughter about a hundred 'political prisoners' in Place Francheville, and to throw their bodies into a pit along with the bodies of horses, dogs and cats.

No: it is not over yet. There will be a lot more German atrocities yet. But Paris is liberated, and we here in the Dordogne are liberated. Is it possible? Is it really true? How are we to take it in, to translate the facts into their immediate and further consequences; how are we to grasp everything, make sense of it, reflect on it, control the tide of thoughts and feelings that sweeps over us from all sides? There are moments when happiness can be as impossible to assess in all its consequences as sorrow; moments when one may be numbed by joy just as much as by pain; moments when the heart understands before the intellect has comprehended. A hope which we sometimes did not even dare to believe in had become reality. A trial which so often threatened to crush us has been overcome. But it is only gradually, bit by bit, that we can take it on board, that we can come to terms with it.

In the afternoon we greet Hélène and Gabriel Rispal, who have rushed up to see us in the little room that we have lived in for nearly two years now. Gabriel is still in his white painter's overalls; he has not yet had time to change. In Belvès, as soon as the great news was heard, a procession formed spontaneously, with Rispal at its head, a Tricolour in one hand and a red flag in the other. They went first to the 'Monument aux Morts', then to the graveyard, to the freshly dug graves of those fallen in the Resistance; and finally to the main square. There Gabriel was lifted onto a table and had to sing them the 'Marseillaise' and 'Paname'. After that, though, he and his wife had left everyone standing to come to us – to share this so deeply longed-for hour with us. And now they are urging us to follow them to Belvès, to spend the evening with them in their house – because now there is nothing to stop us, is there? Now we are no longer clandestines. The iron bolt has been pulled back, we are free. We are assured that we can come and go as we please.

What? Go to Belvès – us? Leave our hiding place, show ourselves on the street? Openly admit that we are still alive? But ... what if we bump into a policeman?

In a sudden flash of lightning I live through it all again – the miracle. The three miracles, that snatched us from the grasp of death. I see barbed wire – row upon row of it. My hut: Hut Number 8. I breathe the aroma of dirt again, and the sweet scent of old straw on the plank-beds. I feel the hunger again – how it bites your insides. Concentration camp. Concentration camp for Jews. There were 1,800 of us at Beaune-la-Rolande. Where are they now, my unhappy comrades? What gruesome death awaited them in one of the Extermination Camps in Germany or Poland? The first miracle is that I am not among their number.

And then: the day after tomorrow – 25th August 1944 – will be the second anniversary of the day when, in the grey of dawn, seven *gendarmes* entered our house in Voiron. The bus to Grenoble. Caserne Bizanet, that sinister antechamber of death. The people – the children playing – waiting to be handed over to the Germans, to death. How we were saved at the very last moment. We: my wife and I, and Sláva, who had taken it upon herself to keep faith with Jews. We were allowed out – 'provisionally'. And then Rosa. Poor Rosa – for her there was no miracle, no 'provisionally': an officer was in a bad mood. We had to abandon her to her fate. What has become of her?

Then an interlude. Our 'escape to Switzerland'. The railway station at Aix-les-Bains; disaster lying in wait all around us. That *gendarme* – our potential ruin – looming towards us. Another episode that could so easily have had irrevocable consequences.

And finally the third miracle: Hélène Rispal. The same Hélène who is now trying to persuade us not to hide any longer. Hélène, who had the brainwave – in the middle of a sleepless night – to hide us here in Labarde. The telegram from her son. The journey here; the arrival.

The whole thing – the whole of the past – rises suddenly before me; and passes again, like a vision. But a vision that is clearer, more vivid, more real than the present. It is the present, rather, whose outlines appear murky, difficult to make out – the present that seems to disappear like a dream.

A triple darkness had to descend on us, so that we could finally disappear under the protective darkness of the clandestine world. And it is only a short time ago that we had to hide ourselves still deeper: in our cavity behind the morgue. Yesterday it would still have been a possibility that the Germans might take us. And now we are assured that it is all over – we are free. We are earnestly encouraged to show ourselves openly. It is too much: too much at once. I look at my friends in amazement.

Try to understand me. Have patience with me. I have not yet absorbed the new reality. I feel like someone who has suffered from hunger too long to be able to take a proper meal, even one composed of the most tempting dishes. I must be aware of my own limits – of what I can take in. And so I beg a little patience – a little time, yet, before we appear once more as human beings among others.

It was three days later, then, on a Sunday, that we made our 'entry' into Belvès. There had been a frenzy of preparation for it. Gabriel Rispal picked us up in a car. The Rispals' charming home had been festively decorated with flowers in our honour, and a beautifully laid table adorned the dining room. Our old friend Pierre Vorms had come from Périgueux (where he had been working at the rank of major on the general staff of the FFI – the Forces Françaises de l'Intérieur*) to celebrate our 'resurrection'.

Emil Kofler had made the journey from Monpazier, although he was beset with a terrible anxiety: his son, who had done outstanding work for the Resistance, had been picked up in the street in Paris and deported to Germany at the end of July.

Vorms had also brought with him two officers, an American and a Yugoslav, who had fought alongside the French in a *maquis* right up to the liberation of the Dordogne. We sat down to eat. The food was exceptional. Only a friendship like that of Hélène Rispal could have performed such a culinary feat in the France of late August 1944.

Now, must I be completely honest?

To find myself here in this company – this was more than just a return to life, a return to light after the years of persecution, of running from one place to another in a deep, dark mineshaft. Alongside our sense of security there was also the feeling that here, with our friends, we had found something like a new home.

Nevertheless, I did not exactly manage to bask in the warm glow of this happiness. I had not regained a sufficient sense of equilibrium; I was too distraught, too wound up, still, by the lack of peace, the perpetual motion. And then, too, there was the effort not to let any of this show, to put on a front of merry good humour; to listen to the conversation of the two foreign officers, who had such interesting stories to tell. In the same moment that I had ceased to be a hunted animal, constantly on the run; that I had, at least to an extent, been received back into the society of free men and women, I nevertheless again felt as though I were excluded from this society – an outsider, a perpetual outsider. And in spite of the care and the affection, the warmth and tenderness that surrounded me, in spite of the heavy, intoxicating wines, I sensed that my whole being was still shot through – like a dull, constant pain – with the dreadful destruction, still being inflicted by the German rabble even on those of us who had been saved, who had survived.

For those Jews who have been able to escape the slaughter, a new tragedy now begins – the tragedy of the soul. Those of us who were rescued have escaped with our lives – our purely physical lives. But how can we rescue that other life, the higher one, the life of feelings and thoughts – the life that actually makes existence worthwhile?

Outside, the street stands invitingly bathed in sun, happiness, oblivion, the carefree cries of children. A street free of the sound of German boots. It is there for me too, now. But at the same time this street fills me with something like a feeling of agoraphobia: I have an overwhelming dread of everyone who might recognise me, might speak to me out there. Fear of the questions that they might ask me; fear of the answers that I would have to give.

> *Yes, we are back in Belvès.*
> *Actually, we have been away for a long time: more than two years.*
> *We were in the Isère, and then back here again – at a place in the country.*
> *My wife and Miss Kolářová are quite well, thank you.*
> *Madame Rose? No, she is not with us ... Goodbye!*

Is that all? Yes, that is all.

What do they know of everything that lies between these questions and these answers – of everything that rises between them like a ghost? And how could I possibly ask them the courtesy of *not* asking – of just walking past in silence? We were away, and now we are here again: let that be enough for you. Your life carried on as before in that period. We – we others – have come back from the dead.

Come back ... to what?

If I had been compelled on that very first day after our liberation to be among people and to answer their questions, I probably would have run away immediately – back to Labarde, back to our 'subnormals', our simpletons, who remain unaffected by the madness, the foulness, of the 'normal' world; back to our nuns, whose universe extends no further than the humble performance of their duty and the peace afforded by their faith. For the frail creatures here, and for the women of the convent, the present is the same as the past, and the future will be the same as the present. For them the chain has not been rent asunder.

To return. To return *where?*

Until now we were prevented by a *force majeure* from even thinking about tomorrow – from making plans beyond the next hour. This *force majeure* no longer exists. The outcome of the War is now a certainty: the monstrosity of Hitler's world will be terminated. All that is uncertain is how long that will take. The hope which at many times seemed little more than a dying ember has become a flame that lights up the sky. We Jews, however – those of us who by a miracle have survived – now stand in the shadow of two enormous, menacing questions. Two anxieties.

The first is: what has happened to all our relatives and friends, and indeed to all those countless individuals about whose fate we at least believe we are uncertain, so long as circumstances prevent us from making any enquiries, or receiving any news. 'Prevent'? I should rather say, so long as circumstances still *allow* us to clutch at a vague hope, a 'perhaps'. Which is like clutching at a straw. Which of the missing might still be alive ... *perhaps* ... ? And what inexorable answers – what irreversible certainties – lie before us. How many mass graves contain the mouldering bones that once bore the name, the life, of a loved one. And alas, even that final resting place – that of a mass grave – cannot be regarded as a certainty. For so many Jews were thrown into those crematoria while still alive, only to then have their ashes used by the Brown Cannibals as manure in their accursed fields. How many bones were so efficiently ground up in mills that were invented especially for that purpose? There is no outrage, no desecration that would have been too much for the Germans – men and women.

The only certainty that we possess is a bald figure. Of the fifteen million Jews scattered all over the world, in Europe six million have been 'exterminated'. So far. It is not over yet.

The second question is: what is to become of us surviving refugees? Are we to return? Where to?

Home? It is true that each of us has a country, which, after payment of the allotted price – spiritual and other – we finally managed to leave. But we no longer have a home. Worse than that: in our 'fatherland' we would be more foreign than we are in a foreign country, more deracinated than we are in our exile. Every face – familiar or unfamiliar – every house, every stone would serve only to bring back to us the bitter memory of the shame, the insults, the betrayal, the humiliation that we were subjected to immediately after the Anschluss took place. With every breath we took we would breathe in the memories like poison gas. Every step would simply throw into greater relief the gaping, unbridgeable abyss between that past and the present. There would be no word, no assurance, no look, no smile, no tear that we could ever trust any more. Behind every mask memory would show its face – the hideous grimace of a monster.

Besides, of those in Vienna who shared our fate, after 10th March 1938 – our relatives, our friends – no one is still there. No one. They are dead; deported – disappeared without trace; or else somewhere far, far away: America, Australia, New Zealand; China ... It is a graveyard, my homeland: a graveyard even for the survivors. We could not even be certain that we would find the graves of those who had the good fortune to die before the invasion. For even these have, we learn, been desecrated and destroyed.

But, wherever it may be, it will mean, for very many of us, starting from the beginning again. 'Recommencer à zéro.'

Starting at zero again; starting with nothing. In both the material and the spiritual sense. Starting, in fact, at a lot less than zero. Many of us survivors, who are already near the end of our lives – are we to begin the struggle again, in spite of age, in spite of exhaustion; in spite of our shattered nerves, of all the incurable wounds that we bear?

Will we find help, or at least justice?

We are receiving such fine promises, at the moment, from all quarters. A golden age will dawn just as soon as the Monster of the Swastika has finally been slain. Punishment of all crimes; reparation for all wrongs; freedom; equality; justice. Every individual will be assured both a life and a death that accord with human dignity. We shall see, of course, which of these wonderful proclamations of human happiness are actually translated into fact, once propaganda has itself become redundant, and once the politicians of all parties no longer need to use the sufferings of others as material for their political games ...

And will those people of goodwill who did not themselves experience Hitler's Germany at first hand – will even these people have enough imagination and energy to keep alive their abhorrence for the guilty and their willingness to help the victims after the War as well? The human heart so easily reverts to oblivion, to routine; human memory is so short, especially as regards other people's troubles. Then, of course, we have the demands of what is known as 'Realpolitik' – that is to say, of the politics that wants to cover up everything, to sweep it under the carpet. And to leave the dead alone.

No. After the incredible quantity of suffering with which the end of the Third Reich was purchased – after *this* war – the dead must not be left as dead, must not be left under the great shroud of forgetting. The dead must arise again, inexorably, in the remembrance, in the conscience of the world, bloody witnesses for all time of an age in which the outrages of a Hitler and of his Germany – outrages of a kind that had never before existed or been imagined – were allowed to happen. The voice of the dead should be louder than all the victory celebrations; stronger than any kind of politics. The voice of the dead demands expiation – in as far as there can ever *be* expiation, given what was done under the sign of the Swastika. Expiation, so that they can have retribution – yes, retribution, because it would be the most blatant hypocrisy, the most abject betrayal, to try to magic away the concept of retribution. Even if applied with the most extreme severity, this would not merely constitute justice, it would actually still represent the most extreme leniency. But the voice of the dead demands expiation as a preventive measure, too, so as to protect future generations from reaping the harvest of the hellish seed sowed by Hitler and his brood. The disappearance of the Third Reich on the surface will accomplish nothing. It must be rendered genuinely harmless.

The most evil and cowardly atrocities were – even before the War – 'only' perpetrated against Jews. 'Only' – that qualification which functions as an excuse, or even as a term of approval. And there are many, I know, who add this 'only', if not aloud, then at least silently. Hitler's proud boast, in one of his speeches, that he would at all events leave behind him an anti-Semitic Europe, was not a vain one.

But do not forget, all you others – even those whom Hitler will have left behind him as anti-Semites – that it concerns you, too. *Vestra res agitur.* Whether in the Occupied or the Unoccupied lands, you should realise that if Germany had been victorious, all of you would have sunk inevitably to the category implied by that 'only'. You would have all become 'only' slaves – you, your children, and your children's children – slaves, whom the Master Race would have felt free to use as they desired, arrogantly and without restraint. Here in France, for example, you would have been 'only' – according to the Führer's own words – despised 'negroids'. I admit that this position is still far from being comparable with ours.

Still, you may certainly believe that your 'only' – that is, the status of serfs belonging to the comrades within the Master Race – would have been fully sufficient to make you wretched for generations, even if the thousand-year Third Reich had not lasted for quite a thousand years. So: do not forget; take retribution; be watchful. Otherwise your children may easily have to endure a Fourth Reich. Hitler is not an incomprehensible accident of history. He was merely a synthesis – an infernal crystallisation – of his own Germany, which freely chose him.

To return – where?

Each of us has a land where he or she was born, but we no longer have a home. We are in exile everywhere – to such an extent, in fact, that we are no longer in exile anywhere. We will be at home anywhere that we are able to find a little love and a bit of bread.

The experiences that constitute our life since emigration – they are coursing round our bodies like a poison that can never, now, be removed. Our other past, meanwhile – before 1938 – might, conceivably, become a memory that does not automatically involve sorrow. It is rather like the grave of a dead person: you occasionally still visit it, but the sorrow has at last become no more than a fleeting aroma – the aroma of a far-off, insubstantial melancholy.

The young are in a better position. They have found a new home, where in their youth they may still put down deep roots. They will be able to forget that they even had something to forget. They may be able to say – even today – that the effect of Hitler was simply to force them into their true homeland.

We old people, on the other hand, have only uncertainty ahead. People tell us that we must stand firm again on our own two feet; they assure us that we will be able to move forward in confidence. But for that to be true we would have to have firm ground beneath our feet. Now we see only sand, sand that gives way with every step we take.

From the first day when, as an immigrant starting from the beginning again with nothing, I had to knock on the doors of strangers, I experienced a great deal of disappointment, disillusionment, depression, ingratitude and unfairness. Later, during the Occupation, I suffered terrible things at the hands of French people. What the Germans were, I knew already: I knew it from what I had seen in Austria. I now got to know their French accomplices and pupils. They were, in many cases, in no way inferior to their teachers.

And yet, at the same time, it has been granted to me in the course of my sorrowful journey in France to meet wonderful human beings – human beings the like of whom I have never encountered before.

Human beings to whom I was a stranger, or very nearly one; who had not the slightest obligation towards me and who, in the midst of the most virulent anti-Semitic witch hunt, declared themselves for the foreign outcast, when, back home, I had been shamefully abandoned, betrayed and denied by so many 'friends' of long years' standing. Human beings who exposed themselves fearlessly to the most dreadful dangers, because they had taken it upon themselves as a conscientious duty to save fugitives from the German murderers. These were Christians in the finest sense of that word, who were concerned to right some of the wrongs that were being perpetrated all about them by 'Aryans' against Jews. Human beings who did not just offer their support, but blessed me with their brotherly affection and devotion.

Human beings who could be admired, in the France of the Resistance, as worthy children of that people who, more than 150 years ago, rose up for freedom and human rights.

French men and French women.

To return ... where?

If only it might be granted to me not to have to part from these human beings, who reached out their hand to me in my hour of need; to find some corner warmed by the fire of their affection, a place where I could stay right to the end – the true end, this time, beyond which we do not have to start again, once more, from zero.

A little love and the little piece of daily bread: those are the true necessities of life. Nourishment for the soul and sustenance for the body – modest as it seems, that is all that one needs for existence. Everything else is deceit and illusion – sound and fury. If I did not know that before, it is a lesson that life has taught me since 10th March 1938.

These years have brought me more than just experiences. I am grateful to them for a realisation – a final realisation that is deeper than everything that one can get from religions, philosophical systems and political ideologies. Religions, philosophical systems and ideologies all bring their own wisdom with them. But the only knowledge which can actually help – the knowledge of love – has disappeared amid all our fantastic intellectual advances. That is why humanity was able to reach such a murderous state.

Well, I have found love. More love than I could measure. More than, in good times, I could even have dreamed of. More than I have deserved.

Will I be able to find the little bit of daily bread, too?

36

Carlos

As EARLY AS 1943, in Labarde, I had heard the name 'Carlos',* spoken in tones of respect. Carlos and Soleil were the two best-known *chefs* of the *maquis* in the Dordogne. But while Soleil was the archetype of the impetuous daredevil, Carlos, for all his courage and resourcefulness, was also a thoughtful individual, who would conscientiously weigh up all his strategic and tactical options. Also, Soleil liked to be in the forefront of events, and he had an absolute talent for self-publicity. Carlos preferred to remain behind the scenes.

In September 1944 I met him at Gabriel Rispal's house in Belvès.

Carlos is very slim, almost weedy. He looks the complete intellectual – his blue-grey eyes peep out through a pair of glasses that seem to have become part of his face. He has the natural, gentlemanly courtesy of a man of the world. Even in his immaculately turned-out captain's uniform Carlos looks rather like some scholar who has reached the post of professor very early in life, around the age of thirty. Only occasionally does one notice, suddenly, that hard set of the chin, the dark, fierce look in the eyes, which betray his experience of worlds beyond the study or the laboratory.

Carlos speaks in a very calm, measured way; his is the modesty of a man who only seeks the validation of his own judgement. He never raises his voice, even when speaking of things which would amply justify an emotional reaction. And he steers the conversation away from his own personal life with an unshakable discretion.

Yet behind everything that he says, as well as behind everything that he implies without saying it; behind the level-headed matter-of-fact manner, you sense the power of a pent-up fanaticism – a fanaticism that could only be shifted by death itself. Fanatical conviction and fanatical hatred. There is no obstacle, no disappointment, no setback which could ever dent the conviction; and there is no let-up, no slackening of the hatred. The only force that could be stronger than them is death.

But even death would not stop them. Carlos has a phrase, which he utters very simply and without any sense of drama: 'If I fall ...' The conclusion is clear: 'My death would only affect me, not the cause that I serve. Wherever I had to stop, another would continue the work in my place. All other considerations are irrelevant.'

' ... No, I am not a Spaniard, I am a Catalan. I was unable to complete my studies in engineering in Barcelona, and did not qualify. Even at sixteen I belonged to the secret "movement"; you could say that I grew up as a clandestine. In those days we were working for the Catalan cause in particular, as well as fighting Fascism in general. Study only took place in our spare time.

' ... We have nothing to do with the Spanish anarchists, who have created a lot of negative publicity for us. The political programme of those desperadoes is simply destruction; we are interested in construction. For us revolution is merely a means to an end; they, on the other hand, are only interested in the means, and they will consider any means, even collaboration with the enemy.

'... In '39 we had to abandon the struggle against Franco. Temporarily. On 14th February my group – which consists entirely of university students – managed to get across the French border. Finally we reached the camp of Argelès.

'"Camp" is a euphemism here, for it consisted of a little bit of land surrounded by barbed-wire fencing. Only the earth beneath you, and no roof at all over your head. No blankets, either ... As for the food ... let's not talk about that. The camp commandant was a captain in the *gardes mobiles*. Hitler would have liked him – an SS man by nature, although he was French.

'When war broke out we were formed into a "compagnie de travailleurs" – a labourer company. Twelve hours a day hard grind. For 50 centimes pay.

' ... the food? Fortunately we were sent to Agde, where the Czech army under General Ingr was on training. That saved many of us from starvation; for the Czechs were wonderful comrades. We were forbidden, under threat of the severest punishments, to have contact with them – even to exchange a word with them. But the Czechs were outraged at this treatment of us by our superiors, and they found ways of communicating with us, and in particular of concealing bread and provisions for us in amongst the refuse in the rubbish bins which we had to empty each day. Great men, the Czechs – every last one of them, from general to private.

'Many of us had an agreement from the French régime according to which we were to emigrate to the United States or to Mexico. These people had the visa, the permission to travel – everything. And there were many ships departing for those destinations. But whenever a liner sailed, the relevant people were always informed one day *after* the departure.

'... After the Drôle de Guerre, when Pétain concluded the armistice with Hitler, many of us were handed over to Spain. It is easy enough to imagine what happened to them; it would have been much more humane simply to shoot them immediately. The others were sent to the *départements* of Ariège and Corrèze, and there employed as lumberjacks. We received four francs for one *stère* of wood. We would have starved if we had not used Sundays to do all kinds of jobs for local farmers, who gave us a bit of food in return. In Agde our salvation had been the Czechs; in the Corrèze it was the people of Ussel. It was in Ussel, too, that I got married. My wife is there now, with our eight-month-old son; she lives with her mother. My father-in-law was arrested as a communist by the Vichy police and taken to a concentration camp, after which he was deported by the Germans. Since then we have heard nothing from him.

'... In the middle of 1943 I set up a *maquis* in the Dordogne. To begin with we had basically no weapons; and we were not much better off for clothes, either. At my first engagement with the Germans there were eighteen of us and fifty of them. All we had was one rifle. They even had a tank.

' ... In my company there are not just French but Spanish, Portuguese, Czechs, Austrians, Poles and Belgians. Many of them are Jews.

'... There is, of course, a certain xenophobia towards us in some quarters. We have very often heard the statement "We don't need these foreigners!" But, if we had not joined the *maquis*, these same people would have accused us, as foreigners, of being parasites and not taking part in the struggle to liberate France – of not doing our duty to the country that has given us protection. The loudest voices raised against the "foreigners" belong to those persons who came over to the Resistance at the very last minute, when the Germans had already more or less lost; or those who managed to find their way to us only once there was no longer any danger for them. Back at Égletons, where I had ten dead – eight Spaniards and two Poles – many of these *chauvinistes* were still doing good trade with the Germans.

'... The *miliciens*,[13] the French Gestapo, and all connected with them, were in no way preferable to the Germans. It was betrayal by a *milicien* that led to fifteen of my men being tortured and executed. But I got my hands on him. Oh, yes.

' ... As I have said, there are many going about in the Resistance now, who only a short time ago were hedging their bets, and who were risking only other people's necks. We see some people parading themselves amongst us, who would have paraded with the Germans just as happily if *they* had been the victors. People who are now using the Resistance not just as a cover for their previous shady dealings as collaborators, but also as springboard for their career. While on the other hand you have the little people – ordinary working-class people, who are not asking for anything, are not demanding any reward, and are now returning humbly to normal life – and these are the people who risked their lives a hundred times in the service of the Resistance. Look – in this notebook I have noted down a few people that would seriously deserve to be household names throughout the country. Here, for example, is a humble publican, Madame Magnanon; or there is Monsieur Salon in Siorac, or Brigadier Chataigneau of the *gendarmerie* in Monpazier ...

' ... My men no longer need me; and so I have dissolved my *maquis* here. But my work is not over. I shall go to the Spanish border, now. We need to be very attentive there: Franco takes great pleasure in welcoming the fleeing Germans with open arms.

' ... I do not believe that we shall remain long at the border. Franco's time – the time of the Spanish Fascists – will be up soon, too. I shall leave my wife and child here in France. If I fall, my son will one day know why I have fallen.'

That, then, is Charles-Henry Ordeig, known as Carlos. The Germans had placed a bounty of a million francs on his head.

---

13. The *milice* was the French military police, which acted in collaboration with the Nazis.

37

In memory of my comrades from the concentration camp at Beaune-la-Rolande

MY COMRADES IN HUT 8 – and all of you, 1,800 lost souls, whose ordeal began in the Jewish concentration camp of Beaune-la-Rolande, to be concluded in unimaginable horror somewhere in Germany or in Poland – oh, my unhappy brothers, I must come to you once more, I must return to you in spirit.

It is not that I wish to say farewell to you. No. Since the moment that I left you on the other side of the barbed wire, not a day has gone by on which I have not thought of you; and up to the moment of my last breath not a day will come when I will ever forget you.

I know that there are no words for what I should like to say to you. There can only be silence; a reverent silence in your honour and sorrow in your memory. Nevertheless I, as a survivor, would feel it was a sin against you at this time – a terrible abandonment – not at least to try and stir the memory of you in others. In others who *would* be able to forget – but must never be allowed to forget – what was done to you.

I am writing these lines in a beautiful, remote village of the Périgord on a mild, enchanting day in late autumn. Autumn of the year 1944 – the first autumn since the Liberation. My window is wide open, outside all is peace and tranquility, as soothing as the caress of a gentle, old mother. It is possible for me to sit in a room with friends, who bestow care and affection on me. And nothing, now, is to prevent me from going out, from breathing the fresh air, in freedom.

You, meanwhile, my comrades ... I do not even know where – to which final hell – they took you, when they came one day at dawn, more than two years ago now, to remove you from Beaune-la-Rolande to some unknown 'Extermination Camp'. Auschwitz, Buchenwald, Belsen, Dora? Different names which all conceal the same, nameless horror. I do not even know if a single one of you is still alive; nor what outrages they perpetrated upon you even after your deaths. All I do know is that you must have had to endure a thousand torments, in your body and in your soul, before at last – at last – death came to take pity on you. And all this, not because there was a war – not because you were fighting to defend your fatherland, your freedom, your lives and indeed the honour of your death. No. The reason that you had to drain the cup of sorrow and humiliation to the bottom was quite simply that you were Jews. Jews who by virtue of that fact stood entirely outside the law; who were delivered, unarmed, defenceless, to the sadistic pleasure, the mocking laughter, of your slaughterers. There was no trace of humanity there, that might have reached you in your final abandonment. They left you with nothing – not even a hidden scrap of paper, an old letter, a picture, nothing that might have given you a little support in your long, endless agony. Before revelling in the tortures to which they subjected you, they stripped you bare, in soul every bit as much as in body.

I left you behind; I was reunited with my wife and Sláva; and by a miracle we were able to experience the hour of the Liberation. We, too, had our sufferings, along the way. But what were they, compared with your sufferings?

I feel that I ought to ask your pardon; that I ought to bow humbly before you and say, very softly: 'Forgive me – forgive me for not having had to share your destiny.'

Where are you, my comrades from Hut 8?

Where are you, Ernst Friedezky? You who were my 'hut chief', but in truth also my brother – constantly concerned to show me some token of friendship – even if it were just a word, a smile, a look, a clasp of the hand, a cigarette. You were constantly trying to spread comfort and confidence about you – even though all the while your own pain was so terrible, that you often had to exert the most superhuman effort in order not to collapse under the weight of your own sorrow. And yet that silent – silenced – suffering of yours only redoubled your desire to help, your goodness.

I read your last farewell letter to your wife – written when they were already beckoning you towards the gas chambers and the ovens. Your handwriting, always so clear, so firm, wavered just a little – like a voice which is threatening to crack. This letter, though, in its strength, in its power, is not only a devastating testament of greatness and of love; but also a monument to you, a worthier one than any writer or sculptor could have made. Why on earth did I not transcribe this letter when your wife gave it to me to read ... ? And yet how could I have known that she would herself be deported only a month later. She was the equal of you, on that last night when we took our leave of her in the prison. 'At least I will share the same fate as my husband.' Those were the only words that she wasted on her own behalf. Where is she now?

Where are you, Alois Stern – you who once, when I seemed about to collapse from hunger, put your last, precious bit of sugar in my mouth? Where are you, Helfand, with your bright smile and your indomitable zest for life? Where are you, little Herschel, whose ears began to burn when you showed anyone your child's picture – and where is he, the little boy? Where are you, Bilder, Schleuderer, Wachsberger, Gruenbaum – you and all my other comrades? Where are your families – all those whom you wept for, and who wept for you, in the sleepless nights? Where are the millions of the murdered – the millions of men, women and children whose only crime was that they were born Jews?[14]

My comrades from Beaune-la-Rolande and all you others who shared the same fate – there is only *one* answer to the despairing question, 'Where are you?' There is only *one* prayer for the dead, *one* prayer for you eternal rest, only *one* legacy that you have left to us, if your martyrdom is not to be turned into the most despicable cynicism, the most terrible blasphemy.

And that is that we take care that your remembrance is not reduced to idle words, to well-sounding phrases that are forgotten as soon as they are spoken.

It is not just that we must not forget. We must convert everything that we owe to your memory into active hatred: unstinting, holy hatred for everything that the notion of Hitler and of Hitler's Germany carry with them; hatred for that quintessence of evil. It is a hatred that must be passed down like a religion from generation to generation. Because the end of Hitler and of the Third Reich will not also mean the end of that mentality that gave rise to the likes of Hitler, of Himmler, of Goering,

---

14. The bald answer is that the vast majority of the inmates of Beaune-la-Rolande were deported to Auschwitz in 1942 (see Chronology) and killed there. I have not been able to trace all the names mentioned, but have found the following records. Ernst Friedezky (born Czechoslovakia, 1890), died at Auschwitz, September 19th 1942. Leon Schleuderer (born Austria, 1891), deported to Auschwitz, June 28th 1942. Alois Stern (born Czechoslovakia, 1896), died at Auschwitz, August 10th 1942. Oscar Wachsberger (born Czechoslovakia, 1896), died at Auschwitz September 2nd 1942.

of Goebbels – and of countless others whose accursed names may or may not be known to us. This mentality will continue to live on, like a sleeping demon, within many millions of German people and even like-minded members of other nations. It is not enough simply to dodge out of the way of that demon; not enough to eliminate – temporarily eliminate – the product of that mentality. It is necessary to stamp out the mentality itself. To stamp it out as thoroughly as the Germans would have stamped out the last of the Jews, if they had had enough time.

There is a great deal of talk these days of the 're-education' of Germany. It is rather as if one were to talk of a degenerate individual being put right again by a spell in a sanatorium: it might be doubted whether such re-education would have a lasting effect. Even if that possibility did exist, it could only happen after a very, very long time. Until such time, the Swastika-Mentality will always risk reverting to type, even after the disappearance of the Swastika itself – just like a habitual criminal, to whom wrongdoing has become second nature, if not first nature, and whose instincts are unlikely to be altered either by a stay in a sanatorium or by 're-education'.

My comrades from the concentration camp of Beaune-la-Rolande, my comrades from all the camps – I have already confessed that I feel something like guilt towards you. Since the day on which I was first able to venture outside again, I have more than once encountered the criticism that I do not seem sufficiently to appreciate this good fortune; that I seem not to have grasped what it means not to be a hunted animal any more – to have survived.

Oh, no. You, my unhappy comrades – you may all be my witnesses, that they do me an injustice. Not grasped it? It is precisely because I have grasped it so well that I cannot give way to anything like unalloyed happiness. There is a bitter aftertaste that stays with me. It is the thought of you that will not leave me alone. And it should not leave me alone. If it were to leave me alone, even for one single day, I would feel that to be a betrayal of you.

If I knew that you had been saved, then I would not regret my experience of a concentration camp. On the contrary – I would regard it as a test which led to spiritual enrichment. Because it was with you, in our Hut 8, that I learned what that word 'comradeship', which is so often and so thoughtlessly bandied about, really means. The fortunate can never learn that. Only the most unfortunate of the unfortunate can learn its true significance.

In the straw of Hut 8 we shared everything: sorrows as well as pieces of bread, the darkness of our nights as well as the fleeting glimpses of hope, our humiliation as well as our last cigarette. If, now, I were able also to share with you my liberation, then, I assure you, no one would be able to criticise me for not appreciating the miracle to the full.

And so, this is not a farewell that I address to you. I just wanted to tell you, that without you my liberation seems to me incomplete – almost unreal. Whenever I want to breathe deeply of this air of freedom, to drink it in, then I taste the ashes that that air brings with it: your ashes.

And yet, at the same time, this freedom defines the place that you occupy in my life. What this freedom signifies is, first of all, the presence of you who have departed, the voice of you who were made silent. This freedom is one more bond that binds me indissolubly to you – with you, and with the hatred for your murderers. No vow could ever be stronger or more unbreakable than this bond.

A great writer once said: 'The mystery of love is stronger than the mystery of death.' May the deeds of Hitler's Germany at least have the consequence that, throughout the whole world, the mystery of hatred, too, shows itself stronger than the mystery of death – of that death which is called 'forgetting'.

38

The undeserving survivors

In France, the overwhelming majority of the Jews who have been fortunate enough to survive Hitler's extermination programme are not foreigners, not immigrants 'sans feu ni lieu', without a hearth or a home. They are mainly Jews who, being established French families – resident here for generations – had previously thought that they had all possible citizen rights.

It was the Germans, and their Vichy accomplices, who began the process whereby these Jews were demoted from *français israélites* (French people of the Israelite religion), first to *juifs français* (French Jews), and in the end simply to *juifs* (Jews) pure and simple. The net of persecution grew tighter and tighter around them, until finally they too were at the mercy of any arbitrary action, just like the immigrants. They too became hunted animals, who were forced to seek shelter in the darkness of clandestinity.

And now these Jews are back again – and, would you believe it, they want to reassert their rights! They are not content with simply having saved their lives; they refuse to regard their entire social and material fabric of their past as something that has gone forever, or to regard their future as a problem whose solution must be left to chance and to the goodwill of others. Instead of considering every breath they take an undeserved boon, and every hard-earned bit of bread as generous gift – as well as every humiliation as an unalterable fact; instead of accepting that they must start again from zero, this kind of survivor is so presumptuous as to want to carry on from the same place from which he was violently snatched away! They have the temerity, these survivors, to make claims on things which belong to them; claims on everything that they were viciously robbed of, in both the moral and the material sense. They stubbornly refuse to take account of the fact that, if things had been done in the proper Hitler way, they would be long dead and gone, just like all the others.

To put it bluntly: they shouldn't have survived. And there is a whole host of people who cannot do enough to show their resentment of that.

I do not mean here just the born anti-Semites, who proudly boast that they 'did not wait for Hitler before they became anti-Semites'; nor just the anti-Semites by training, in whom the poisonous seed of Nazi propaganda found a particularly fertile environment for germination; nor, indeed, just the professional anti-Semites, the exploiters – big and small – of Jewish suffering, of Jews' fear of death; the hyenas in the office of the *Banditariat aux affaires juives* and the countless private gangsters and graverobbers of all kinds, for whom the cessation of the great witch-hunt against the Jews meant the end of a quite unprecedented period of prosperity, the termination of a fabulous age of bounty, a time when the plentiful riches to be had from plundering the Jews simply fell into waiting 'Aryan' laps.

No. This sense of outrage is shared by another category of anti-Semites, too. Let us call them the neo-anti-Semites.

The fact that Jews who have been guilty of the impropriety of escaping the cut-throats – the fact these lucky beggars are no longer prepared to be satisfied with hiding timidly in a hole, but actually demand to take their place like everyone else, and alongside everyone else, is unforgivable to many even of those who previously prided themselves on not being anti-Semites in the German mould, those who previously were even so generous as to accept that Jews are after all human beings – human beings with a right to life. Especially those Jews who were thought to be dead. These were the fine, tolerant principles they had in the past – that is to say, as long as that right to life could not be exercised by any actual survivors.

But, as I have said, we now see Jews suddenly popping up – Jews who one had every right to believe had gone forever; and they have the extraordinary presumption to want to return to their previous rank and position, or to want to repossess the dwellings and workplaces that were stolen from them. They want to be master in their own house once again, and again to enjoy the fruits of their own labour. This is all the thanks they show for having been allowed to survive: they have the gall to go looking for their own spiritual and material possessions in the hands of those who stole or received them – to demand compensation, or even a full rendering of accounts. It really is going too far. And quite apart from any of these other grievances, they are bringing competition back again; we thought that that, at least, had been stamped out once and for all. Everything could be so nice, so simple, so comfortable if only they had not reappeared from nowhere – these troublemakers, these spoilsports, who should by rights have been dead long ago. It really has to be said that the Gestapo and the Extermination Camps did not complete their task.

That is the position of many people who have taken advantage of Jewish misfortune – people who had thought that at least this inheritance that they had come into from the missing Jews was incontestably theirs. Now they are bitterly disappointed; now – just imagine it – they are expected to give back some part of the bounty that fell into their laps without any effort on their part. And so they react with outrage, and start up the hue and cry: we can see the Jews in action all over again: worming their way in, pushing themselves forward, getting everywhere, grabbing everything for themselves without taking account of anyone else. The 'Jewish Question' – these people assert – must be considered afresh: it is more pressing than ever.

After the unspeakable sufferings that were visited on them, it would perhaps have been understandable – even justified – if the survivors had been granted some kind of favourable treatment – or at least a bit of goodwill. For – without in any way wishing to minimise the sufferings of the 'Aryan' populations of the occupied countries – it cannot be repeated often enough: what was done to the Jews had nothing to do with the War itself.

Witness the events which took place, long before the War, first in Germany itself, then in Austria and Czechoslovakia, and which were allowed to take place without any obstruction. From the Nuremberg Laws onwards, the Jews were accorded the negative privilege of an anti-Semitic extermination plan. They might, perhaps, have been accorded a positive privilege, for once.

But we do not demand any privilege, or any special treatment. All we demand is justice, in other words precisely and objectively the same rights and duties as all other people; to be subject to the same criteria of judgement, whether on the positive side or on the negative side. What is really sad is that something as self-evident as this needs to be stated in the first place. We do not demand any *pro*-Semitism. All we want is that everyone be judged as an individual, without prejudice, according to his merits, his strengths and his weaknesses, rather than as part of a collective and according to an accident of birth. For any kind of anti-Semitic discrimination is by its very nature also an *incrimination.*

We are, of course, very far from being perfect. Just like everyone else. We too – of course – have among our number the normal percentages of good and bad human beings – the better element and the not-so-good element – with every gradation in between the extremes. Just like everyone else. And each of us, of course, has his good and his bad characteristics; his virtues and his vices. Just like everyone else. And we of course want these eternal, universally valid human norms (which are only not relevant in the case of the Nazi *non*-humans) to be applicable to us too.

Far be it from us to claim any special treatment or recognition for any positive qualities or achievements. We do not labour under the illusion that we are more intelligent, more talented, more able, cleverer than everyone else.

But when Mr X, say, who happens to be a Jew, is guilty of some misdemeanour, then it should be enough to say, 'Mr X was guilty of a misdemeanour,' instead of adding the self-satisfied term of emphasis, 'The *Jew* X ...,' let alone the spiteful statement, 'Of course: all Jews are like that.' It would not occur to anyone to say that the Catholic, the Protestant or the Muslim X had been guilty of a misdemeanour, let alone 'There you are, that's what they are all like, the Catholics/Protestants/Muslims.'

This self-evident truth – that each person is answerable for his own actions, and that a whole people cannot be made answerable for the actions of individuals, nor be taken as a kind of hostage for them; that one's religious allegiance should be regarded as a private matter, not a criterion for other people's judgement – this most basic truth is all that we wish to be observed.

In any case, if you want to make such judgements – and to use those absurd, pejorative anti-Semitic terms of reference – it would be easy enough to show that there are many Jews who are far more 'Christian' than many Christians, and many Christians who are far more 'Jewish' than many Jews.

In day-to-day life one is often tempted to pose the question: If a Herr Bloch or a Monsieur Lévy had behaved like this Herr Brand or this Monsieur Dupont, what a terrible uproar would there be against the *Jew* Bloch, the *Jew* Lévy, in particular, and against Jews in general?

Among the surviving Jews there are, naturally, some whose behaviour is not beyond reproach. A less worthy individual remains a less worthy individual before and after the Liberation. But is there anyone who could seriously deny that for every such Jew there is, at least, a corresponding number, proportionally, of 'Aryans', who would attract, at least, the same level of reproach? And these 'Aryans' cannot even bring forward as extenuating circumstances for their behaviour the mistreatment and humiliation that every one of us survivors, without exception, has experienced – the best as well as the worst of us.

What, then, of the so-called 'Jewish Question'? It is a fiction. The Question only ever existed because it was raised, rather than being raised because it existed; indeed, it was raised *in order* that it might exist. Its existence was a necessary precondition for the outrages committed in the name of anti-Semitism. It served the purposes of Hitler and his 'Comrades of the People' in their performance of the most ghastly – and also the most cowardly – crime in world history.

There is, and always has been, one extremely simple solution to the 'Jewish Question': to admit that it does not exist. Wherever Jews have not been prevented, either by the force of written laws, or by the more insidious unwritten laws, from rising out of the Ghetto, from bettering themselves, from entering into society – from assimilating, rather than merely adapting themselves to pressure and oppression; wherever they have been granted full equality, not just on paper but in reality too, there has been no 'Jewish Question'. The most striking example of this is Soviet Russia – the same country that a relatively short time ago (within a few decades, in fact), was the Tsarist Russia of the pogroms and the anti-Semitic laws of exclusion. (Still, of course, an utter paradise compared with even the early days of the Third Reich.)

In Soviet Russia the entire 'Jewish Question' was removed from the equation with a single stroke of the pen. And if one is to judge from results, it would appear that Russia has had no cause to regret this action of Lenin's. (I should note here, just to avoid any possible insinuations, that I neither belong to nor ever have belonged to any political party.)

And so, for the Russian Jews, their country was transformed – at a single stroke of the pen – from the land of their birth to their fatherland. A fatherland, as any of us would dream of it: a place that you could feel that you belong to, that you can devote yourself to with all your strength, without being humiliated and rejected for your pains. A land in which you feel rooted, in good times and in bad, in life and in death, along with your children and your grandchildren. Your beloved soil, which means security, constancy, permanence, and no longer the perpetually foreign road trodden by Ahasuerus;[15] and into which you may return even after your death, as it were into the arms of a mother.

It is hardly surprising, then, that so many Jews even outside Russia have become grateful adherents of an ideology that knows of no 'Jewish Question'.

This, of course, provides another God-given opportunity for those anti-Semites who specialise in anti-communist propaganda too to accuse the Jews of a double crime: Judaeo-

---

15. Ahasuerus: although this is the name of various kings in the Bible (and in fact etymologically the same name as 'Xerxes'), the name was also applied to the mythical figure of the 'Wandering Jew' from medieval times onward: a Jew who is cursed (probably as a result of mocking Jesus on his way to the Crucifixion) to wander the earth until the Second Coming. This mythical figure is often used as a symbol for the general fate of 'the Jew' in the diaspora.

communism. An accusation which of course dates from the time of Hitler's invasion of Russia. Before that these same Jews were branded – by these same anti-Semites – 'Judaeo-plutocrats'.

It is not clear whether this term 'Judaeo-communists' is intended to malign Jews for being communists or communists for being Jews. All that is clear is that no distinction is to be made between the two categories – communists and Jews.

The Russians adhere to the same principle, albeit in a different sense. They also make no distinction, for example, in their attitude to war criminals. The many hundreds of thousands of Jewish men, women and children who were brutally pursued to their deaths in Russia will not be forgotten any more than their 'Aryan' counterparts. Here, too, Russia acknowledges no 'Jewish Question'.

In many other countries, meanwhile ... There, I fear, the Jewish victims will have been 'only' Jews; and the question of their fate will be a Jewish question, which here means a question without importance. A Jewish question which one passes over with a shrug of the shoulders. They are dead; why waste any more time talking about it?

The other 'Jewish Question', on the other hand, is a live one, for those who have survived but should not have. Because they have the impertinence, not just to go on living, but to want to go on living like everyone else.

Yes – and to die like everyone else, too: to die a natural death. Instead of doing what they should have, which was to meet a painful end, long ago, in the persecution camps, the gas chambers, the ovens – these citadels of Germanic culture and civilisation; to follow the excellent example of those six million Jews who can never again be accused of wanting anything, of demanding some kind of position. Not even a grave.

39

Still in Labarde: but free

DOWN IN THE VALLEY, where a path turns off from the main road from Belvès to Ste-Foy, a path which climbs up a hill towards a rambling building, half hidden by lime trees and chestnuts, there is a primitive wooden signpost. The inscription it bears is half worn away by age, wind and weather. ASILE DE LABARDE.

Throughout the entire period of our first stay in Belvès we never heard anyone speak of Labarde. It was only in November 1942, on a bleak, wet, cold morning, that we deciphered the inscription for the first time.

Labarde is, of course, well-known to the neighbours in the various farmhouses dotted around the nearby area. Most other people who pass by the signpost have no idea of the identity of this 'asylum'. They continue on their way without a second thought. And even those who may have heard that it is a Franciscan convent, with a hospital for the mentally and physically disabled and for epileptics – even these people have no further curiosity and prefer to move on and think of something more pleasant.

Hospital. Mentally ill. Disabled – deficient – dementia ...
They are not things that one likes to dwell on. A person finds
himself unconsciously quickening his step, anxious to get away.
And besides, this war has brought about quite different things,
which one has long since got used to.

For nearly two years Labarde was our hiding place, out of which
we could not dare to stray. Even to go down to that wooden
signpost in the valley – even this would have been an adventure of the most foolhardy kind. If we had been noticed by a
gendarme who had happened to be there – or even by a casual
passer-by – it could have had the most disastrous consequences.
Any encounter could have sealed our fate. We were at the mercy
of any random individual that we might come across.

Well – since the day of the *Libération*, we may come and go as
we please. Nothing was to stop us leaving Labarde – with all
the pain and infirmity that it hides within itself – that very day.
And yet we have remained. And every time that we return from
a trip 'outside', and find ourselves once more at the wooden
signpost, we glance at that half-eroded inscription, with a look
of tenderness and gratitude. A look that pauses for a moment
and says: 'How good to be back.'

We have remained in Labarde. Not just because it would
have seemed to us ungrateful – treacherous, even – to turn our
backs on the place that offered us refuge, as soon as it had
served its purpose. Not just because we would have been unable
to repress a feeling of shame, as if we were betraying a friend
who had shown us unconditional loyalty in times of trouble.
Not just because we wanted to avoid giving the impression that
our humble lodging here was suddenly not good enough for us,
when we had for so long found there what the most spacious
and magnificent palace could not have given us: protection
and warmth. So much warmth. In Labarde Hélène Rispal had
found an 'asylum' for our cold, homeless spirits, too.

But it is not just because of such scruples as these that we have stayed. For, ever since the *Libération*, every time that we have returned to Labarde, and taken that turning off from the main road, we have felt a kind of inner bond with the house on top of the hill – a house which probably seems so grim and forbidding to many. A house of mental derangement and of sorrow, but also of light and compassion.

As soon as they see us in the distance, they run – limp, hobble, stagger – towards us, our 'poor in spirit'. Our *enfants*. They gesticulate, wave, cry, laugh, stammer. For anyone seeing them for the first time it would be a grotesque crowd of madwomen, provoking feelings more of revulsion than of sympathy.

Are these creatures really so revolting, though, in their ugliness, their disfigurement – with their grimaces, their atrophied, deformed limbs? To us it is not so clear. Not any more. We no longer see the face, the outward appearance of these 'weak-minded', these 'cripples', these misshapen creatures. We only see their dependence, their need of affection, expressing itself laboriously through the babbling of their spirit. We understand their language. It is the eternal language of the creature who requires a little love – requires to receive it, and to give it.

And here again are our nuns, too, in their brown Franciscan habit with the white-edged black wimples.

Not once in all the time that we had to hide here did they make us feel that they were our benefactors, that they were offering asylum to outcasts. Not once – even when the Germans were in the immediate vicinity of Labarde – did they indicate to us even by the slightest hint that our presence was putting them in serious danger. Even at the most critical moments they never attempted to get rid of us, although this would have been humanly quite understandable. On the contrary: the Mother Superior wished under no circumstances to allow us to leave the house.

And now, every time that we go away from Labarde, even for a couple of days, we are always welcomed back with such warmth that we feel like people returning after a long voyage.

There she is, our dear Soeur de l'Annonciation, with her strict, and yet terribly delicate, expression. She always takes advantage of her first free moment to come to us, and to sit for a while with us in our room. Soeur de l'Annonciation does not say much; she is a woman of few words, who does not like to show her feelings. The strength of her friendship is felt in her silence, though – a friendship in which she has been our faithful companion and in which she shares everything with us, our freedom, now, as much as our oppression, then. We think of the time that the Sister found us that hollow behind the morgue ...

Soeur de l'Annonciation, who speaks so little, once told us that she prays for us a lot. It is not necessary to have faith oneself to feel that, for this Christian woman, her prayers have been a path to God.

It is now the seventh year that we have been without a home; and we do not know where destiny may yet drive us, before we are finally received by that earth which will no longer be foreign to us, wherever it may be, as it is the mother of all the dead. But every day in the present is a good day, as long as we know that, even apart from our nearest and dearest, there is one door which is always open to us – even if it is the door of a house of the sick.

Asile de Labarde. To us this was a place, too, where in the past the nights brought dreams of choking panic in which we imagined ourselves back in the clutches of the Germans. We started out of our sleep in horror. What relief, what a release, then, to realise, to be able to say: 'Thank God, it was only a nightmare; we are here in our Labarde, all three of us – here in our room, here in our beds.'

At moments like that, the house of the sick was a veritable paradise ...

There is another reason, too, that we are happy whenever we return from outside, and find ourselves back within the confines of our convent.

Outside – there is the world. Not yet the post-War world; but at least the post-Liberation world. It is already possible to draw certain conclusions from one's experience of it; it is already necessary to abandon certain illusions. Already. The portion of the world outside that comes within our vision is a very small one; it is nonetheless big enough for us to recognise the whole. And the whole is not how one might have hoped it would be.

I am sometimes tempted to pose the question: What would have had to happen to the human race to make it change a little? What further kind of trials would there have to be to make it stop for a moment – to make it pause for thought – to make it better, more human, in reality and not just in empty phrases? You would think that what had already happened would be enough. You would think that it would be a thousand times more than enough.

After more than four years, we are finally free of the Germans. The terrible consequences of their actions remain, and are everywhere to be seen. But they themselves are gone. Their potential for wrongdoing is gone.

It honestly seems that many do not fully realise what this means. It seems as though many do not deserve this miracle. Otherwise they would have other thoughts in their head than those which stem from a monstrous selfishness; from greed, from vanity, from ambition. Otherwise they would think of something other than haggling, of ducking and weaving, of intrigues and partisan battles. Activities which are all too often carried on by people who make a tremendous show of their patriotism – a patriotism which, however, waited cautiously for the removal of the Germans before becoming visible. Otherwise, too, so many would not have to starve; mothers would not have to see their children waste away, while at the same time anything can be had on the black market by those who can afford to pay for it, and while racketeers and spivs of every variety parade their wealth shamelessly for all to see. Otherwise so many honest individuals would not see all their efforts come to nothing. Otherwise so many who cheerfully risked their lives in the heroic days of the Resistance and the Insurrection would not now be so disheartened and sickened as to give up the struggle against the enemy within – against those whose only use for the holy flame was to cook themselves some soup with it.

The *épuration*, or cleansing, which is spoken of more and more the less it is put into practice, ought to be carried out by many people first and foremost upon themselves. Then France would – after the glorious beginning that she has made – have the power to rediscover her inner greatness, and not just her superficial prestige.

Much could be said, too, about the systematic work of subversion, the malicious pleasure taken by Hitler's French followers (who cleverly managed to slip the net of *épuration*) in thwarting and sabotaging the great project of reconstruction of their country.

But it is better to return to Labarde.

Here in Labarde we scarcely hear or see anything of what goes on 'outside'. It is a situation which can sometimes feel extraordinarily beneficial – like the unpolluted air that we breathe up here on our hilltop.

Our 'poor in spirit' are not bothered by the 'outside'; their very infirmity protects them from that. Theirs is the Kingdom of Heaven. And within the walls of the convent our nuns are able to remove themselves from anything which does not immediately affect the microcosm in which they move.

Life lived in the convent is admittedly not free of imper-
fections and weaknesses; it has its ups and its downs – its
'human, all-too-human'. But this life, dedicated to renunciation, to self-denial, to the cheerful performance of tasks which
bring no thanks and no earthly reward; this life is a life that
still involves faith; it reverently follows the dictates of a higher
power – as if they were the eternal harmonies of a heavenly
music; it still discerns the voice of a God within a Godless
age – an age which remains horribly deaf, empty, desolate in
the face of the murderous sound and fury that afflict it, in the
face of all the suffering and tears, in the face of all the vows
and fine words.

Up until the Liberation our room in Labarde was a hiding
place. Now, when we return there from outside, it sometimes
seems to us like an island – a tiny islet in the middle of a tur-
bulent, hostile sea. And one day, sooner or later, we shall have
to set out upon that sea.

That day is not yet upon us. Yet I should like to take my
leave of Labarde before that becomes too hard for me – before
the actual hour of our parting. Because when that day comes,
when I walk down the hill for the last time, on that path that
leads to the main road, then I shall carry straight on, quickly,
without turning my head, without looking again at that sign
down there in the valley, with its worn-away letters that spell
LABARDE.

Labarde, March 1945

Afterword

THIS BOOK WAS COMPLETED in March of this year. Since then we have seen the collapse of the Third Reich, the apparent death of Hitler, the cessation of hostilities, and the day of the official declaration of victory. The post-War period has begun.

Much of what appears in this book may perhaps seem not merely superseded, but actually out of date. Life has moved on in the meantime, with all the superficial process of change, of washing away; life in its eternal as well as its transitory nature; life with its wonders and its horrors. And even now, a survivor already tends to be regarded as the remnant of a past age.

Nonetheless, I did not want either to alter or to add to a single sentence of this book. Any such revision would have seemed false. All I have done is to delete certain statements that have already proved to be groundless or excessively naive.

I know that I run the risk of appearing as a defeatist in spite of the victory, and of arousing the displeasure of many who had looked on a happy end to the War as synonymous with an end to the evil that preceded the War, as well as to its causes. These enviable optimists regard the past as dead and buried, while they ignore the present and build for the future.

For one who saw the end of the War because, one might say, he survived the past against all probability, things do not appear so simple. Many things which should have been automatic consequences of the victory have not happened, and, conversely, much has taken place that one would not have believed possible. The dead are dead, and the living distance themselves from them with a haste, sometimes, that lacks even the slightest modicum of decency. And it is these living for whom those dead died.

The places where the Germans constructed the most famous of their torture-hells will, sooner or later, become a lucrative part of the tourist industry – attractions marked with stars in the guidebook. In Weimar the Germans will be able to point, not just to Goethe's house, but also to the temple of a quite different spirit: the Extermination Camp of Buchenwald.

It is true: the dead ride fast. But the living ride even faster. Everything else is just politics – politics as politics always has been. Business is business and politics is politics. All the dead in the world – all the persecuted – cannot alter the fact that politics remains so dreadfully alive. That it remains politics.

The victory has been celebrated everywhere in the appropriate manner. Everywhere there has been the march past, the parties, drinking and dancing. People everywhere have been impressed by festivities and by beautiful speeches. All the time, though, one has had the feeling that something was not quite right. There were too many who had to mourn alone, for their dead or for themselves. There were too many who were already too busily engaged in exploiting the economic opportunities provided by the victory to find time to interrupt their business for the historic event. There were, finally, too many who had believed that they were contributing to an ideal, and were forced to realise somewhere along the way that they were only there to allow cleverer individuals to profit by their contribution.

The victory over Hitler's Germany was achieved at the cost of unprecedented sacrifices and sufferings. To be worthy of this victory, however; to be able to celebrate a victory which – alongside all the political and diplomatic measures, alongside the reconstruction and restarting of the destroyed buildings and industries – might bring with it another kind of reconstruction, might lead to the unveiling of a better, a purer world … the celebration of *that* victory may, perhaps, be the lot of the generation to come. If, that is, they do not actually find themselves engaged in a new war, against a new Third Reich.

Labarde, July 1945

The Sisters of the Convent of Labarde, c.1945.

The Rispals: Gabriel (top); and, below, Hélène (left) with Grete
and her son Konrad, after the War, in Belvès.

Translator's epilogue

Moriz Scheyer's wish 'not to have to part from these human beings, who reached out their hand to me in my hour of need' was granted; he did, indeed, 'find some corner warmed by the fire of their affection ... right to the end'.

At some point after the War he, Grete and Sláva moved into the 'maisonette' (as it was known to us on family visits), a house outside the centre of Belvès, with a garden sloping down steeply towards the valley below. The house belonged to Hélène Rispal and it was given to them as their home for the rest of their lives. Another spectacular act of generosity on the part of Hélène. Soon after the War, too, Grete learned the fate of the nineteen members or family who had perished, mostly in Auschwitz.[16]

Moriz Scheyer never returned to Vienna, though he did acquire a new Austrian passport. He had suffered from a chronic heart condition even before the events related above; he died in 1949.

Sláva Kolářová died in 1948. She had returned briefly to her Czech homeland, suffered a stroke and returned to Belvès to be looked after by the Scheyers at the end.

---

16. With the exception of one brother, Egon, who escaped to England without his wife, and one brother-in-law, Jenö Kurz, who survived a concentration camp, all of Grete's siblings (and their spouses), nephews and nieces died in the persecution, some at Terezín, the majority at Auschwitz. Her eldest brother, Leo, who had succeeded his father Sigmund as head of the Jewish community in their Czech home town, was executed for political opposition.

The 'Maisonette' in Belvès given to the Scheyers by Hélène Rispal;
and, below, Sláva (left) and Grete (right) reunited there, after the War,
with Grete's son Konrad, and his first wife Jutta.

The other main protagonists in Moriz Scheyer's narrative survived much longer. Gabriel Rispal died in 1970. Grete died in the summer of 1977; Hélène just over a year later, in 1979. Jacques Rispal, who lived in the 'maisonette' for some time after Grete's death, followed them in 1986.

Moriz and Margarethe Scheyer are buried in the Rispal family grave, alongside Gabriel, Hélène and Jacques Rispal; Sláva Kolářová is buried in the same graveyard, though in a different plot. It seems that after the War Grete formally converted to Catholicism, possibly in fulfilment of a promise she had made to one of the Sisters of the Convent.

Memories of Konrad Singer: the years up to 1938

Before discovery of Moriz Scheyer's manuscript, in the early 2000s, I had begun to interview my father, Konrad Singer (Grete's son, Moriz's stepson), wanting to preserve a record of his memories of his early life; he had by this time produced a brief written memoir too. When the manuscript came to light, there were some further interviews: I was keen, now, to fill out Moriz Scheyer's written account – frustratingly brief, on certain persons and events – with whatever my father could remember of them after the passage of more than sixty years.

I give here a brief summary of those memories, communicated in both written and interview form, inasfar as they add to the picture of Moriz, of Grete and of Sláva, of the family's life more broadly, and of the dramatic events of 1938.

My father's earliest memories were of Salzburg, where he and his elder brother Stefan lived with his parents – Grete and her first husband, Dr Bernhard Schwarzwald – and his nanny 'Veili', the Sláva of this book; and also of Jindřichův Hradec, a picturesque town in southern Bohemia (now in the Czech Republic), where Grete's father, a successful businessman, lived with a large extended family. The Czech side of the family had made the transition, within living memory, from the status of *Pinkeljude* – a humble door-to-door salesman

The Singer family textile factories in Bohemia and Moravia, 1921.

with a bag of goods – to that of successful industrialists: Sigmund Singer, Grete's father, owned two factories producing textiles.[17] He was head of the Jewish community in the town, and prided himself on his position in the synagogue; at the same time, the family were assimilated Jews, Czech-speaking and regarding themselves as Czechs.

Summer holidays – as well as the first two years of my father's life, before the move to Salzburg – were spent at his grandfather's house with this extended family (about whose eccentricities there were a number of family legends). From the earliest years onward, my father was largely brought up by Sláva, whom he remembered with great tenderness, and to whom he was much closer than to his actual parents.

Grete had met Bernhard Schwarzwald, her first husband, during a year at a *Pensionat* – a finishing school – in Dresden, a favoured location for such purposes for those who could afford it. Bernhard was a brilliant and charismatic, but emotionally erratic, young doctor. The match was not – or would not have been – approved by Sigmund, and the couple in effect eloped, travelling in 1912 on a cruiser to Celebes (now Sulawesi) in the Dutch East Indies, where Bernhard had succeeded in getting a post as a doctor with the Dutch colonial authorities. Two years –

---

17. The textile industry was a major Jewish success story in early 20th-century Bohemia (the Zweig family's prosperity, for example, had similar roots). One source of the firm's growth had been the demand for industrially knitted garments for soldiers during the First World War – a fact which in turn led to the accusation from anti-Semitic sources that the owners of such successful factories were 'Kriegsverdiener' (war profiteers).

and one child, Stefan – later, war intervened, and Bernhard felt it his patriotic duty to return and enlist. His active service, however, turned out to be brief. The couple lived for a short time at Jindřichův Hradec, where Konrad (my father) was born in 1917. Then, shortly after the War Sigmund set Bernhard up in practice, buying him a large property in open country, on the outskirts of Salzburg, which he ran as a sanatorium for sufferers from nervous disorders. Among the guests was Sigmund Freud's wife Martha, who stayed at the sanatorium for a rest cure – and was briefly visited by the great man himself – in the summer of 1919.

It was in this idyllic location that the family lived in the years immediately after the First World War; and my father's memories of the period include meeting Stefan Zweig and his adoptive daughters: the famous author had retreated from mainstream Viennese literary society, living on a hill just outside the centre of Salzburg; within the small intellectual community of Salzburg, he and the Schwarzwalds had evidently made social contact. It seems likely that it was at Salzburg, too, and also through Zweig, that Grete met her second husband, Moriz, who was an old friend of the great author.

The Singer family around 1920: Grete (standing, third from right) with her father (seated, centre), her seven siblings and two of their wives.

Bernhard Schwarzwald had died suddenly, on a trip to Vienna, from a cause which at the time was described as a heart attack. My father was seven at the time; he understood later, from conversations with other relatives, that this was in fact a suicide – a suicide possibly connected with debts, or with a love affair, and almost certainly with the consequences of what would now be called a bipolar condition.

With Grete's remarriage came the move to Vienna, where Moriz Scheyer was a successful theatre and book reviewer, and eventually editor of the arts pages, for one of Vienna's two main daily newspapers (the *Neues Wiener Tagblatt*). The contrasting characters emerge in my father's account: Moriz, the respected but hypersensitive literary man, jealous of his privacy,[18] liable to cut off contact with friends or colleagues at some perceived slight, never free of the feeling of 'stage fright' as he approached the weekly writing task for his paper; Grete, the confident and extrovert society lady, playing bridge with Alma Mahler and meeting family members in cafés for convivial gatherings which Moriz would strenuously avoid.

My father recalled arguments between his mother and stepfather, and even an intervention of his own, as a teenager, advising them that if they made each other unhappy they should split up; but it seems impossible to judge whether the level of disharmony in the family was any more than 'normal'. One episode caused a definite crisis, when Moriz conceived an infatuation for a minor opera singer – a drama which was brought to a head by Grete taking pills and then ringing to say goodbye. A doctor was called, and the immediate crisis averted.

The circles in which Moriz Scheyer moved included the most distinguished musicians and writers of the time in Vienna: the Mahlers, Bruno Walter, Stefan Zweig, Arthur Schnitzler, as well as a host of literary figures less well-known today; to many he was a person worth cultivating, in view of his ability to place reviews in the paper.

---

18. A habit of Moriz's that my father recalled was that of getting up to open the windows at a certain point in the evening, during social gatherings in their apartment. This was a clear signal, understood by all his guests, that it was time for them to leave.

Grete in the early 1920s with her children, Konrad (left) and Stefan.

From 1934, the Austrian government under Chancellor Schuschnigg was authoritarian, with a command economy and no real democracy, but it was desperate to avoid being taken over by the two more powerful – and fascist – neighbours, Germany and Italy. Political parties, including the National Socialists, were banned. The political culture, for liberal-leaning as well as for Jewish people, was unpleasant, but not threatening.

Families like that of my father did not consider themselves as belonging to a distinct group, the Jews; they thought of themselves as Austrians who happened to be Jewish by faith – although the faith itself, even in the generation before my father, consisted only of a few minimal traditional observations. My father recalls having separate instruction in

263

Hebrew at his school (actually a Catholic establishment, the Piaristengymnasium); and he had a bar mitzvah ('you couldn't do that to my grandfather – not have a bar mitzvah!').

Families like the Scheyers 'had nothing to do with' the orthodox, Hassidic community, regarding its visible display of separateness and traditional religious practice as liable to provoke 'active' anti-Semitism. 'Passive' anti-Semitism – manifested, for example, in the difficulty of Jewish people rising to higher ranks in the civil service or army – certainly already existed. But to the rise of Hitler and fascism there was a range of attitudes: supporters were not always ideological fanatics. Many were entranced by the 'economic miracle' which Hitler seemed to have conjured in Germany; a student acquaintance told my father: don't worry about the anti-Semitism, that's just to appeal to the masses, once they're in power that will all be forgotten.

The Anschluss, however, brought Hitler literally to the family's door: on 14th March 1938 his cavalcade entered Vienna down the Mariahilferstrasse, the busy street, leading into the city from the south-west, on which the Scheyers lived. How urgent, or desperate, was the situation for a young Jewish student in Vienna in March 1938? He sought advice from his head of department, Hermann Mark;* wait until after the break, he was advised (Hitler's invasion had coincided with a mid-term holiday at the university): perhaps it will not be as bad as we fear. At the end of the break, Mark – who had one Jewish parent – had already been dismissed from his post. The acts of violence and humiliation started immediately, too: Jewish students who attempted to return to the university might be grabbed by party activists and forced to clean the streets; my father was 'fortunate' in suffering no worse personal humiliation than to be told to move from a park bench, now designated as not for Jews, where he was sitting with a girlfriend.

While his parents made their way from Vienna to Paris in the way described in Moriz's manuscript, my father found a route to Zurich – bizarrely enough, through Germany: he had learned from a cousin that it was still possible, in Leipzig, to acquire a visa for Switzerland by making an unscrutinised claim to be a 'German businessman'. In Zurich, as a guest of family friends, he spent the summer writing letters in the attempt to be able to continue his studies at a university in Britain, and finally succeeded in doing so, at Glasgow.[19]

Belvès, Rispals, Resistance

The following section tells more about the characters encountered in Belvès in Moriz's account: about the Rispal family, especially, but also about their and others' Resistance activity in that region. It is based again partly on my father's (and to a limited extent my own) recollections, and partly on those of Georges Rebière,* a schoolfriend and Resistance comrade of Jacques', whom I met and interviewed in Belvès in 2008 (and who also wrote a personal memoir of the Resistance).

Gabriel Rispal was a 'larger-than-life' character; a joker; a bon vivant; and a committed communist. A handyman and decorator, he was also an artist in his spare time, a *peintre de dimanche*, whose paintings hang in many a Belvès house – as indeed they did in my childhood home in Surrey. Hélène, also a committed communist, was by contrast the quiet one. Her generosity, and emotional attachment, were obvious to anyone who met her; her steely determination – the acts of courage and self-sacrifice – were rather, as also emerges from Moriz's account, carried out by stealth.

Jacques Rispal – Gabriel and Hélène's son – was, as Moriz mentions, 'talent-spotted' by Pierre Vorms, and he went on,

---

19. Two things were necessary for the would-be student immigrant: first, a British citizen prepared to act as financial guarantor; secondly, the offer of a place – and more particularly, of subsistence – at a university. The first service was provided by Marian Dunlop, one of a number of individuals who volunteered themselves in this way, apparently via a Quaker organisation, without having ever met the persons they were assisting; the second, by the Glasgow branch of the International Student Service. This, in effect, involved a whip-round amongst other students, organised by Alec Cairncross (later Sir Alec, a distinguished economist) to enable him and a handful of other refugees to be funded, at the minimal level of board and lodging with a local landlady. To both Marian Dunlop and Alec Cairncross my father retained a lifelong sense of his indebtedness.

Les copains: Jacques Rispal and his friends in a pre-war theatrical production (Jacques is seated, right; on the left are Jean Despont and, standing, Liliane Despont), and in Belvès (Jacques on the bike, Georges Rebière second left).

after the War, to have a considerable career as an actor, as well as dramatic experiences as a political activist. In the small-town community of pre-war Belvès, Jacques ('Jacquot') and his friend Georges Rebière were part of a close-knit band of *copains*: their leisure activities included various kinds of musical and theatrical activity, on which the political and military turmoil of 1940 had an unexpected side effect.

Pierre Vorms was a friend of Moriz's from Paris: Jewish, but a French citizen, he was serving as an officer in a regiment which found itself retreating through Belvès after the débâcle. He decided to remain in Belvès rather than return to German-occupied Paris. In the Paris art world, Vorms ran a gallery supporting avant-garde artists, known especially for the work of the Flemish artist Frans Masereel. Now in Belvès, struck by the range of talents amongst the *copains*, Vorms suggested the formation of a theatrical troupe – the Cercle Théâtral de Belvès – with the charitable aim of raising money for French prisoners-of-war in Germany (at the time an enormous number).

The performances seem to have consisted of song-and-dance numbers in the first half and a play in the second. Both Vorms and Jacquot played the piano, the latter also singing and acting; Georges specialised in the Clown; Gabriel painted the sets; prominent members were Jean and Liliane Despont, presumably son and daughter of the postmaster Antoine, who set up the clandestine telecommunications network. In retrospect the artistic significance of these productions must be the theatrical debut of Jacques Rispal. Rebière paints a vivid picture of him in grotesque drag, complete with a necklace of onions, as Marguérite in a spoof Faust.

Of course, the Cercle Théâtral was destined for a fairly short career; other concerns soon became more pressing. Men like Vorms, Rebière and Rispal, after observing the events of 1940 with increasing horror – the débâcle, the Armistice, the according of absolute power to Pétain, the series of anti-Semitic edicts – were soon drawn to resistance, even though the organisation of 'the Resistance' as a coherent force, acknowledging de Gaulle as its head and liaising with London, took longer.

At the same time, Jacquot's generation soon had a more immediate worry: the *chantiers de la jeunesse*, military-style youth labour camps, set up in 1940 to replace national service. Rebière's call-up came in 1942, Rispal's the following year. Worse still: in June 1942, Prime Minister Laval offered a French labour force to assist in German factories depleted by the workers' absence at the front (Germany would release prisoners of war in exchange). 'La Relève' was intended as a voluntary scheme; but lack of take-up meant that conscription was soon envisaged. By a law of February 1943, the 'Service du travail obligatoire' made possible the conscription of entire years of *chantiers* – those of 1940, 1941 and 1942, to begin with.

The policy, ironically, gave a boost to the Resistance: *réfractaires* – men who went into hiding to avoid the call-up, with its attendant prospect of forced labour in Germany – frequently at the same time joined the Resistance. When Jacquot's turn came, he, like others, gave his *chantier* the slip and joined a *maquis* – a Resistance cell hiding out in the country.

On the specifics of Jacques Rispal's Resistance activities, it is difficult to uncover any details beyond what emerges from Moriz's account, until the summer of 1944. By then, the various Resistance groups operating within France were fused together in the FFI (Forces Françaises de l'Intérieur), run more like a conventional army, formed into units and given training with weapons, with the aim of engaging and delaying German tanks moving across France from the east towards Normandy, and whose activities were coordinated with those of the regular army in the liberation of France. Jacquot and Georges were now billeted together, and the latter has a fairly full account of this last stage – including, around this time, the loss of a number of friends from their circle. Their war ended in Bordeaux, where they had had the responsibility of liberating the city from the remaining German troops (and where, incidentally, Rebière describes Jacquot engaging in some less heroic escapades, 'borrowing' the colonel's car for night-time activities and then leaving it in a ditch).

Before this final stage, security dictated that Resistance members knew nothing of activities outside the assignments on which they were directly involved. Rebière tells us something of the structure of the Resistance at Belvès: his own father Jean apparently made up the first 'trio', alongside Georges Marty (a neighbour of the Rispals) and his brother, Jean. These three would then recruit three more, and so on. Gabriel Rispal appears in Rebière's account on a number of occasions: arriving to warn someone of an impending arrest, for example, and picking up weapons from a British parachute drop. The 'Carlos' who so impressed Moriz – Charles Ordeig – also appears: he became head of a *Main d'oeuvre immigrée*, a Resistance group formed from immigrants.

Jacquot's official position in the organisation had, perhaps, been similar to that of Rebière: a member of the Forces Françaises Combattantes in the network of 'Hilaire-Buckmaster', whereby there was liaison between London and the overall head of the Armée Secrète for the southern Dordogne.

It is difficult to know to what extent the rescue of my grandparents was part of an organised action, rather than a spontaneous act of personal heroism – as my father always portrayed it, and indeed as Moriz presents it in the book. In November 1942 Jacques Rispal was not yet in hiding; presumably, though, he was already involved in the Resistance. The provision of false documents for the train journey sounds like part of an organised Resistance activity; yet this too is presented by Moriz as a personal initiative carried out by René Mathieu (who did the same for several others). Moriz is very clear in representing the plan as being hatched entirely by Hélène, who then drew on favours from a range of friends, family and acquaintances to make it a reality. Perhaps one thing that the episode serves to demonstrate is how informal and improvised much Resistance activity was, especially when it came to the saving and concealing of refugees.

Nor were the Scheyers the only refugees to live clandestinely in Belvès during the War and settle there afterwards. After the War, the Scheyers' next-door neighbour at the Maisonette was a man called Elias Magaran, who had been a refugee involved in the Resistance in Belvès, and subsequently married there.

The apparently shared idealism of the Resistance – although there were already political tensions within it – was quickly fractured after the War, when the same de Gaulle who had, at least nominally, led the Resistance struggle, headed a

Jacques the young actor: a publicity shot inscribed to
Grete, Moriz and Sláva, around 1948.

government attempting to preserve French colonial power in Indochina and Algeria by military force. Resistance veterans who opposed French colonialism – and in many cases became involved in the active campaign against it – were thus in a practical state of civil war with their ex-comrades-in-arms.

Virulently opposed to colonialism and to what he described as 'Nazi methods being used, in my name, under the French flag', against the Algerian people, Jacques Rispal was among a group – including a number of fairly prominent artists – who, in the 1950s, aligned themselves with the 'terrorist' Algerian independence movement, the FLN, headed by Francis Jeanson. Jacques' involvement was active; and he was arrested and tried as a 'bag-carrier' (*porteur de valises*) for the movement, in a high-profile case in 1960. He served nearly three years in prison. The above quotation comes from a letter from Rispal to a former Resistance colonel, André Malraux, whom he had met during *maquis* activities in the Dordogne and who was now a government minister, and is printed in a book Rispal wrote about his trial and imprisonment.[20] For Rispal – as for others in France at the time – the struggle for Algerian independence was quite simply a continuation of the wartime struggle.

Rispal had been active on the Paris stage from the early 1950s, especially at the Théâtre de l'Atelier, where his avant-garde work included early productions of Pinter. His film career began in earnest somewhat later, after the above political drama. It is a career which in a way reflects the political tribulations of the period. Through the 1960s to the 1970s, Rispal played characters who in a variety of registers – by turns sombre, doom-laden, satirical, playful – reflect the themes of shattered idealism, moral ambiguity, conflict or nihilism of their authors' films. In *La Guerre est finie* (1966), for example, Rispal is a melancholic loyalist in a communist group in Spain, very much on its last legs, very slowly beginning to realise that the Revolution is in fact not about to happen. There are cameos in Buñuel's satirical *La Voie lactée* (1969) and *Le Charme discret de la bourgeoisie* (1972); and the Truffaut connoisseur

---

20. Jacques Rispal, *De la DST à Fresnes ou trente et un mois de prison* (1990).

271

may remember the eccentric upstairs neighbour in *Domicile conjugal* (1970), refusing to leave his house until Pétain is given an honourable burial at Verdun. In Louis Malle's controversial *Lacombe Lucien* (1974), Jacquot plays a landlord exploiting the precarious situation of a Jewish tenant in wartime France. And it seems that the hesitant acceptance of a role in Costa-Gavras' *L'Aveu* (1970) – a film dealing with torture in communist Czechoslovakia – represented a decisive rejection of Stalinism, on the part of Rispal as well as of others on the Left in France.

In later years, Georges Rebière told me, he had often begged Jacquot to leave the pressures of his life in Paris and retire to Belvès to his true home and friends. This, indeed, he eventually did, to the same 'maisonette' of the Scheyers' residence and my childhood holidays; though he died shortly afterwards.

Belvès, 1970s: my memories of Grete and Hélène

Throughout my childhood, each summer, we would make the long car journey from Surrey to Belvès in the Dordogne, to visit 'Granny Grete'.

White-haired, gold-toothed, upright, smoking cigarettes in a holder, Grete seemed to belong to a distant world, a mysterious past. She was surrounded – in what was then, long before the middle-class English invasion of the area, a real backwater in the middle of rural France – by remnants of a different life. The 'menagerie' of Venetian glass; the Austrian playing cards, which would be laid out on the vine-shaded patio table in a 104-card game of patience; items of jewellery, pearls and diamond brooches – a range of objects and accoutrements that completed the picture of a grand lady belonging in some salon of a great city. Occasional remarks would hint at that past: Mahler might be mentioned, or Bruno Walter – or the cousin who had emigrated to the States and ran the Metropolitan Opera. There were curious old photographs and artefacts dating from the sojourn in the Dutch East Indies, with her first husband, and – though I do not remember Moriz ever being mentioned – a writing desk, some old pens, some traces of writerly presence.

With my grandmother, Grete, 1960s.

And then there was Hélène. By the time of my earliest memories of our visits, she and Grete had become inseparable; and we understood that she was in a way as much a part of the family as our grandmother. We would visit Hélène, and until his death her husband Gabriel, in their flat above their hardware shop, or she would come to the 'maisonette' – often bringing pastries – every day. We would have many of our meals together. Occasionally, we also met Jacquot, on a visit from Paris. My main memory is of him performing a knife-swallowing trick for the amusement of us children.

Gradually, in later years, we children began to understand the extraordinary story that lay behind the friendship with Hélène. It was, in a sense, our family legend – oft repeated by my father, albeit only in dim outline. The key points of that outline – points which, especially in later life, my father

273

could not get past without a crack in the voice – were the actions of the two women: how Hélène had 'risked the life of her only son' to save them; how Veili (Sláva) had been prepared to join them in a concentration camp, though she was not Jewish.

The story of the book: the survival of 'A Survivor'

By my late teens I had become increasingly fascinated by my family past – the pre-war Viennese culture, the estate in Bohemia, the dramatic and terrible stories of tragedy or of escape. It was, I think, around 1980, that my father came out with what was, to him, a casual revelation: 'My stepfather,' he said, 'wrote some account of his experiences during the War, but I found it so full of self-pity that I threw it away.'

And it seems that he genuinely had done that. My disappointment, even anger, at such an action – its failure to understand my fascination with the family history – faded to resignation. There was nothing to be done: that manuscript, whatever exactly it had been, was long gone.

Then, in 2005, my father moved house, and my brother and I were faced with the task of clearing out the attic. Amid the accumulated stuff of forty-three years of family life – books, toys, garden furniture – there were a number of suitcases that must have been deposited there at some point by Grete: suitcases predominantly full of Czech linen, silver or other family possessions. Some of the suitcases also contained papers, for example, folders with copies of Moriz's newspaper articles, reviews of his books, and so on. And there, suddenly, amid the lace tablecloths and monogrammed dressing gowns, it was. A sheaf of fragile papers, typed in German: 'Ein Ueberlebender' (A Survivor) by Moriz Scheyer. It was the long-lost manuscript – the carbon copy of the destroyed original.

The fact that the story of the above pages had lain hidden, above us, for all those years – literally hanging over us – was an extraordinary one. More troubling, though, was the fact that my father had apparently destroyed it.

My father, Konrad Singer, shortly after the War.

I tried, subsequently, to make sense of my father's reaction. The charge of 'self-pity' is one I remember clearly, from that first revelation of the book's existence (and of its destruction). It is perhaps significant that in later conversations – and he had not reread the manuscript in between – he did not repeat that charge, but focused rather on the book's strident 'anti-German' sentiment. Perhaps, with increasing years, even my father had come to feel that the judgement of 'self-pity' was a harsh one to make in relation to such an account.

There was a conflict in experience and attitude – a conflict that went far beyond the content of the actual book, although certainly an impatience with his stepfather's emotionalism, an aesthetic abreaction to its tone, formed part of his negative attitude to it. One must, I think, consider that broader conflict in experience and attitude. My father, too, was uprooted from his family home – but at the age of twenty, to a country which did not become occupied, and with the opportunity to continue his career from more or less the point at which it had been interrupted. He did not personally witness any horrors, let alone live in daily fear of arrest or deportation.

One might, for sure, see a lack of imagination, or empathy, in his reaction to Moriz's account as either 'self-pitying' or 'anti-German'. When I asked him, in an interview after the manuscript's discovery, when it was that he first realised what his parents had gone through, he responded: 'Well, what they had to go through was really nothing compared with what other people had to go through.' When probed as to what it was that he objected to so strongly in the book, he talked of the incident Moriz recounts of the young German soldiers delighting in peeing through the fence in the direction of the Jewish prisoners. Two things were particularly objectionable here: his dwelling on something – the action of some stupid boys – that he should have been able to 'rise above'; and his dwelling on things likely to spread anti-German feeling, to give a blanket condemnation of all Germans as evil. He associated Moriz's focus on this incident with his habitual tendency to talk in sweeping, condemnatory terms of the actions and character of 'the Boche'.

My father's attitude seems harsh, unrealistic, unsympathetic. But it was in some ways, I think, not uncharacteristic of the younger generation in 1945. They wanted to look forward, not backwards; the attitude – in my father's case, as in others – was one of rationalist idealism. They would build a new world in which the irrationalities of religion, nationalism and racialism that had shattered Europe – and of course, destruction and bereavement were everywhere to be seen: they had not affected only Jewish communities – would cease to be relevant. They did not want to dwell on those irrationalities. There is, in this, too, perhaps, some of the typical 'second generation' attitude to the survivors' experience. It was, to put it simply, a long time before people wanted to know.

It is interesting to set alongside that attitude Moriz Scheyer's own pessimism about the audience for his book: that no one would ever be interested in 'what had happened to Jews'. The perception might seem an extraordinary one today, after the publication of so many survivors' accounts and Holocaust histories, let alone of related films and television documentaries, as well as the very high consciousness of these events in school education. Yet this would all happen much later. It is one of the most valuable, near unique, features of Scheyer's account that it was written at the time, in the heat of events. By the same token, that account – completed before the beginning of the Nuremberg trials and decades before the publication of most survivors' accounts – is evidence of a moment in history where it was quite plausible to believe that anti-Semitic atrocities – especially those of the National Socialists – would never be widely studied, or taken as seriously as their other crimes.

And the generational conflict, or conflict of attitudes, took a more concrete form. too. My father was involved actively in certain projects or re-education – in particular, giving lectures to Germans in British prisoner of war camps, and volunteering in emergency relief work in destroyed post-war Germany. The former project, presumably part of the post-war programme designed to prepare prisoners for life in de-Nazified Germany, and which my father himself described as 'preaching the doctrine of reason', was something that Moriz disliked and disapproved of. There was, to him, no point in trying to reason with these people.

Memories ... and memories

Working on this book has emphasised fragility of memory, in a number of ways.

As already mentioned, I had interviewed my father about his early memories before the manuscript came to light, and then carried out some further interviews after that discovery. By the time of these further interviews, not only his short-term memory but his long-term memory, too, had started to become less secure: increasingly, I would draw a blank in asking for further information about this or that individual; I would notice, too, that an identical form of words would be used to describe two completely different persons or events, so that it was impossible to tell to whom it originally belonged;

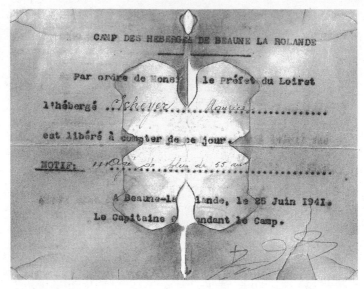

The document, dated 25th June 1941, certifying Moriz Scheyer's liberation from imprisonment at the concentration camp at Beaune-la-Rolande. The reason for his release is given as 'over the age of 55'.

perhaps most worryingly, I realised that a tentative suggestion made by me in a question – 'Was it perhaps person X who did that?' – would be fed back to me a few minutes later in the conversation, as a certainty: 'Of course, it was person X who did that.'

I was faced with a striking contrast in forms of memory. On the one hand, I had the written account, the last letter typed in 1945, unchanging, in no way vulnerable to false memories or later confusions or suggestions, but unable to respond to my questions. On the other, I had my father's living memories – theoretically an infinite resource, but fragile, subject to confusion and increasingly suggestible.

One hopes, in such a project as this, that one is rescuing something from oblivion, preserving for future generations something that came so close to being destroyed forever. Yet working on such a book brings home how fragile and tenuous the process of preserving past memories is – and how arbitrary and selective the 'history' that is in the end preserved.

It has been fascinating to delve into the past, to discover some hidden facts and recover long-forgotten personal histories. But the process has made me more intensely conscious than ever of the transience, the short lifetime of human memories. Without some written record, the actions and characters of individuals – individuals as intensely important to those around them as a Gabriel or Hélène Rispal – are largely, if not entirely, forgotten within a generation or two, at most three.

But even when there is some written record, some trace which invites one to want to know more, in the overwhelming number of cases it is just that: a trace. How soon all but a very few individuals disappear even beyond the reach of research and the trawling of archives – to the point where it is impossible to recover more than at best dates and places of birth and death, impossible to recover something of their personality or actions. I went in search of oral accounts to supplement the written document, and delved in libraries and archives to clarify or expand on what people had told me ... but so often the oral account was hazy, and the relevant written account impossible to find. Before long there would be a tantalising impasse, a dead end beyond which I could not proceed.

Of course, it cannot surprise us that many of the characters in this drama – the inmates at Beaune, many of the people met at Belvès, even the Koflers – have vanished beyond the point where one might hope to add anything to the brief information contained in Scheyer's pages. It is perhaps more surprising – again something that emerges from Scheyer's writing – to realise how extraordinarily transient are artistic reputations. The name of Scheyer himself, a substantial figure in Viennese literary life in the 1930s, hardly appears even in specialist accounts of the literature and intellectual life of that period. And the reversal of fortunes is even more striking in the case of some of the much more famous individuals of whom he talks. Stefan Zweig, it is true, has undergone a recent revival; but the name of Romain Rolland, for example, an absolute giant of the political-intellectual culture of the inter-war years, hugely influential through his pacifism and his promulgation of the ideas of Tolstoy and Gandhi, and a virtual god to many (not just to Zweig and Scheyer), is now scarcely known; still less so a whole series of names of (then) major French literary figures, mentioned throughout the book.

Another very striking thing I discovered in the research on this book was that, even in the case of the persons in this story who do leave some historical record, that historical record does not contain the events of this story itself. Jacques Rispal, for example, is known, and sometimes locally celebrated, for his theatrical career and even for his Resistance activity; but his role in saving the lives of three – maybe many more – refugees is not recorded, even by Georges Rebière, who was his childhood friend and wrote a book about the period. Marian Dunlop – my father's and uncle's benefactor in enabling them to enter Great Britain – was a much loved and respected individual, who founded a school of Christian meditation which had a considerable following. There exists a biography, but it shows no awareness of her activity in enabling Jewish refugees to come to England. The youthful role of the distinguished economist Sir Alec Cairncross in raising the funds to enable refugee students to continue their lives in Glasgow was something of which even his immediate family were unaware.[21]

They are acts worth remembering.

Labarde today

At the Convent of Labarde, today, there is no memory that three refugees were sheltered there by the nuns during the darkest days of the Nazi Occupation. The convent is as Moriz Scheyer describes: remote from the bustle of normal life, secluded, difficult to find. One might be walking back into the pages of his narrative: more than sixty years on, the place

---

21. It provides a curious footnote to the story that my (secular Jewish) grandparents owed their survival to the combined exertions of the communist atheist Rispals and the Catholic Sisters, while my father and his brother owed theirs to the charitable activities of the rationalist Alec Cairncross, the Quakers who set up offices to assist refugees in Vienna, and the Christian spiritual teacher Marian Dunlop.

The back building at Labarde, where Moriz, Grete and Sláva
were given asylum.

is still, as he depicts it, a haven – a home for sufferers from
mental disabilities. Visiting in 2009, we meet a few of them
taking the air, walking with a relative or helper in their calm
detachment. But there is no memory here, either personal or
institutional, of the individuals or events related in Scheyer's
narrative. The story has not been passed down; no record has
been kept. The 'convent', in fact, was long since deconsecrated
and the internal architecture reorganised. Precise locations
are impossible to find; even the extraordinary hiding place
behind the chapel, related so vividly by Moriz, can only be
reconstructed with a deal of guesswork and imagination.

Peering into the woods and fields of the Dordogne stretching
away below, one wonders how many other extraordinary tales
– tales of terror and of ordinary people's heroism – remain forever hidden and forgotten in that huge landscape. The chance
discovery of a typescript like this one does not tell all; in a way
it raises more questions and makes one want to know so much
more. But it does open up a vista, a world of experience which
would otherwise be closed.

Moriz Scheyer: writer

Moriz Scheyer is a forgotten name of pre-war Viennese culture. However, he belonged to an important literary and cultural milieu, in which he played a significant role, with an active career as a critic, essayist and travel writer.

Early life and literary career

Moriz Scheyer was born in Focşani in Romania on 27th December 1886, the son of a businessman. But by the time of his secondary education the family had moved to Vienna, where they lived in Hietzing, a pleasant suburb to the south-west of the city. At school, he recalled, he was a 'reasonable classicist', able to feed answers in Latin and Greek exams to his friend, who would perform the same office for him in mathematics. He studied law at the University of Vienna, graduating in 1911; and started work on the staff of the *Neues Wiener Tagblatt* in 1914. This was one of Vienna's two 'quality' daily newspapers, with a high reputation in the arts.

A lover of French culture and literature, Scheyer lived in Paris in the early 1920s, working as a cultural foreign correspondent for the paper – a role he continued on a more short-term basis, for a month a year, after his return to Vienna in 1924. He also spent some time as a correspondent in Switzerland.

In fact, he was quite a traveller; and this played a major part in his early literary activity. In 1918–19 he made a sea

The young Moriz Scheyer.

voyage via Egypt to South America – a voyage involving weeks on a cruise ship, and encounters with a number of then exotic locations, as well as exotic individuals. The experience inspired a number of writings, which are collected in his first three published books: *Europeans and Exotics* (*Europäer und Exoten*, 1919), *Tralosmontes* (1921) and *Cry from the Tropical Night* (*Schrei aus der Tropennacht*, 1926).

The books consist of vignettes, vivid depictions of unusual places, events and, in particular, characters. For example, we meet Saadi ibn Tarbush, a young Egyptian boy who acted as Scheyer's guide in Cairo, and to whom the glimpse given by Scheyer of the glamour of the European's life turns out corrupting and fatal. Then there is Gly Cangalho, a morphine-addicted 'Creole' character who spends all her time travelling on cruises, and is known to all captains. Gly is a recurrent, apparently semi-fictionalised character in these early books, and seems to be the focus of some obsession on Scheyer's part. Then, there are the parodic Englishmen – themselves almost exotic creatures in their ability to be at home everywhere and lacking any emotional response to the exotic all around them. Or, there is Mr Dronnink, a Dutch musical genius ruined by a woman and by drink, 'burnt out' and reduced to playing the piano on cruise ships. And we have vivid pictures painted of the experience of a tropical night on the ship; of storms, of cockfights, of the 'coffee coast'. The characters seem straight out of the world of Agatha Christie; we only need an unexplained body or two to transform the already eerie atmosphere of the memoirs to that of 1920s crime fiction.

'Chef de feuilleton'

From 1924, in Vienna, until his dismissal at the Anschluss, Scheyer was arts editor of the *Neues Wiener Tagblatt*.[22] He was in charge of 'Theater und Kunst' – the review section – and thus held a position of some cultural influence. He himself regularly reviewed for one particular theatre, the Josefstädter, and organised the reviewing of the others. He also contributed many book reviews. His literary activity, though, has to be understood in the particularly continental context of the *feuilleton*. The term refers both to the arts pages of a newspaper and to a distinct type of article. Typically, a *feuilleton* takes a particular cultural event, such as a book publication or exhibition, as its starting point, but goes beyond mere review to offer a broader, essayistic reflection – a retrospective on an author, a historical reflection on the subject of a biography, or on a genre; *feuilletons* may also include reflections of a more personal or imaginative kind.

The writing of *feuilletons* became Scheyer's main literary activity. Such writing has certain typical characteristics: the creation of mood in a short span; the miniaturist's attention to detail; succinct, punchy summing-up of an argument, or

---

22. After 1938, and its 'Aryanisation' by the Nazis, the *NWT* was amalgamated with other titles; it appeared for the last time in 1945.

character; typically, some kind of emotional or 'sentimental', rather than purely analytic, response to the subject. Scheyer was at home with this miniaturist's art; and he surely brought some of it to the present book. Chapters like 'In place of a chapter on the Resistance', 'Carlos', 'The undeserving survivors', read rather like *feuilletons* – though with very different themes from the ones written for his paper.

Scheyer's three further published books were collections of such essays, previously published in the *NWT*. They are: *Escape to Yesterday* (*Flucht ins Gestern*, 1927); *Human Beings Fulfil Their Destiny* (*Menschen erfüllen ihr Schicksal*, 1931); *Genius and Its Life on Earth* (*Erdentage des Genies*, 1938). The titles in themselves are indicative of certain moods or attitudes. The last two reflect the author's preoccupation with the notion of the 'great man' (or, occasionally, woman), and especially with that of the great artist. The first betrays his capacity for nostalgia.

Scheyer in his milieu: early 20th-century Vienna

Such preoccupations were characteristic not just of Scheyer but also of Viennese writing of the early twentieth century much more broadly. They are attitudes which Scheyer shared, not least, with his almost exact contemporary (1881–1942) and friend, Stefan Zweig.

Much of Zweig's literary output – his most substantial books, in fact – consisted of biographies of historical, literary or intellectual figures; his subjects included Balzac, Dickens, Romain Rolland, Dostoevsky, Casanova, Stendhal and Tolstoy. Scheyer shared with Zweig the fascination with biography and with the great men of history, as well as a tendency to see in the literary or artistic genius some more-than-merely-mortal individual. But he also shared a fascination with his specific subjects. Each of the above figures was the subject of a *feuilleton* by Scheyer – in most cases, it seems, inspired by the Zweig publication. Scheyer's last two books consist largely of essays dramatising the life stories of such 'greats'; to the above names are added those of Verlaine, Victor Hugo, Baudelaire, Rembrandt.

It could be said that nostalgia was something of a Viennese literary speciality in the early years of the twentieth century. The obsession with transience, with a vanishing, unrecoverable world, recurs in the opera librettos of Hugo von Hofmannsthal, in the novels of Joseph Roth[23] (*Radetzky March*, *The Emperor's Tomb*),* obsessed with the loss of the Old Empire and its traditions, and in the short stories of Stefan Zweig. In Zweig's *Buchmendel*, an unemployable but irreplaceable man of letters is ejected from the café where he has for years resided by the harsh utilitarian attitude of the new management; in *Chess Story*, the mental breakdown of the brilliant amateur chess player is in a sense the breakdown of the old world which he represents against the uneducated, machine-like character of his opponent. *Letter from an Unknown Woman* is redolent with the sense of a lost past; and *The World of Yesterday* provides the title of one of Zweig's last books, in which he recalls in nostalgic detail the era of his parents' generation.

So, too, Scheyer – in an essay on his older contemporary Arthur Schnitzler – writes of 'the reflection of a city, that has since lost its own "I".' Schnitzler's Vienna – that world of tradition and culture, of clear social orders and customs, of elegant love-affairs – is gone; it is a 'disappearing dream, the resonance of a memory'. One seems here to be involved not so much in a nostalgia-fest as in a potentially endless nostalgic regress. The focus on transience, and the desire to revisit the past, are prominent features of Schnitzler's characters, for example in his best-known play, *Reigen* (*La Ronde*, or *Merry-Go-Round*), an interlocked chain of sketches depicting sexual encounters at all levels of Viennese society. Nostalgia is already an essential element in this poetic world for which Scheyer experiences nostalgia.[24]

In the context of the present book, of course, Scheyer had good reason to be nostalgic. 'Once upon a time ...,' he begins, and proceeds to talk of the lost innocence of the world of 1944,

---

23. Scheyer, incidentally, wrote an obituary of Roth – the only article that I have been able to discover published during his time in Paris.
24. It is not for nothing that Freud admired Schnitzler: the sexual or erotic dimension of the recall of early memories is a central theme in Schnitzler's male-female encounters.

the impossibility of still enjoying nature, and the summer, as one used to before the War intruded. But it is striking that he here quite closely echoes words he had written in 1927, in the preface of *Escape to Yesterday*; there, already, summers are not what they were.

Again, when he talks in *Asylum* of how it is the present that seems ghostly, and only the past seems real, the notion recalls perspectives in his previous writing:

> Yesterday ... it seems so many years since there still was a yesterday. It has become something so distant, so improbable, that – even if you have actually experienced it – you think of this yesterday as of a lost dream ... The time of expectations is past. Beyond the realm of hope, of fulfilment, of beauty and excitement, we watch unmoved as a present which is at once harsh and ghostly passes us by – a present which is nothing but discontented noise and emptiness.
>
> (*Escape to Yesterday*, pp. 9–11)

And nostalgia was a theme Scheyer had elaborated even in his first published book, *Europeans and Exotics*: 'I have sought, again and again, to take refuge from the desolate reality of the last years in the only truth that still makes existence tolerable, opening wounds but at the same time healing them: memory'.

War and depression

It is tempting, perhaps, to see Scheyer, not just as buying into Viennese literary nostalgia, but as a permanent malcontent. An extremely sensitive individual, easily hurt and nervous; though clearly, too, equally sensitive to the beauty, the excitement, of moments – of books, of musical experiences, of paintings, of relationships. In my father's doubtless unsympathetic view, he was someone who simply found it difficult to be happy – a permanent pessimist. But it is worth pausing to consider the concrete reasons for pessimism, in the volumes published up to 1927.

One (about which I can only speculate) may be unhappiness in love. Moriz met Grete, presumably in 1925 or 1926, after the death of her first husband. A previous romantic obsession seems to be hinted at in *Tralosmontes*; and unhappiness in love is a submerged theme in *Escape to Yesterday* ('There is only one solution: to love. You can only rediscover that sunken island, your homeland, in the heart of another – no longer in yourself'). In *Europeans and Exotics*, the end of the preface – talking of the comforts to be had from travel, and from the memory of it – suggests a profound loneliness. Another kind of misery is easier to document – namely that related to the Great War and its aftermath. Alongside more general expressions of the dullness and emptiness of the present, the prefaces to both *Europeans and Exotics* and *Escape to Yesterday* contain some comments which are more historically specific.

> These pieces were mostly written during the War ... but without belonging to that moment, with its debased, mendacious language. I felt it my duty as a 'good European' to keep as far as possible away from any officially sanctioned 'mindset'.
>
> (*Europeans and Exotics*, p. 5)

> They have disappeared without trace – vanished in a puff of dull, suffocating smoke – those wonderful castles in the air, those bright Palaces of the Grail that were pointed out to us by cunning deceivers on the Horizon of Peace ... Dynasties were overthrown; oppressors put aside; but in their place came a thousand other dynasties, a thousand other oppressors, each with a well-polished lie at the ready – a lie which was quite cynically deposited in the dustbin just as soon as the 'last' fluctuation on the stock exchange of world history had turned the weaker into the stronger. People babbled of progress, made proclamations of freedom – but in reality every solemn phrase, every programme, every attack on the status quo – every form of progress – only really had the purpose of enabling the onward march of the Market.
>
> (*Escape to Yesterday*, pp. 10–11)

DIREKTION DER STAATSOPER

Eintritts-Karte Nr. ▓15▓

zu den Generalproben in der
WIENER STAATSOPER
für die
SPIELZEIT 1937/38

Nur gültig für

Herrn
Frau *Moritz Scheyer*

Parkett
Eingang in der Operngasse

Ohne Stempel der Staatsoperndirektion ist
die Karte ungültig.

Scheyer's press pass for the Vienna Opera for the 1937–38
season belied any sense that he would be forced to leave the
city before the programme's end.

The remarks attest to the profound disillusionment and despair that resulted, not just from the War itself, but from the disastrous Depression that followed it, in Austria in particular. Scheyer is speaking of the illusory hopes that political leaders raised for the post-war world. There is a nostalgia for the 'old order' in preference to rampant capitalism; but it would also be possible to interpret the words in a more definitely socialist manner. It is interesting here to consider Scheyer's political attitude to the First World War itself. A poem, *Lonely Battlefield*, was published by Scheyer in the *Arbeiter-Zeitung* (the organ of the Austrian Social Democratic party) on 17th November 1914:

Lonely Battlefield

Under the pale first snow
Many a young sorrow lies buried.

The late moon, indifferent and cold,
Shines down like a funeral torch.

The night utters prayers for the dead.
In the east there glimmers a distant light.

Scheyer (like Zweig) had been an ardent admirer of the pacifist Romain Rolland, and of the anti-nationalist philosophy of
the 'good European'. There seems insufficient evidence as to
whether he remained a committed pacifist during Austria's
involvement in the War; however, the above poem, written so
early on in the hostilities, makes a powerful statement.

It is also noteworthy and horribly ironic that Scheyer's last
published volume, completed in 1937 and published in 1938,
has much less sense of the 'terrible times', and the 'need to
escape', than any of the others. But this too is revealing. Life
was pretty good: he had a stable, respected professional position and was economically comfortable. And the advent of
Hitler in Austria, though feared, was simply not anticipated as
an immediate threat. Moreover, in early 1938 that latest book
was receiving considerable critical acclaim, including an enthusiastic letter from Stefan Zweig, then resident in London.

Music

Scheyer's attitude to and involvement with music also have to
be understood in relation to their time and place. It is perhaps
difficult for us to understand how fundamental music was to this
culture, not just in artistic but also in social and intellectual terms.
In Vienna classical music and its practitioners and institutions –
especially the opera – were the focus of enormous popular fame,
rivalries and press interest; but, more than that, to intellectuals
music was a pursuit with a moral, even religious, dimension, its
practitioners, in particular the composer and conductor, godlike
figures, whose realm of activity lifted them far above normal
human endeavour. It is noteworthy that Scheyer, though not
actually a music critic, had a pass to attend dress rehearsals at the
Opera. A family anecdote has him addressing Gustav Mahler in
the street, and he seems to have been friendly with Bruno Walter;
for both of whom he clearly had enormous admiration.

Music recurs as a metaphor in his writing, too: the sound
of Nazi boots provides 'the new theme tune of Parisian life';
and in the camp at Beaune there is the 'nightly symphony of

Moriz Scheyer's French residence permit, issued in July 1947.

misery and sorrow, with the rustling of straw running through it like a pedal note on the organ'. (Such elaborate metaphors could also be paralleled from the writings of Zweig.)[25]

The rediscovery of music at Labarde, via the radio, is one of the most vivid emotional experiences in the book. Nowhere is his nostalgia more real than in the evocation of the vanished faces of Mahler – 'the noble, illuminated face … the devotee at the altar of genius' – and of a previous generation of performers at the Vienna Opera. Music has the capacity to take him back, but also to take him completely outside normal reality. An otherworldly vision, as he says, which at the same time can shed light on this world.

Scheyer's work: historical and real-life experience

There seems a terrible retrospective irony, as one reads through Scheyer's collections of essays, with regard to two of the recurrent themes of his work: that of 'becoming great

---

25. Zweig's musical obsessions extended to his acquiring manuscripts of the great composers, as well as (prominent in his Salzburg villa) a desk that had belonged to Beethoven.

through suffering' and that of women who sacrifice themselves for the men in their lives. Tolstoy, Wilde and Verlaine, for example, are characterised as achieving their true potential – fulfilling their destiny – through suffering. It was, very specifically, Verlaine's period of imprisonment that brought out his greatness; Wilde's turned him into a poet.

As for the women whose lives of self-sacrifice excite Scheyer's interest, they include Mata Hari, the Empress Eugenie, Lady Hamilton (who inspires Nelson to greatness but dies lonely and unknown), Rachel (a famous French actress exploited mercilessly by her family), two literary figures, Mariana Alcoforado and Marceline Desbordes-Valmore, whose sorrows are sublimated in poetry, and Anna Grigorievna and Sophie Andreevna, who sacrifice their lives to Dostoevsky and Tolstoy respectively. (There are, conversely, various female villains or 'adventuresses' – Verlaine's wife, the Tsaritza Catherina.)

On the one hand, all this may seem to belong to the realm of outdated and historically unreal romanticisations of the great personalities of history and literature – and of a decidedly pre-feminist 'harridan-or-heroine' attitude to women. On the other, it may seem too horribly close to the bone, in relation to the very real suffering, heroism and female self-sacrifice that are so central to this book.

At least it must be said that that in his historical account Scheyer is acutely conscious of the real-life heroism and self-sacrifice of two women in particular – Sláva Kolářová and Hélène Rispal; and also – though less explicitly, and though he never mentions her by name – of his own wife, Grete.

Also that, again with the cruel judgement of hindsight, Scheyer's main literary output, consisting of some 250 *feuilletons*, as well as sundry theatre and book reviews, all for immediate publication and consumption, may seem to today's reader like a literary preparation, a honing of the talents required for the present work. The one which struggled to make it from writing to publication – indeed, to survive at all – but which, surely, provides his most enduring testament.

People mentioned in the text

Below are notes on people (and organisations) mentioned in the text. Page references are to further discussion in the Translator's Epilogue, Moriz Scheyer: Writer *and* Further Reading.

Abetz, Otto (1903–58). Appointed German ambassador to France in 1940, and as such theoretically at the head of the political wing of the Occupation, although in practice the SS and the Gestapo seem to have dominated. Abetz was, however, energetic both in the field of the promotion of German culture and, for a period in 1940, in 'safeguarding', i.e. confiscating, French works of art, especially those under Jewish ownership.

Cairncross, Alec (1911–98). Distinguished economist and later Chancellor of Oxford University. He was in 1938 the representative of the International Student Service in Glasgow. **> pp. 265, 280**

'Carlos': see Ordeig.

Cassou, Jean (1897–1986). Museum curator, art critic, literary critic and, during his incarceration in Toulouse for Resistance activities in 1941 (he had been active in propaganda), author of a set of poems, *33 Sonnets Composés au Secret*, composed and memorised in the absence of pen and paper.

Crémieux, Benjamin (1888–1944). Author and intellectual who was in a position to help Moriz Scheyer during his time in Paris; however, he himself was to end up in Buchenwald. A French Jew, he became involved in Resistance activities and anti-Vichy publications, and was arrested and then deported to the camp, where he died. **> p.305**

Crucy, François (1875–1958). Journalist and socialist politician. He had been head of information in the left-wing Front Populaire government of 1936–37 under Léon Blum, and was a central figure in the Agence France-Presse after the Liberation.

Darquier, Louis (1897–1980). Extreme fascist and anti-Semite. He succeeded Vallat as head of Vichy's *Commissariat général aux questions juives* in May 1942 (immediately before the first mass deportations from France to the death camps); he was replaced in February 1944, apparently for excessive greed and incompetence.

Dunlop, Marian (1880–1974). Inspirational teacher, writer and founder (in 1932) of the Fellowship of Meditation, developing a technique of Christian meditation which still has adherents. She acted as guarantor for Scheyer's stepsons, Konrad and Stefan Singer, enabling them to come to Britain in 1938. **> pp. 265, 280**

'Exposition Juive'. The notorious exhibition 'Le juif et la France', mounted at the Palais Berlitz in Paris from September 1941 to January 1942 as Nazi anti-Semitic propaganda.

FFI (Forces Françaises de l'Intérieur). Body formed in early 1944 through merging of several armed Resistance groups in France. **> p.268**

de Gaulle, Charles (1890–1970). Head of French government in exile, 1940–44, as leader of Free France and the Free French Forces, and head of Provisional Government, 1944–46. He returned to lead the government in 1958, at the height of the Algerian War, where a bitter struggle against the FLN eventually gave way to negotiations and independence. **> pp. 267, 270**

Gerlier, Pierre-Marie (1880–1965). Archbishop of Lyon and primate of Gaul from 1937. Although he avowed support for Pétain, and seems not to have been unequivocal in his condemnation of anti-Semitic policies, he did something to raise concern publicly about both deportations and inhumane conditions in French camps; he also gave support to Glasberg and the Amitié chrétienne. In September 1942 (after Saliège) he sent a pastoral letter, to be read in churches, condemning the deportations more openly.

Glasberg, Alexandre (1902–81). Catholic priest (and by birth a Ukrainian Jew) who led the formation of the charity Amitié chrétienne in 1941, comprising both Catholic and Protestant laypersons, aiming to help Jews under persecution. One activity was the establishment of shelters to house Jews released from French internment camps. After the mass arrests of 1942, the activities of Glasberg and Amitié Chrétienne became clandestine.

Herriot, Édouard (1872–1957). Politician of the French Radical

294

party, three times Prime Minister and for a long period President of the Chamber of Deputies. He was exiled from 1942 to 1945 for his opposition to the Vichy régime.

'Hilaire-Buckmaster'. Hilaire was the codename of George Starr, who ran Britain's SOE (Special Operations Executive) in south-western France, in sabotage operations, etc., from 1942. There was clearly some friction with de Gaulle. Starr is credited with uniting communist and non-communist elements in his outfit. Maurice Buckmaster was from July 1941 head of the French (F) section of SOE and worked with the communist FTP, the Francs-Tireurs Partisans. The immigrant wing of this was the FTP-MOI (Main d'Oeuvre Immigrée). **> p.269**

International Student Service. Geneva-based organisation active in assisting student refugees in the 1930s; it was run in conjunction with, and funded by, local universities. **> p.265**

Kofler, Edgar. Son of Emil Kofler (see below). Konrad Singer recalls: '[Emil] Kofler had a son, who was quite friendly with us, about two years older than me; he joined the Resistance in Paris and was captured by the Germans, or by the Vichy French, and killed, shot. I knew him quite well – we were very friendly … he was a nice boy!' He is commemorated by a street name in Voiron: Bd Edgar Kofler. **> p.279**

Kofler, Emil. Romanian compatriot of Moriz Scheyer who settled in France before the War. Konrad Singer recalls: 'Kofler was a friend from Bucharest … who had a business in Paris and once, twice a year would pass through Vienna from Bucharest to Paris and visit us.' **> p.279**

Kolářová, Sláva (born Jindřichův Hradec, Czechoslovakia, 1893; died Belvès, France, 1948). Moriz and Grete Scheyer's housekeeper and companion, and Konrad Singer's beloved nanny 'Veili'. **> pp. 257–60, 270, 274, 281, 292**

Laval, Pierre (1883–1945). A socialist leader of two French governments in the 1930s, before playing a prominent role in the Vichy government in 1940. Pétain, however, disliked him and dismissed him at the end of that year. He was brought back as Prime Minister in 1942. The nature of his collaboration with the Germans – negotiating with them the precise numbers and categories of Jews to be deported, and assisting in the process, but thus arguably reducing the overall total that might have been deported – remains highly controversial. **> p.268**

Lenormand, Henri-René (1882–1951). French playwright, known for works exploring subconscious psychological motivation and influenced by Freud's theories.

Mahler, Gustav (1860–1911). A legendary conductor as well as composer, Mahler presided over the Vienna Opera from 1897 to 1907. The cast remembered in the narrative by Scheyer is almost identical to that of the production of *Fidelio* in 1904, a famous musical-dramatic event; and each of the musicians mentioned was part of the Mahler 'team': Anna von Mildenburg (1879–1947), a dramatic soprano, with whom Mahler had a close personal relationship; Leopold Demuth (1861–1910), a baritone; Wilhelm Hesch, a Czech bass; the Danish tenor Erik Schmedes. Arnold Rosé (1863–1946) was concertmaster of the Vienna Philharmonic (and Mahler's brother-in-law); Friedrich Buxbaum the first cello (and cello in the Rosé quartet). The first ever recording of Mahler's *Lied von der Erde* was conducted by Bruno Walter. **> pp. 262, 272, 290–1**

Malraux, André (1901–76). Novelist and art theorist who fought on the Republican side in the Spanish Civil War and was active in the French Resistance; he also served as Minister for Cultural Affairs in de Gaulle's government, from 1958 to 1969. **> p.271**

Mark, Hermann (1895–1992). Born to a Jewish mother and gentile father in Vienna, he had a successful career both in industrial chemistry and academia, as a pioneer of polymer science. Professor of Physical Chemistry at Vienna until 1938, after the Anschluss, he managed a dramatic escape (smuggling out his assets in the form of platinum concealed in coathangers) to Switzerland, from where he travelled eventually to the US, where he completed his career at the Polytechnic Institute of Brooklyn. **> p.264**

Masereel, Frans (1889–1972). Flemish artist who worked especially in woodcut, sometimes in graphic-novel form, depicting the brutality of the modern world. He was a pacifist, and an artist much admired by Stefan Zweig; indeed there were published collaborations between the two. He was persecuted by the Nazis as 'decadent'. **> p.267**

Mathieu, René and **Henriette**. Both teachers, and the latter mayor, at St-Cernin-de-l'Herm, near Belvès. They saved at least two other Jewish families (one introduced to them by the Rispals), by providing them with false identity papers and finding them secure hiding places. **> p.269**

Mauriac, François (1885–1970). Distinguished French novelist, awarded the Nobel prize for literature in 1952.

Maurras, Charles (1868–1952). Writer and political theorist, founder of a journal influential in right-wing and, later, fascist circles: *Action Française*. Though opposed to Germany, he was virulently anti-Semitic.

Musikverein. The historic venue for orchestral concerts in Vienna. Franz Schalk was its head from 1904–21; both he and Felix Weingartner, another distinguished Austrian conductor, were also at different periods heads of the Vienna Opera.

Neues Wiener Tagblatt (NWT). One of the two 'quality' dailies in Vienna in the 1930s, for which Scheyer wrote *feuilletons* and was the arts reviews editor.
> pp. vii, 262, 282, 284–5

Ordeig, Charles-Henry, known as **Carlos**. **> p.269**

Pétain, Philippe (1856–1951). The French general was the 'hero of Verdun' in World War I. In June 1940 he sought an Armistice with Germany and was then voted absolute powers as head of state, leading the Vichy régime in 'Unoccupied' France but collaborating closely with the German authorities. **> pp. 267, 272**

Rebière, Georges. Resistance fighter and native of Belvès. Later the author of a history of Belvès and a Resistance memoir, *Aimez-vous cueillir les noisettes? (Do You Like Chestnuts?)*. Now in his 90s, he runs a museum in Belvès of local culture and traditional musical instruments of his own construction.
> pp. vi, 265–9, 272, 280

Reinhardt, Max (1873–1943). Austrian-Jewish theatre director, and founder in 1920 of the Salz-

burg Festival (with a production of Hugo von Hofmannsthal's *Everyman*, which is still repeated every year). Also a significant film director, including in the US, where he ended his career after emigration in 1938.

Rispal, Gabriel (1875–1970); **Hélène** (1903–79); **Jacques** (1923–86). The Rispal family were Resistance organisers in Belvès and were responsible for the survival of Moriz Scheyer, Grete and Sláva. **> pp. vi, 256-9, 265–9, 271–2, 279, 280, 292**

Rolland, Romain (1866–1944): French author, thinker and pacifist admired by Scheyer and Stefan Zweig. **> pp. 279, 285, 290**

Romains, Jules (1885–1972). Well-known literary figure of the period, whose major work was a 27-volume cycle of novels, *Les Hommes de bonne volonté*. He was sufficiently close to Scheyer that he gave him a number of signed copies of his novels.

Roth, Joseph (1894–1939). Austrian-Jewish novelist, best known for *Radetzky March* (1932), about the decline and fall of the Austro-Hungarian Empire. **> p.286**

le Roy, Eugène (1836–1907). French writer, known for his nonconformist lifestyle and political outlook, and author of a number of Republican and anti-clerical writings as well as the novels mentioned by Scheyer.

Saliège, Archbishop Jules-Gérard (1870–1956). Archbishop of Toulouse and the first senior cleric in the Unoccupied Zone to appeal publicly, in a pastoral letter of August 1942, against the mass deportations and treatment of Jews in camps. His letter is seen by some as having had a profound effect on French opinion and contributing to the saving of many Jewish lives.

Sax, Victor. Konrad Singer recalls: 'he was a rich Swiss and was regarded as a good friend by my stepfather … he asked [Victor and his wife] to look after my upkeep while in Zurich.' The couple are also remembered in one of Scheyer's *feuilletons*, published in his 1919 book *Europeans and Exotics*, which tells the story of a dog they had that wanted its freedom.

Schaumburg, Ernst (1880–1947). German Lieutenant-General, from 1941 Commandant of 'Greater Paris' and effective second-in-command to Stülpnagel.

Scheyer, Margarethe (Grete), née Singer (1892–1977). Grete married Moriz Scheyer in 1927, after the death of her first husband, Bernhard Schwarzwald. **> pp. vi, viii, x, 257–63, 270, 272–4, 281, 288, 292**

Schnitzler, Arthur (1862–1931). Austrian playwright and prose writer acquainted with Moriz Scheyer. **> pp. vii, 286**

Schuschnigg, Kurt (1897–1977). Chancellor of Federal Republic of Austria from July 1934 (after the assassination of Dollfuss) until March 1938. **> p.263**

Schwarzwald, Dr Bernhard. First husband of Grete Scheyer and father of Stefan and Konrad Singer. **> pp. 259-62**

Seyss-Inquart, Artur (1892–1946). Nazi sympathiser appointed to the cabinet of Dollfuss in 1933 and made Minister of the Interior by Schuschnigg as part of his attempt to compromise with Hitler. He was temporarily Chancellor on Schuschnigg's resignation at the Anschluss; he subsequently served the Third Reich as administrator in Poland and in the Netherlands. He was convicted at the Nuremberg trials, in particular for his extreme repression in the Netherlands, and executed in 1946.

Sieburg, Friedrich (1893–1964). Nazi journalist who had worked in France and was author of a well-known book, *Gott in Frankreich* ('Is God a Frenchman?'), celebrating the 'French' ideals of devotion to pleasure and freedom from commercial values. Sieburg allied himself to Pétain. As Scheyer suggests, the 'love of France' that Sieburg professes actually conceals the Nazi contempt and desire to dominate. (It is interesting to compare the attitude described in the 1942 novel *Le Silence de la Mer*, by Verors (pseudonym), where the notion of the 'musical' German with a love of French culture is replaced by the dawning realisation of the Nazi reality.)

Singer, Konrad (1917–2013); **Singer family**. > pp. vi-vii, 259–65, 273–8

Stülpnagel, Otto von (1878–1948). World War I veteran, recalled to active service by Hitler and made Military Commander of France from October 1940. Carried out mass executions of hostages in obedience to Hitler's orders, although he protested this and attempted to mitigate the violence of German policy in France. He resigned in 1942, was succeeded by his cousin Carl-Heinrich, and committed suicide in prison in 1948.

Thil, Georges (1897–1984). Lyric-dramatic tenor with a huge international profile in the 1930s, he is considered by some the greatest of French tenors.

Vallat, Xavier (1891–1972). Committed anti-Semite. From March 1941, he was Commissioner of the Vichy *Commissariat général aux questions juives* but was replaced, apparently for being too moderate, in 1942.

Vorms, Pierre. An old friend of Moriz Scheyer, resident in Paris where he published art books (especially those of Frans Masereel). After the débâcle he settled in Belvès, where he seems to have remained after the War;

he was also actively involved in the Resistance. Konrad Singer recalls: 'he visited us even in Vienna before; lived in Paris; then in Belvès he also had a house, very close to the maisonette [of Hélène Rispal] ... he was regarded by my parents as a good friend'. > pp. 265, 267

Walter, Bruno (1876–1962). A major figure in the European music world from the early 1900s to the 1930s, Walter was a charismatic conductor and protégé of Mahler's. He moved to Vienna in the mid-1930s when it became impossible for him to perform in Germany, and his association with the Vienna Philharmonic and the Salzburg festival both gave rise to legendary recordings. After the Anschluss he was offered and accepted French citizenship; he subsequently emigrated to the United States, where he continued an active career until his death in 1962. He seems to have been at least an acquaintance of Moriz Scheyer's. > pp. vii, 262, 272, 290

Wessel, Horst (1907–30). Nazi activist and 'martyr' (he was killed in Berlin by two Communist Party members) who wrote the lyric of the eponymous song, also known from its first line as 'Die Fahne Hoch' ('The banner high'), which was the marching-song of the storm-troopers and functioned as a Nazi national anthem. The incident Scheyer describes may remind one of the famous episode in the film

Casablanca, where, however it is 'The Watch on the Rhine', rather than the Horst Wessel song, which provides the Nazi competition to the Marseillaise.

Weygand, Maxime (1867–1965). French Major-General, under Foch, at the end of the First World War, and involved in the armistice negotiations at Compiègne. He was recalled from retirement in 1939 to head French operations in the Orient, then to France as commander-in-chief in May 1940 after the German breakthrough had begun; from September 1940 he served in Pétain's government.

Zweig, Stefan (1881–1942). Austrian-Jewish writer with an enormous international reputation in the 1920s and 1930s, for his short stories, essays and biographies. A friend of Moriz Scheyer's from early days in Vienna, he emigrated, first to England, then to the US and finally to Brazil, where he died in a suicide pact with his second wife in February 1942. **> pp. vii, 260-2, 279-80, 285-6, 290-1**

A chronology of events 1933–45

1933 Hitler achieves absolute power in Germany.

1934 Schuschnigg succeeds Dollfuss as Chancellor of the Federal State of Austria. His policies are authoritarian and undemocratic, but pro-independence.

1933–39 Large numbers of Germans, especially Jews, flee to France.

9 March 1938 Schuschnigg announces plebiscite for 13th March to decide between Austrian indepedence and absorption in greater Germany.

12 March 1938 Anschluss: German annexation of Austria. Seyss–Inquart appointed puppet Chancellor; implementation of anti–Semitic policies, with dismissal from jobs and acts of violence against Jews, followed by appropriation of assets and 'Aryanisation' of businesses.

30 September 1938 Munich agreement, followed directly by German invasion of western and northern Czechoslovakia ('Sudetenland').

November 1938 'Kristallnacht': widespread looting and destruction of Jewish businesses and synagogues, supposedly in response to assassination of a German diplomat in Paris.

1938–39 Anti–immigrant legislation in France in response to influx of refugees.

March 1939 German Occupation of remainder of Czechoslovakia.

August 1939 'Molotov–Ribbentropp Pact' signed (non-aggression treaty between Germany and USSR).

September 1939 Invasion of Poland by Germany (and USSR); Great Britain and France declare war on Germany.

September–October 1939 Arrest of 'German' Jews in France, interned as aliens; most are freed by May 1940.

May 1940 Germany invades Luxembourg, Netherlands, Belgium and France.

14 June 1940 Fall of Paris; beginning of 'Exodus'.

22 June 1940 Armistice: division of France into German-occupied region in north and west, and 'zone libre' (Vichy France).

July 1940 French senators vote full powers to Marshall Pétain to negotiate with German authorities; massive movement of people south, especially from Paris.

1940–41 Series of anti–Jewish orders by German authorities and *Statuts des Juifs* by Vichy régime.

October 1940 First French *Statuts des Juifs* excludes Jews from range of occupations. German ordinance requires Jews to declare assets and appoint 'temporary administrators' of their businesses and finances. Systematic appropriation of Jewish assets in France (administrated by Otto Abetz).

1940 Militarist–traditionalist 'National Revolution' led by Prime Minister Laval; inception of Chantiers de Jeunesse – youth camps replacing military service.

1940–41 Beginnings of French Resistance activity.

March 1941 Creation of *Commissariat général aux affaires juives* under commissioner Xavier Vallat in Vichy.

May 1941 6494 Austrian, Czech and Polish Jews in Paris (aged eighteen to sixty) requested to attend police station 'pour examen de votre situation'; those who do are taken to concentration camps at Beaune–la–Rolande and Pithiviers.

June 1941 Second 'Statut des Juifs' extends definition of 'Jewish'; requires census in Unoccupied Zone. German invasion of USSR.

August 1941 Further roundup of Jews in Paris, taken to Drancy.

December 1941 Roundup of 743 French Jewish professional men in Paris.

March 1942 First deportation from French concentration camps to Auschwitz; the deportations continue regularly and systematically from this time onward.

April 1942 Laval offers German authorities 'La Relève' – a voluntary French workforce for Germany in exchange for the return of prisoners of war.

May 1942 Jews in Occupied France must wear yellow Star of David with word 'Juif'.

June 1942 First deportations from Beaune–la–Rolande to Auschwitz.

July 1942 Roundup of Jews in Paris, sent to Drancy, Beaune-la-Rolande or Pithiviers (the usual end destination from these camps is Auschwitz).

August 1942 Second deportation from Beaune–la–Rolande to Auschwitz.

Summer 1942 Roundups and deportations of Jewish immigrants in Unoccupied Zone; some protests and clandestine assistance operations from church figures.

Autumn 1942 The voluntary French workforce becomes the forced 'Service de travail obligatoire'; this provokes defection (*réfractaires*) and swells ranks of Resistance and *maquis* operations.

November 1942 Allied invasion of North Africa ('Operation Torch'); Germany responds by occupying previously Unoccupied Zone in France.

1942–44 German occupying authorities and French military police jointly involved in roundups and deportation of Jews.

June 1944 Allied landings in Normandy.

August 1944 Liberation of Paris. German forces retreat through France; some commit atrocities.

May 1945 Final defeat of Hitler's Germany; end of war in Europe.

Further reading

A brief selection of books giving further historical background and survivors' accounts from the period covered in this book:

Austria and the Anschluss

Sir Malcolm Bullock, *Austria 1918–38: A Study in Failure* (1939). Chronicles the years leading up to the Anschluss.

Oswald Dutch, *Thus Died Austria* (1938). Analytical account of the period by a Viennese journalist.

G.E.R. Gedye, *Fallen Bastions* (1939). Vivid, emotive eye-witness account by a foreign correspondent.

France 1938–45, Nazi occupation, camps and survivors' experiences

Saul Friedländer, *When Memory Comes* (1978); *Memory, History and the Extermination of the Jews of Europe* (1993). Pierre

Vidal-Naquet, *The Jews, History, Memory and the Present* (1996). Interesting not just for the memories that parallel some of those in this book, but also for their analysis and reflection on questions of Nazi-period history.

Susan Zuccotti, *The Holocaust, the French, and the Jews* (1993). French wartime history as it affected Jews, detailing the phases of anti-Semitic legislation and persecution.

Renée Poznanski, *Jews in France during World War II* (1994). The author covers Belvès in the War, mentioning several individuals in Scheyer's account.

Arthur Koestler, *The Scum of the Earth* (1941). Koestler's gripping tale of arrest, imprisonment, and escape to London from Nazi-occupied France.

David Rousset, *A World Apart* (1945). One of the earliest accounts of the Nazi camps, by a French non-Jewish prisoner and Resistance fighter. The book mentions Benjamin Crémieux, an acquaintance of Scheyer's.

Claudine Vegh, *I Didn't Say Goodbye: Interviews with Children of the Holocaust* (1979). 14 brief monologues by French Jewish children, who survived the Nazis through being adopted by non-Jewish families.

J. Crémieux-Dunand, *La Vie à Drancy* (1945). Vivid account by internee, documenting horrific conditions at the notorious Paris holding camp, from which nearly 70,000 people were deported to their deaths.

Georges Wellers, *L'Étoile jaune à l'heure de Vichy: de Drancy à Auschwitz* (1973).

Survivor's account documenting persecution of French Jews and especially life at Drancy.

Robert Antelme, *L'Espèce humaine* (1947). Important testimony and reflection on Nazi concentration camps and their victims by Resistance fighter and survivor of Buchenwald and Dachau.

French Resistance

H. R. Kedward, *Occupied France: Collaboration and Resistance, 1940–44* (1985). Fine account of the French Resistance.

Georges Rebière, *Aimez-vous cueillir les noisettes?* (2006). Wartime memoir of a Belvès Resistance fighter and friend of the Rispal family.

Translator's acknowledgements

I have incurred a number of debts in the course of my work on this book, which it is a pleasure to acknowledge. In particular, my sincere thanks go to Jonathan Coe, Mark Geller, Thomas Rütten and Tamsyn Barton for their support, advice and encouragement at various stages of the project; to Georges Rebière for answering my questions on persons and experiences of the Resistance in Belvès, as well as for sharing with me his photographs from that time, and to Cherith Beglan for introducing me to him; to my cousin, Hilary Fawcett, for sending me her photographs of Gabriel and Hélène Rispal and of the portrait of Grete Scheyer; to my brother, Michael Singer, who actually first pulled the typescript out of a long-neglected suitcase; to the Wingate Trust, whose financial support allowed me time to complete the translation and research the background to the book; and last but by no means least to Mark Ellingham at Profile Books for his enthusiasm and for his meticulous and sensitive editorial input.

My greatest debt remains that to my father, Konrad Singer. It is, of course, a debt that goes far beyond his specific contribution to this book; yet that contribution was itself – ironically – a huge one. In spite of his personal rejection of his stepfather's work, he spent many hours, both before and after the discovery of the typescript, patiently sharing his own memories of and perspectives on the people and events of this narrative, as well as their historical, moral and political background. He has undoubtedly shaped the book, as far as my own contribution to it is concerned, at least as much as its main author.

P. N. Singer